Charleston

JIM MOREKIS

Contents

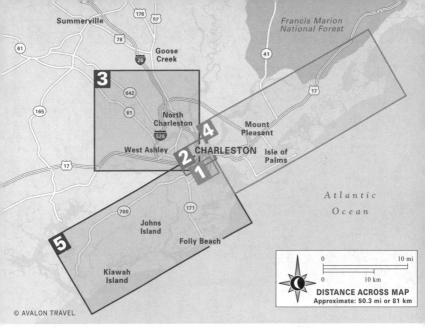

Maps

🟠 SIGHTS

2	SOUTH CAROLINA AQUARIUM	79 DOCK STREET THEATRE
3	FORT SUMTER NATIONAL MONUMENT	81 FRENCH HUGUENOT CHURCH
5	PHILIP SIMMONS GARDEN	82 OLD SLAVE MART MUSEUM
19	KAHAL KADOSH BETH ELOHIM REFORM TEMPLE	86 WATERFRONT PARK
20	WILLIAM RHETT HOUSE	92 FOUR CORNERS OF LAW
25	ST. MARY OF THE ANNUNCIATION CHURCH	93 ST. MICHAEL'S EPISCOPAL CHURCH
32	OLD CITY MARKET	101 RAINBOW ROW
37	CONFEDERATE MUSEUM	102 THE OLD EXCHANGE AND PROVOST DUNGEON
50	OLD CITY JAIL	104 CABBAGE ROW
52	UNITARIAN CHURCH	105 HEYWARD-WASHINGTON HOUSE
61	GIBBES MUSEUM OF ART	106 NATHANIEL RUSSELL HOUSE
62	CIRCULAR CONGREGATIONAL CHURCH	107 MILES BREWTON HOUSE
64	OLD POWDER MAGAZINE	108 THE BATTERY
65	ST. PHILIP'S EPISCOPAL CHURCH	109 CALHOUN MANSION
		110 EDMONDSTON-ALSTON HOUSE

🔴 RESTAURANTS

16	JESTINE'S KITCHEN	56 DIXIE SUPPLY CAFE AND BAKERY
21	CIRCA 1886	59 HUSK
24	CHARLESTON GRILL	60 POOGAN'S PORCH
26	HYMAN'S SEAFOOD	67 HIGH COTTON
27	FIG	68 MAGNOLIAS
29	CRU CAFÉ	71 SLIGHTLY NORTH OF BROAD
33	PENINSULA GRILL	73 CYPRESS
34	KAMINSKY'S	83 MCCRADY'S
40	CITY LIGHTS COFFEEHOUSE	91 GAULART & MALICLET
41	FULTON FIVE	103 CAROLINA'S
42	IL CORTILE DEL RE	
51	QUEEN STREET GROCERY	

🟣 NIGHTLIFE

22	VICKERY'S BAR AND GRILL	70 SOCIAL WINE BAR
55	TOMMY CONDON'S IRISH PUB	84 ROOFTOP BAR AND RESTAURANT
		97 BLIND TIGER

🟢 ARTS AND CULTURE

13	THE HAVE NOTS!	87 CITY GALLERY AT WATERFRONT
47	THE AUDUBON GALLERY	94 ANNE WORSHAM RICHARDSON BIRDS EYE VIEW GALLERY
54	SYLVAN GALLERY	95 PINK HOUSE GALLERY
63	PURE THEATRE	96 ANN LONG FINE ART
66	THE FOOTLIGHT PLAYERS	99 CHARLESTON RENAISSANCE GALLERY
72	ROBERT LANGE STUDIOS	100 HELENA FOX FINE ART
80	CHARLESTON STAGE	
80	CHARLESTON SYMPHONY ORCHESTRA	

🟠 SPORTS AND ACTIVITIES

1	SPIRITLINE CRUISES	39 ORIGINAL CHARLESTON WALKS
4	SANDLAPPER WATER TOURS	48 ARCHITECTURAL WALKING TOURS
35	BULLDOG TOURS	76 CHARLESTON STROLLS
36	ED GRIMBALL'S WALKING TOURS	98 CHARLESTON ART TOURS

🟢 SHOPS

6	BOB ELLIS SHOE STORE	38 CITY MARKET
7	OOPS!	43 GEORGE C. BIRLANT & CO.
8	PHILLIPS SHOES	44 A'RIGA IV
9	COPPER PENNY SHOOZ	53 JOINT VENTURE ESTATE JEWELERS
10	ART JEWELRY BY MIKHAIL SMOLKIN	57 PRESERVATION SOCIETY OF CHARLESTON BOOK AND GIFT SHOP
11	CROGHAN'S JEWEL BOX	58 ALEXANDRA AD
12	THE TRUNK SHOW	69 CHARLESTON COOKS!
14	STELLA NOVA	74 INDIGO
15	HALF MOON OUTFITTERS	78 SHOPS OF HISTORIC CHARLESTON FOUNDATION
17	RANGONI OF FLORENCE	90 BERLINS MEN'S AND WOMEN'S
18	WORTHWHILE	
23	PAULINE BOOKS AND MEDIA	
30	BELMOND CHARLESTON PLACE	

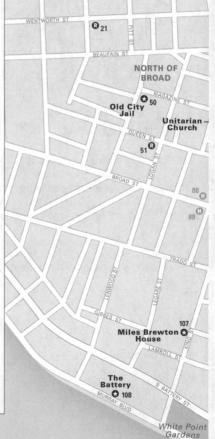

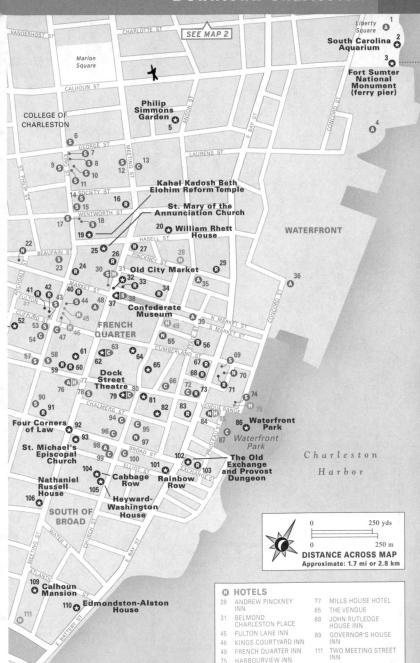

VANDERHOST ST
CHARLOTTE ST

Liberty Square 1
South Carolina Aquarium 2
Fort Sumter National Monument (ferry pier) 3

Marion Square

CALHOUN ST

4

COLLEGE OF CHARLESTON

Philip Simmons Garden 5

GEORGE ST
6
7
9
8
10
12
13
11

Kahal Kadosh Beth Elohim Reform Temple

SOCIETY ST
14
16
15

WENTWORTH ST
17
18

St. Mary of the Annunciation Church

19

William Rhett House 20

WATERFRONT

22
BEAUFAIN ST
23
25
26
27
HASELL ST
PINCKNEY ST
28
29

24
30
31
Old City Market
35
36

41
42
40
MARKET ST
32
33
34
FULTON ST
43
44
48
38
37

Confederate Museum

52
53
CLIFFORD ST
45
46
FRENCH QUARTER
39
N. MARKET ST
S. MARKET ST

CONCORD ST
E BAY ST
ANSON ST
MEETING ST
KING ST
ST PHILIP ST
ARCHDALE ST

54
47
49
55
56

57
58
61
63
CUMBERLAND ST
67
69
59
60
62
64
65
66
68
70
71

76
77
Dock Street Theatre
80
72
73
74
75

90
78
79
81
82
83
84
85

91
CHALMERS ST
VENDUE RANGE
86
Waterfront Park

Four Corners of Law 92
94
95
96
97
87
Waterfront Park

St. Michael's Episcopal Church
93
98
99
100
101
102
103
BROAD ST
ELLIOT ST
EXCHANGE ST

Charleston Harbor

104
Cabbage Row
Rainbow Row
The Old Exchange and Provost Dungeon

Nathaniel Russell House
105

106
Heyward-Washington House

SOUTH OF BROAD

MEETING ST
WATER ST
CHURCH ST
E BAY ST

ATLANTIC ST
109
Calhoun Mansion
110
Edmondston-Alston House

111
E BATTERY ST

0   250 yds
0   250 m
DISTANCE ACROSS MAP
Approximate: 1.7 mi or 2.8 km

HOTELS

28	ANDREW PINCKNEY INN	77	MILLS HOUSE HOTEL
31	BELMOND CHARLESTON PLACE	85	THE VENDUE
45	FULTON LANE INN	88	JOHN RUTLEDGE HOUSE INN
46	KINGS COURTYARD INN	89	GOVERNOR'S HOUSE INN
49	FRENCH QUARTER INN	111	TWO MEETING STREET INN
75	HARBOURVIEW INN		

GROVE ST
DUNNEMANN AVE
SAINT MARGARET ST
HIGH AVE
8TH AVE
7TH AVE
JAY ST
9TH AVE
11TH AVE
12TH AVE
RUTLEDGE AVE

GRIER AVE

JENKINS AVE

MARY MURRAY DR

GROVE ST
FRANCIS ST
KING ST
ST GODS ST
1   **R** **N**   2
CLEVELAND ST

HAMMOND AVE
JONES AVE

Hampton Park

MAVERICK ST

RUTLEDGE AVE

3   4
C **A**
The Citadel

LEE AVE
ELMWOOD ST
KENILWORTH AVE
PARKWOOD AVE
PRESIDENT ST
MOULTRIE ST

HAGOOD AVE

ASHLEY AVE

HUGER ST

CONGRESS ST

Joseph
P. Riley Jr.
Park
A 5

Stoney
Field

RACE ST

SUMTER ST

**HAMPTON
PARK**

SUMTER ST
CAROLINA ST

ORRS CT
JAMES ST
PERRY ST

Hammon
Field

FISHBURNE ST

Brittlebank
Park

LINE ST

NUNAN ST

Mitchell
Playground

17

LOCKWOOD DR

ALLWAY ST

BOGARD ST

ASHE ST
PERCY ST

R 9

8   **H**

SPRING ST

17

CANNON ST

C 15
16 **S**

17 **18**
R
ANN ST
N 19
N 20

WRAGG SQUARE

Wragg Mall

10 **H**

11 **R**

12 **S**

RADCLIFFE ST

21
Children's
Museum
of the
Lowcountry

ANN ST

MEETING ST

ASHLEY AVE

RUTLEDGE AVE

KING ST

A 22

23
Charleston
Museum

24 **R**

WARREN ST

JOHN ST

25 **C** **A** 26
R
27, 28

29
Joseph
Manigault
House

ST PHILIPS ST

33
Old Bethel
United Methodist
Church

31 **S**
30 **S**

32 **R**

VANDERHORST ST

HUTSON ST

Cannon
Park

© AVALON TRAVEL

✪ SIGHTS
- 3 THE CITADEL
- 14 AIKEN-RHETT HOUSE
- 21 CHILDREN'S MUSEUM OF THE LOWCOUNTRY
- 23 CHARLESTON MUSEUM
- 29 JOSEPH MANIGAULT HOUSE
- 33 OLD BETHEL UNITED METHODIST CHURCH
- 34 COLLEGE OF CHARLESTON
- 37 MARION SQUARE

ℝ RESTAURANTS
- 1 MOE'S CROSSTOWN TAVERN
- 9 TRATTORIA LUCCA
- 11 HOMINY GRILL
- 13 INDACO
- 17 BASIL
- 24 JUANITA GREENBERG'S NACHO ROYALE
- 27 39 RUE DE JEAN
- 28 COAST BAR AND GRILL
- 32 KUDU COFFEE

ℕ NIGHTLIFE
- 2 MOE'S CROSSTOWN TAVERN
- 6 THE RECOVERY ROOM
- 18 DUDLEY'S
- 19 MUSIC FARM
- 20 CLUB PANTHEON
- 39 TRIO CLUB

ℂ ARTS AND CULTURE
- 15 REDUX CONTEMPORARY ART CENTER
- 25 GALLERY CHUMA

𝔸 SPORTS AND ACTIVITIES
- 4 CITADEL BULLDOGS
- 5 CHARLESTON RIVER DOGS
- 22 ADVENTURE SIGHTSEEING
- 22 CHARLESTON'S FINEST HISTORIC TOURS
- 22 GRAY LINE OF CHARLESTON
- 22 SITES & INSIGHTS TOURS
- 26 GULLAH TOURS

𝕊 SHOPS
- 7 CHARLESTON GARDENS
- 12 MAGAR HATWORKS
- 16 HAUTE DESIGN STUDIO
- 30 BLUE BICYCLE BOOKS
- 31 ALLURE SALON
- 36 SPA ADAGIO
- 38 ARTIST & CRAFTSMAN SUPPLY

ℍ HOTELS
- 8 NOT SO HOSTEL
- 10 ASHLEY INN
- 35 FRANCIS MARION HOTEL

Cool Blow Park

Martins Park

SEE DETAIL

Wragg Mall

UPPER KING

14 ✪ Aiken-Rhett House

34 ✪ College of Charleston

35 ℍ

37 ✪ Marion Square

36 𝕊 Marion Square

38 𝕊 ℕ 39

0   250 yds
0   250 m

DISTANCE ACROSS MAP
Approximate: 2 mi or 3.2 km

SEE MAP 1

To  **1 Colonial Dorchester State Historic Site**

2 A

RICHARDSON AVE

DORCHESTER RD

DOTY AVE

W 5TH N ST

R 4

H 5

MAIN ST

6 R

78

Summerville

Summerville-Dorchester Museum

7

CENTRAL AVE

CAROLINA AVE

8 **Azalea Park**

9TH S ST

BERLIN G MYERS PKM

LINCOLN AVE

9 R
10
Middleton Place

H 11

Ashley River

642

DORCHESTER RD

61

Magnolia Plantation and Gardens

12

13 Drayton Hall

ASHLEY RIVER RD

REES FERRY RD

GLENN MCCONNELL PKY

MAIN RD

17

← To **22 Caw Caw Interpretive Center**

SIGHTS

1 COLONIAL DORCHESTER STATE HISTORIC SITE
7 SUMMERVILLE-DORCHESTER MUSEUM
8 AZALEA PARK
9 MIDDLETON PLACE
12 MAGNOLIA PLANTATION AND GARDENS

13 DRAYTON HALL
15 NORTH CHARLESTON AND AMERICAN LAFRANCE FIRE MUSEUM AND EDUCATIONAL CENTER
19 CHARLESTON NAVY YARD

20 *CSS HUNLEY*
21 MAGNOLIA CEMETERY
22 CAW CAW INTERPRETIVE CENTER
23 CHARLES TOWNE LANDING
30 THE COBURG COW

RESTAURANTS

4 ALEX'S RESTAURANT
6 GUERIN'S PHARMACY
10 MIDDLETON PLACE RESTAURANT

18 EVO PIZZERIA
24 FIERY RON'S HOME TEAM BBQ
25 GENE'S HAUFBRAU

27 GLASS ONION
29 AL DI LA

NIGHTLIFE

17 MADRA RUA IRISH PUB

26 GENE'S HAUFBRAU

28 VOODOO LOUNGE

SPORTS AND ACTIVITIES

2 CAROLINA ICE PALACE
16 SOUTH CAROLINA STINGRAYS

32 CHARLESTON SCUBA
33 WEST ASHLEY GREENWAY

SHOPS

3 THE GUITAR CENTER

14 TANGER OUTLET

31 ESD, ELIZABETH STUART DESIGN

HOTELS

5 WOODLANDS RESORT & INN

11 THE INN AT MIDDLETON PLACE

0   1 mi

0   1 km

DISTANCE ACROSS MAP
Approximate: 13 mi or 21 km

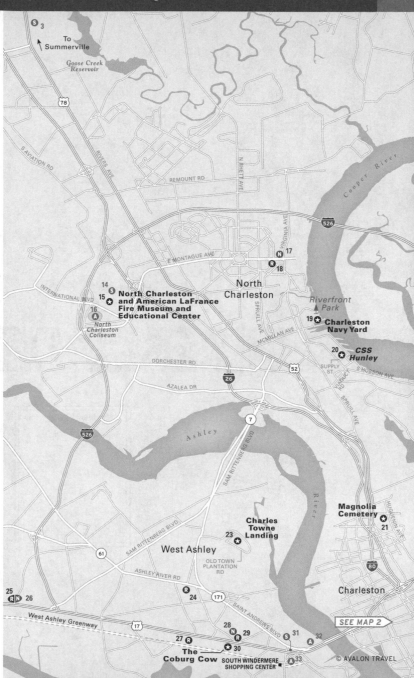

S 3
To Summerville
Goose Creek Reservoir

78

S AVIATION RD

RIVERS AVE

REMOUNT RD

N RHETT AVE

Cooper River

526

E MONTAGUE AVE

VIRGINIA AVE

N 17
R 18

North Charleston

INTERNATIONAL BLVD

14
15 S North Charleston and American LaFrance Fire Museum and Educational Center

16 A
North Charleston Coliseum

SPRUILL AVE

Riverfront Park

19 Charleston Navy Yard

MCMILLAN AVE

20 CSS Hunley

DORCHESTER RD

SUPPLY ST

S HOBSON AVE

26

AZALEA DR

52

VIADUCT RD

SPRUILL AVE

526

Ashley

7

SAM RITTENBERG BLVD

River

Magnolia Cemetery
21

HUGUENIN AVE

Charles Towne Landing

23

West Ashley

OLD TOWN PLANTATION RD

80

61

ASHLEY RIVER RD

R 24   171

Charleston

SAINT ANDREWS BLVD

SEE MAP 2

25
R N 26

West Ashley Greenway   17

28
N R 29

S 31

32

27 R
30
The Coburg Cow   SOUTH WINDERMERE SHOPPING CENTER

A 33

MAP 4

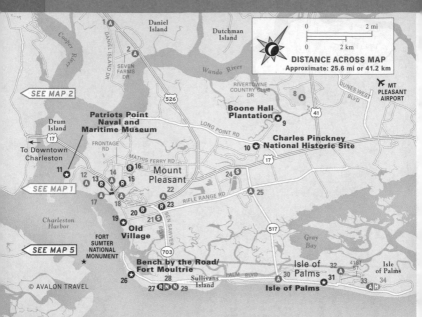

SEE MAP 2

Daniel Island

Dutchman Island

Drum Island

To Downtown Charleston

SEE MAP 1

Patriots Point Naval and Maritime Museum

Mount Pleasant

Charleston Harbor

FORT SUMTER NATIONAL MONUMENT

SEE MAP 5

© AVALON TRAVEL

DISTANCE ACROSS MAP
Approximate: 25.6 mi or 41.2 km

MT PLEASANT AIRPORT

Boone Hall Plantation

Charles Pinckney National Historic Site

Old Village

Bench by the Road/ Fort Moultrie

Sullivans Island

Isle of Palms

Isle of Palms

Isle of Palms

MAP 5

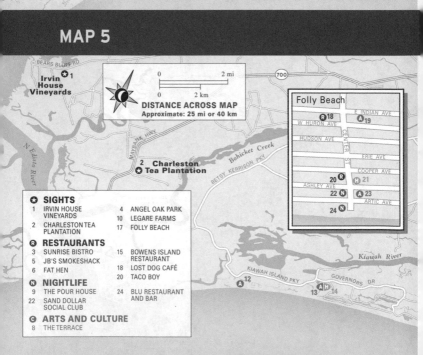

BEARS BLUFF RD

Irvin House Vineyards

DISTANCE ACROSS MAP
Approximate: 25 mi or 40 km

Charleston Tea Plantation

Folly Beach

Bohicket Creek

Kiawah River

KIAWAH ISLAND PKY

GOVERNORS DR

O SIGHTS

1	IRVIN HOUSE VINEYARDS
2	CHARLESTON TEA PLANTATION
4	ANGEL OAK PARK
10	LEGARE FARMS
17	FOLLY BEACH

R RESTAURANTS

3	SUNRISE BISTRO
5	JB'S SMOKESHACK
6	FAT HEN
15	BOWENS ISLAND RESTAURANT
18	LOST DOG CAFÉ
20	TACO BOY
24	BLU RESTAURANT AND BAR

N NIGHTLIFE

9	THE POUR HOUSE
22	SAND DOLLAR SOCIAL CLUB

G ARTS AND CULTURE

8	THE TERRACE

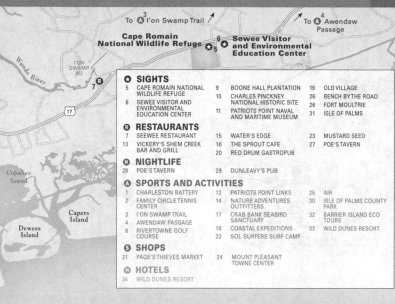

To ❸ I'on Swamp Trail

To ❹ Awendaw Passage

Wando River

I'ON SWAMP RD

Cape Romain National Wildlife Refuge ❺ ❻

Sewee Visitor and Environmental Education Center

17

Copahee Sound

Capers Island

Dewees Island

❶ SIGHTS
- 5 CAPE ROMAIN NATIONAL WILDLIFE REFUGE
- 6 SEWEE VISITOR AND ENVIRONMENTAL EDUCATION CENTER
- 9 BOONE HALL PLANTATION
- 10 CHARLES PINCKNEY NATIONAL HISTORIC SITE
- 11 PATRIOTS POINT NAVAL AND MARITIME MUSEUM
- 19 OLD VILLAGE
- 26 BENCH BY THE ROAD
- 26 FORT MOULTRIE
- 31 ISLE OF PALMS

❶ RESTAURANTS
- 7 SEEWEE RESTAURANT
- 13 VICKERY'S SHEM CREEK BAR AND GRILL
- 15 WATER'S EDGE
- 16 THE SPROUT CAFE
- 20 RED DRUM GASTROPUB
- 23 MUSTARD SEED
- 27 POE'S TAVERN

❶ NIGHTLIFE
- 28 POE'S TAVERN
- 29 DUNLEAVY'S PUB

❶ SPORTS AND ACTIVITIES
- 1 CHARLESTON BATTERY
- 2 FAMILY CIRCLE TENNIS CENTER
- 3 I'ON SWAMP TRAIL
- 4 AWENDAW PASSAGE
- 8 RIVERTOWNE GOLF COURSE
- 12 PATRIOTS POINT LINKS
- 14 NATURE ADVENTURES OUTFITTERS
- 17 CRAB BANK SEABIRD SANCTUARY
- 18 COASTAL EXPEDITIONS
- 22 SOL SURFERS SURF CAMP
- 25 AIR
- 30 ISLE OF PALMS COUNTY PARK
- 32 BARRIER ISLAND ECO TOURS
- 33 WILD DUNES RESORT

❶ SHOPS
- 21 PAGE'S THIEVES MARKET
- 24 MOUNT PLEASANT TOWNE CENTER

❶ HOTELS
- 34 WILD DUNES RESORT

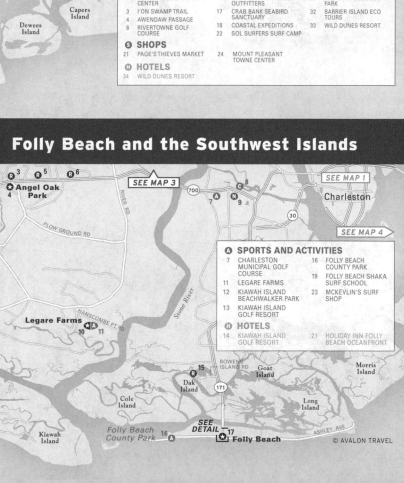

❸ ❺ ❻

Angel Oak Park 4

SEE MAP 3

700

SEE MAP 1

Charleston

RIVER RD

PLOW GROUND RD

30

SEE MAP 4

STONO RIVER

HANSCOMBE PT. RD

Legare Farms 10 11

BOWENS ISLAND RD

Goat Island

Morris Island

15

Oak Island

171

Long Island

Cole Island

Kiawah Island

Folly Beach County Park 16

SEE DETAIL 17

Folly Beach

ASHLEY AVE

© AVALON TRAVEL

❶ SPORTS AND ACTIVITIES
- 7 CHARLESTON MUNICIPAL GOLF COURSE
- 11 LEGARE FARMS
- 12 KIAWAH ISLAND BEACHWALKER PARK
- 13 KIAWAH ISLAND GOLF RESORT
- 16 FOLLY BEACH COUNTY PARK
- 19 FOLLY BEACH SHAKA SURF SCHOOL
- 23 MCKEVLIN'S SURF SHOP

❶ HOTELS
- 14 KIAWAH ISLAND GOLF RESORT
- 21 HOLIDAY INN FOLLY BEACH OCEANFRONT

DISCOVER
Charleston

Everyone who spends time in Charleston comes away with a story to tell about local hospitality. Mine came while walking through the French Quarter and admiring a handsome old single house on Church Street, one of the few that survived the fire of 1775. To my surprise, the woman chatting with a friend nearby turned out to be the homeowner. Noticing my interest, she invited me, a total stranger, inside to check out the progress of her renovation.

To some eyes, Charleston's hospitable nature has bordered on licentiousness. From its earliest days, the city gained a reputation for vice. Charleston's nickname, "The Holy City," derives from the skyline's abundance of church steeples rather than any excess of piety among its citizens.

Don't mistake the Holy City's charm for weakness, however, for within Charleston's velvet glove has always been an iron fist. This is where the colonists scored their first victory over the British in the Revolution. This is the place where the Civil War began. It's the city that survived the East Coast's worst earthquake in 1886 and one of its worst hurricanes a century later.

Charleston is a liberal enclave (by Southern standards, anyway) within a very conservative state. While many visitors come to see the Charleston of Rhett Butler and Pat Conroy, they leave impressed by the diversity of Charlestonian life. It's a cosmopolitan mix of students, professionals, and longtime inhabitants—who discuss the finer points of Civil War history as if it were last year, party on Saturday night like there's no tomorrow, and go to church on Sunday morning dressed in their finest.

Under the carefully honed tradition and the ever-present ancestor worship, Charleston possesses a vitality of vision that is irrepressibly practical and forward-looking.

Clockwise from top left: carriage tour; Arthur Ravenel Jr. bridge; hitching post; aerial view of Charleston.

Stroll through the Battery and view the historic homes.

Planning Your Trip

Neighborhoods

SOUTH OF BROAD

As one of the oldest streets in Charleston, the east-west thoroughfare of Broad Street is not only a physical landmark, it's a mental one as well. The first area of the Charleston peninsula to be settled, the area south of Broad Street—often shortened to the mischievous acronym "SOB" by local wags—features older homes, meandering streets (many of them built on "made land" filling in former wharves), and a distinctly genteel, laid-back feel. It also features more affluent residents, sometimes irreverently referred to as "SOB Snobs."

WATERFRONT

Charleston's waterfront is a place where tourism, history, and industry coexist in a largely seamless fashion. The centerpiece of the harbor area is Waterfront Park, up toward the High Battery. Farther up the Cooper River is Aquarium Wharf, where you'll find the South Carolina Aquarium, the Fort Sumter Visitor Education Center, and the dock where you board the various harbor ferries, whether to Fort Sumter or just for a calming ride on the Cooper River.

FRENCH QUARTER

The French Quarter is Protestant in origin and flavor. Though not actually given the name until a preservation effort in the 1970s, historically this area was the main place of commerce for the city's population of French Huguenots, primarily a merchant class who fled religious persecution in their native country. Today the five-block area—roughly bounded by East Bay, Market Street, Meeting Street, and Broad Street—contains some of

the Dock Street Theatre in the French Quarter

Charleston's most historic buildings, its most evocative old churches and graveyards, its most charming narrow streets, and its most tasteful art galleries.

NORTH OF BROAD

The tourist-heavy part of town that's north of Broad Street is sometimes called the Market Area because of its proximity to the City Market. Its mix of local shops and chains attracts all types, and a four- or five-star restaurant is just a stroll away.

UPPER KING

For many visitors, the area around King Street north of Calhoun Street is the most happening area of Charleston, not only because its proximity to the visitors center makes it the first part of town many see up close. On some days—Saturdays when the farmers market is open, for instance—this bustling, active area of town seems a galaxy away from the quiet grace of the older South of Broad area. Its closeness to the beautiful College of Charleston campus means there's never a shortage of young people around to patronize the area's restaurants and bars and to add a youthful feel. And its closeness to the city's main shopping district, King Street, means there's never a shortage of happy shoppers toting bags of newly purchased merchandise.

HAMPTON PARK

Expansive Hampton Park is a favorite recreation spot for Charlestonians. It's entirely bordered by streets that can be fairly heavily trafficked because this is the main way to get to The Citadel. But the park streets are pedestrian-only Saturday mornings in the spring so people can enjoy themselves without worrying about the traffic.

replica of the CSS *Hunley* outside the Charleston Museum

WEST ASHLEY

Charleston's first postwar automobile suburb, West Ashley also has roots back to the first days of the colony's settlement and was the site of some of the antebellum era's grandest plantations. The biggest draws are the plantations and historic sites along the west bank of the river.

NORTH CHARLESTON

More and more artists and young professionals are choosing to live in North Charleston—actually a separate municipality from Charleston. Some of the most exciting things going on in the metro area are taking place right here. The former U.S. Navy Yard is transforming into a hip mixed-use shopping and residential area, as well as being home to the raised submarine CSS *Hunley*. North Charleston offers a lot for the more adventurous traveler, and, as they're fond of pointing out up here, there aren't any parking meters.

SUMMERVILLE

Summerville got its name for its role as a summer getaway for Charleston's elite, and today it plays the same role as a relaxing day trip from the city.

MOUNT PLEASANT AND EAST COOPER

The main destination in the East Cooper area (the east bank of the Cooper River) is the island of Mount Pleasant, primarily known as a peaceful, fairly affluent suburb of Charleston. Going through Mount Pleasant is the only land route to access Sullivan's Island, Isle of Palms, and historic Fort Moultrie. Shem Creek, which bisects Mount Pleasant, was once the center of the local shrimping industry, and while there aren't nearly as many shrimp boats as there once were, you can still see them docked or on their way to and from a trawling run.

sunset at Folly Beach Pier

FOLLY BEACH AND THE SOUTHWEST ISLANDS

Folly Beach is Charleston's beach town, with the requisite windswept funkiness. James Island and Johns Island are old South, primarily residential areas with deep roots and a surprisingly strong restaurant tradition with an emphasis on hearty Southern classics in humble settings.

HILTON HEAD AND THE LOWCOUNTRY

The Lowcountry's mossy, laid-back pace belies its former status as the heart of American plantation culture and the original cradle of secession. Today it is a mix of history (Beaufort and Bluffton), natural beauty (the ACE Basin), resort development (Hilton Head), military bases (Parris Island), and relaxed beaches (Edisto and Hunting Islands).

When to Go

Springtime is for lovers, and it's no coincidence that springtime is when most love affairs with the region begin. Unless you have severe pollen allergies—not a trivial concern given the explosion of plantlife at this time—you should try to experience this area at its peak of natural beauty during the magical period from mid-March to mid-May. Not surprisingly, lodging is the most expensive and most difficult to secure at that time.

The hardest time to get a room in Charleston is during Spoleto from Memorial Day through mid-June. Hilton Head's busiest time is during the RBC Heritage golf tournament in mid-April. While last-minute cancellations are always possible, the only real guarantee is to secure reservations as far in advance as possible (a full year in advance is not unusual for these peak times).

Spring produces an explosion of blooms in Charleston.

Activity here slows down noticeably in July and August. But overall, summertime in the South gets a bad rap and is often not appreciably worse than summers north of the Mason-Dixon Line—though it's certainly more humid.

My favorite time of year on the southeastern coast is the middle of November, when the tourist crush noticeably subsides. Not only are the days delightful and the nights crisp (but not frigid), but you can also get a room at a good price.

What to Pack

Unless you're coming in the winter to take advantage of lower rates or to enjoy the copious seasonal cheer, there's not much need for a heavy jacket. A sweater or windbreaker will do fine for chillier days. Also note that the ocean and the larger rivers can generate some surprisingly crisp breezes, even on what otherwise might be a warm day.

Because of the area's temperate climate, perspiration is likely to be a constant travel companion; pack accordingly. Whatever you wear, stay with natural fabrics such as cotton. The humidity and generally warm weather combine for a miserable experience with polyester and other synthetic fabrics.

Unless you're coming in the hottest days of summer or the coldest part of winter—both unlikely scenarios—plan on a trip to a drugstore or supermarket to buy some bug spray or Skin So Soft, an Avon product that also keeps away the gnats.

monument in the Battery

The Best of Charleston

Charleston has never lost its abiding respect for social manners and mores or its taste for good food and strong drink. Despite having one well-shod foot firmly in the global future, history is never far away. The city's charms are compact and serendipitous, making it one of the most walkable anywhere. The outskirts contain some of the most interesting chapters in Charleston's long history.

Day 1

Begin your journey in Charleston, the Holy City, named not for its piety but for the steeples in its skyline. First, feel the pulse of the city by going to its bustling heart, Marion Square. Maybe do a little shopping on King Street and at Old City Market afterward. Take a sunset stroll around the Battery and admire Rainbow Row before diving right into a great meal at one of the city's fine restaurants.

Day 2

Today you put your historian's hat on and visit one of Charleston's great house museums, such as the Aiken-Rhett House or the Edmondston-Alston House. Have a hearty Southern-style lunch, then take an afternoon trip to Fort Sumter. After another fantastic Charleston dinner, take a stroll or carriage ride through the French Quarter to close the evening.

Day 3

After a hearty breakfast, make the 20-minute drive over the Ashley River to gorgeous Middleton Place, where you'll tour the gardens. Then stop at adjacent Drayton Hall and see one of the oldest and best-preserved plantation homes in the nation. Make the hour-long drive into Beaufort and spend the afternoon walking around the beautifully preserved historic district.

Southern Cooking: High-Style and Homestyle

Fresh Seafood

The best seafood places put a premium on freshly harvested fish and shellfish.

- **Bowens Island Restaurant,** Charleston—Gloriously unpretentious.
- **39 Rue de Jean,** Charleston—Amazing mussels and fish.
- **Red Fish,** Hilton Head Island—Stylish but always fresh.
- **Saltus River Grill,** Beaufort—Meeting and eating place.

New Southern

The area is home to some adventurous chefs offering an updated take on Low-country classics.

- **FIG,** Charleston—Three words: tomato tarte tatin.
- **McCrady's,** Charleston—Chef Sean Brock's creations are almost too good to be true.
- **Glass Onion,** Charleston—Farm-to-table goodness in an informal setting.

Classic Southern

Your best bets for fine old-school Southern cooking:

- **Hominy Grill,** Charleston—Comfort-food hit with locals and visitors alike.
- **See Wee Restaurant,** Charleston—Possibly the best she-crab soup on the planet.
- **Dixie Supply Bakery & Café,** Charleston—Diner-style brunch faves.

Barbecue

The pleasures of the pig are never far away in this region. Here are the best coastal 'cue joints:

- **Fiery Ron's Home Team BBQ,** Charleston—My favorite barbecue spot in the world, believe it or not.
- **JB's Smokeshack,** Charleston—Lowcountry classic on James Island.
- **Po Pigs Bo-B-Q,** Edisto Island—Great 'cue on a friendly island.

Fiery Ron's Home Team BBQ

Drayton Hall

Day 4

Go over the bridge 15 minutes to St. Helena Island and visit historic Penn Center. From there, drive on to nearby Hunting Island State Park, where you can climb the lighthouse and enjoy the beach. A half hour away, make a late-afternoon stop in Old Bluffton to shop for art, see the beautiful Church of the Cross on the May River, and have a light dinner.

African American Heritage

The cities and Sea Islands of the Lowcountry are integral to a full understanding of the experience of African Americans in the South. More than that, they are living legacies, with a thriving culture—called Gullah in South Carolina—whose roots can be traced directly back to West Africa. For a deeper look, try a guided African American history tour of downtown Charleston.

South of Broad

Make sure to walk by Cabbage Row, inspiration for "Catfish Row" of the African American-themed George Gershwin opera *Porgy and Bess.*

Waterfront

Take the ferry out to Fort Sumter, where the Civil War began. From the fort you can see nearby undeveloped Morris Island, scene of the 1863 Battle of Battery Wagner. That battle included the first all-African American regiment in the U.S. Army, the 54th Massachusetts, whose tale was recounted in the film *Glory.*

the historic Aiken-Rhett House

French Quarter

Visit the Old Slave Mart Museum and learn more about the Middle Passage and how Charleston's African American population overcame the legacy of slavery.

North of Broad

Shop in Old City Market; it never hosted a slave auction, but during its heyday, it was home to a number of African American entrepreneurs and vendors.

Upper King

At the College of Charleston, browse the research library at the Avery Research Center, one of the main repositories of Gullah culture and history.

Visit the wrought-iron garden of the noted Charleston artisan Philip Simmons.

Tour the Aiken-Rhett House, with its excellently and respectfully preserved artifacts of the African American servants who made the historic property run.

West Ashley

Visit Drayton Hall; take the guided tour and pay respects at the African American cemetery.

Hilton Head and the Lowcountry

While walking around Beaufort's scenic historic district, visit the Robert Smalls House, home of this African American Civil War hero, as well as his burial site at the Tabernacle Baptist Church. Drive by the Barners Barnwell Sams House to see where Harriet Tubman worked as a nurse and helped ferry slaves to freedom on the Underground Railroad. Visit

Beaufort National Cemetery and see the memorial to the African American troops of the 54th and 55th Massachusetts Regiments of the U.S. Army in the Civil War.

Make the short drive to St. Helena Island and visit the campus of the Penn Center, a key clearinghouse for the study and celebration of Gullah culture and the site of activism by Martin Luther King Jr. in the 1960s.

Head on into Hilton Head, stop by the Coastal Discovery Museum, and take an African American heritage tour, visiting the site of Mitchelville, the first community of freed slaves in the United States. An alternate plan is to make the trip inland to Walterboro to visit the Tuskegee Airmen Memorial at the regional airport.

Civil War History

Throughout the region there are plenty of military history sites that highlight the Civil War era.

- Take the ferry out to **Fort Sumter,** where the Civil War began.

- There is also **Fort Moultrie,** which hosted a young Edgar Allan Poe in the years prior to the war.

- See the newly raised **CSS *Hunley*** at the decommissioned Navy Yard (only open Friday-Saturday).

- Visit historic **Drayton Hall,** the country's oldest standing plantation home, saved from the torch only because Union troops thought it might have been used to quarantine smallpox victims.

- Beaufort served as a medical center for Union occupation troops, who even used **St. Helena's Episcopal Church** as a hospital.

Fort Moultrie

Romance by the Sea

Spanish moss, friendly beaches, sunsets over the water, sultry weather, moonlit carriage rides—what more could you ask for? The Lowcountry pretty much wrote the book on romantic getaways. Here's a starter list of the most romantic spots.

Charleston

- Romantic B&Bs include the John Rutledge House and Two Meeting Street.
- Enjoy a quiet Italian dinner at Il Cortile del Re or a fantastic Southern dinner at Circa 1886.
- Don't forget a carriage ride or art gallery stroll through the French Quarter.
- Shopping can be sexy! Visit the great stores on King Street.

Hilton Head and the Lowcountry

- Stroll through the walkable, picturesque Beaufort Historic District.
- Visit the driftwood beach on nearby Hunting Island State Park and enjoy the stunning views from the top of the lighthouse.
- Edisto Island is a wonderful place for a relaxing, quiet, no-hassle beach getaway.

Kayaker's Weekend

The Charleston area is framed by the largest contiguous salt marsh in the world. It's not only a kayaker's paradise, but an amazing natural habitat for indigenous and migratory birds. This weekend trip hits the green highlights.

Day 1

Begin at the Cape Romain National Wildlife Refuge north of Charleston. Bulls Island and Capers Island are highlights of this largely maritime preserve, which comprises 66,000 acres of kayaking opportunities. If you're in town October-March, bird-watchers can visit the 22-acre Crab Bank Heritage Preserve in Charleston Harbor. Tonight relax over a world-class dinner in Charleston's downtown.

Day 2

Today's a full day for kayaking in the ACE Basin, comprising the estuaries of the Ashepoo, Combahee, and Edisto Rivers (the last being the largest and most traveled). Public landings and guided tours abound for trips on these nearly pristine blackwater runs. Serious bird-watchers can visit the Bear Island and Donnelly Wildlife Management Areas within the ACE Basin, as well as at the impounded rice paddies at the Ernest F. Hollings ACE Basin National Wildlife Refuge.

Sights

25

...sur-roundings ... with beautiful views of Cha... for a breathtaking morning (page 28).

★ **Most Colorful Stroll:** Painted in warm pastels, the old merchant homes of **Rainbow Row** near the cobblestone waterfront take you on a journey to Charleston's antebellum heyday (page 30).

★ **Wettest History Lesson:** Hop on the ferry to historic **Fort Sumter National Monument,** where the Civil War began, and take in the gorgeous views along the way (page 38).

★ **Likeliest Place to Think You've Seen a Ghost:** A sublime sanctuary and two historic graveyards await you at **St. Philip's Episcopal Church** in the heart of the French Quarter (page 44).

★ **Best Audio Tour:** There are more ostentatious house museums in Charleston, but none that provide such an intact glimpse into antebellum life as the **Aiken-Rhett House** (page 52).

★ **Best Guided Tour:** Don't miss Charleston's oldest surviving plantation home, **Drayton Hall,** and one of the country's best examples of professional historic preservation (page 55).

★ **Most Inspiring Landscape:** Marvel at one of the world's most beautiful gardens, **Middleton Place,** the first landscaped garden in North America (page 58).

★ **"How Did They Do That?" Moment:** Ensconced in a special preservation tank and available for public viewing, the **CSS *Hunley*** was the first submarine to sink a ship in battle and remains a moving example of bravery and sacrifice (page 63).

One of America's oldest cities and an early national center of arts and culture, Charleston's legendary taste for the high life is matched by its forward-thinking outlook. The birthplace of the Civil War is not just a city of museums resting on its historic laurels. Situated on a hallowed spit of land known as "the peninsula," the Holy City is now a vibrant, creative hub of the New South.

Though most key sights in Charleston do indeed have some tie to the city's rich history, house museums are only a subset of the attractions here. Charleston's sights are excellently integrated into its built environment, and often the enjoyment of nearby gardens or a lapping river is part of the fun.

Although one could easily spend a lifetime enjoying the history and attractions of Charleston itself, there are many unique experiences to be had in the less-developed areas surrounding the city. Generally there are two types of vibes in these areas: isolated close-knit communities with little overt development (although that's changing) or private resort-style communities set amid stunning natural beauty.

Because of the city's small, fairly centralized layout, the best way to experience downtown Charleston is on foot—either yours or via hooves of an equine nature. Thankfully, there's a wide variety of walking and carriage tours for you to choose from. The sheer number and breadth of tour options in Charleston is beyond the scope of this guide. For a full selection of available tours, visit the **Charleston Visitor Reception and Transportation Center** (375 Meeting St., 800/774-0006, www.charlestoncvb.com, Mon.-Fri.

Previous: Pineapple Fountain in Waterfront Park; Rainbow Row.

8:30am-5pm), where they have entire walls of brochures for all the latest tours, with local tourism experts on-site.

South of Broad

Map 1

Wander among these narrow streets and marvel at the lovingly restored old homes, but keep in mind that almost everything down here is in private hands. Don't wander into a garden or take photos inside a window unless you're invited to do so (and given Charleston's legendary hospitality, that can happen). This residential area has no nightlife to speak of and gets almost eerily quiet after hours.

★ The Battery

For many, the Battery is the single most iconic Charleston spot, drenched in history and boasting dramatic views in all directions. A look to the south gives you the sweeping expanse of the Cooper River, with views of Fort Sumter, Castle Pinckney, Sullivan's Island, and, off to the north, the old carrier *Yorktown* moored at Mount Pleasant. A landward look gives you a view of the adjoining, peaceful **White Point Gardens,** the sumptuous mansions lining South and East Battery, and a beguiling peek behind them into some of the oldest neighborhoods in Charleston.

But if you had been one of the first European visitors to this tip of the peninsula about 400 years ago, you'd have seen how it got its first name, Oyster Point: This entire area was once home to an enormous outcropping of oysters. Their shells glistened bright white in the harsh Southern sun as a ship approached from sea, hence its subsequent name, White Point. Although the oysters are long gone and much of the area you're walking on is actually reclaimed marsh, the Battery and White Point Gardens are still a balm for the soul.

Once the bustling (and sometimes seedy) heart of Charleston's maritime activity, the Battery was where "the gentleman pirate" Stede Bonnet and 21 of his men were hanged in 1718. As you might imagine, the area got its name for hosting cannons during the War of 1812, with the current distinctive seawall structure built in the 1850s.

Contrary to popular belief, no guns fired from here on Fort Sumter, as they would have been out of range. However, many thankfully inoperable cannons, mortars, and piles of shot still reside here, much to the delight of kids of all ages. This is where Charlestonians gathered in a giddy, party-like atmosphere to watch the shelling of Fort Sumter in 1861, blissfully ignorant of the horrors to come. A short time later the North would return the favor, as the Battery and all of Charleston up to Broad Street would bear the brunt of shelling during the long siege of the city (the rest was out of reach of Union guns).

But now, the Battery is a place to relax, not fight. The relaxation starts with the fact that there's usually plenty of free parking all along Battery Street. A promenade all around the periphery is a great place to stroll or jog. Add the calming, almost constant sea breeze and the meditative influence of the wide, blue Cooper River and you'll see why this land's end—once so martial in nature—is now a favorite place for after-church family gatherings, travelers, love-struck couples, and weddings (about 200 a year at the gazebo in White Point Gardens).

Still, military history is never far away in Charleston, and one of the chief landmarks at the Battery is the USS *Hobson* Memorial, which remembers the sacrifice of the men of that vessel when it sank after a collision with the carrier USS *Wasp* in 1952.

Look for the three-story private residence where East Battery curves northward. You won't be taking any tours of it, but you should be aware that it's the **DeSaussure House** (1 E. Battery St.), best known in Charleston history for hosting rowdy, celebratory crowds on the roof and the piazzas to watch the 34-hour shelling of Fort Sumter in 1861.

MAP 1: S. Battery St. and Murray Blvd., 843/724-7321; daily 24 hours; free

Edmondston-Alston House

The most noteworthy single attraction on the Battery is the 1825 Edmondston-Alston House, the only Battery home open to the public for tours. This is one of the most unique and well-preserved historic homes in the United States, thanks to the ongoing efforts of the Alston family, who acquired the house from shipping merchant Charles Edmondston for $15,500 after the Panic of 1837 and still lives on the third floor (tours only visit the first two stories).

Over 90 percent of the home's furnishings are original items from the Alston era, a percentage that's almost unheard of in the world of house museums. (Currently the house is owned and administered by the Middleton Place Foundation, best known for its stewardship of Middleton Place along the Ashley River.) You can still see the original paper bag used to store the house's deeds and mortgages. There's also a copy of South Carolina's Ordinance of Secession and some interesting memorabilia from the golden days of Race Week, that time in February when all of Charleston society came out to bet on horses, carouse, and show off their finery. The Edmondston-Alston House has withstood storms, fires, earthquakes, and Yankee shelling, due in no small part to its sturdy construction; its masonry walls are two bricks thick, and it features both interior and exterior shutters. Originally built in the Federal style, second owner Charles Alston added several Greek Revival elements, notably the parapet, balcony, and piazza, from which General P. G. T. Beauregard watched the attack on Fort Sumter.

MAP 1: 21 E. Battery St., 843/722-7171, www.edmondstonalston.com; Tues.-Sat. 10am-4:30pm, Sun.-Mon. 1:30pm-4:30pm; $12 adults, $8 students

Know Your Charleston Houses

a joggling board

Charleston's homes boast not only a long pedigree but an interesting and unique one as well. Here are the basics of local architecture:

Single House: Thus named for its single-room width. With full-length piazzas, or long verandas, on the south side to take advantage of breezes, the single house is perhaps the nation's first sustainable house design. The house is lengthwise on the lot, with the entrance on the side. This means the "backyard" is actually the side yard. Church Street has great examples, including 90, 92, and 94

Church Street, and the oldest single house in town, the 1730 Robert Brewton House (71 Church St.).

Double House: This layout is two rooms wide with a central hallway and a porched facade facing the street. Double houses often had separate carriage houses. The Aiken-Rhett and Heyward-Washington Houses are good examples.

Charleston Green: This uniquely Charlestonian color—extremely dark green that looks pitch-black in low light—has its roots in the aftermath of the Civil War. The government distrib-

★ Rainbow Row

At 79-107 East Bay Street, between Tradd and Elliot Streets, is one of the most photographed sights in the United States: colorful Rainbow Row. The reason for its name becomes obvious when you see the array of pastel-colored mansions, all facing the Cooper River. The bright, historically accurate colors—nine of them, to be exact—are one of the many vestiges you'll see around town of Charleston's Caribbean heritage, a legacy of the English settlers from the colony of Barbados who were among the city's first citizens.

The homes are unusually old for this fire-, hurricane-, and earthquake-ravaged city, with most dating from 1730 to 1750. As you admire Rainbow Row from across East Battery, you're actually walking on what used to be water. These houses were originally right on the Cooper River, their lower stories serving as storefronts on the wharf. The street was created later on top of landfill, or "made land" as it's called locally. Besides its grace and beauty, Rainbow Row is of vital importance to American historic preservation. These were the first Charleston homes to be renovated and

uted surplus black paint to contribute to the reconstruction of the ravaged peninsula, but Charlestonians were too proud to use it as-is. So they added a tiny bit of yellow, producing Charleston green.

Earthquake Bolt: Due to structural damage after the 1886 earthquake, many buildings were retrofitted with one or more wall-to-wall iron rods to keep the house stable. The rod was capped at both ends by a "gib plate," often disguised with a decorative element such as a lion's head, an S or X shape, or some other design. Notable examples are at 235 Meeting Street, 198 East Bay Street, 407 King Street, and 51 East Battery (a rare star design); 190 East Bay Street is unusual for having both an X and an S plate on the same building.

Joggling Board: This long (10-15 ft.) flexible plank of cypress, palm, or pine with a handle at each end served various recreational purposes. Babies were bounced to sleep, small children used it as a trampoline, and it was also a method of courtship. A couple would start out at opposite ends and bounce until they met in the middle.

Carolopolis Award: The Preservation Society of Charleston hands out these badges, to be mounted near the doorway, to local homeowners who have renovated historic properties downtown. On the award is "Carolopolis," the Latinized name of the city; "Condita AD 1670," the Latin word for "founding" with the date of Charleston's inception; and the date the award was given.

Ironwork: Wrought iron was a widely used ornament before the mid-1800s. Charleston's best-known blacksmith, Philip Simmons, worked in wrought iron. His masterpieces are visible most notably at the Philip Simmons Garden (91 Anson St.), a gate for the Visitors Center (375 Meeting St.), and the Philip Simmons Children's Garden at Josiah Smith Tennent House (Blake St. and E. Bay St.). Chevaux-de-frise are iron bars on top of a wall that project menacing spikes. They became popular after the Denmark Vesey slave revolt conspiracy of 1822. The best example is at the Miles Brewton House (27 King St.).

brought back from early-20th-century seediness. The restoration projects on Rainbow Row directly inspired the creation of the Preservation Society of Charleston, the first such group in the United States.

Continue walking up the High Battery past Rainbow Row and find Water Street. This aptly named little avenue was in fact a creek in the early days, acting as the southern border of the original walled city. The large brick building on the seaward side housing the Historic Charleston Foundation sits on the site of the old Granville bastion, a key defensive point in the wall.

MAP 1: 79-107 E. Bay St.

Nathaniel Russell House

Considered one of Charleston's grandest homes despite being built by an outsider from Rhode Island, the Nathaniel Russell House is now a National Historic Landmark and one of the country's best examples of neoclassicism. Built in 1808 for the then-princely sum of $80,000 by Nathaniel Russell, aka

"King of the Yankees," the home is furnished as accurately as possible to represent not only the lifestyle of the Russell family but also the 18 African American servants who shared the premises. The house was eventually bought by the Allston family, who amid the poverty of the Civil War and Reconstruction decided in 1870 to sell it to the Sisters of Charity of Our Lady of Mercy for use as a school for young Catholic women.

Restorationists have identified 22 layers of paint within the home, which barely survived a tornado in 1811, got away with only minimal damage in the 1886 earthquake, and was damaged extensively by Hurricane Hugo in 1989 (and has since been repaired). As with fine antebellum homes throughout coastal South Carolina and Georgia, the use of faux finishes is prevalent throughout, mimicking surfaces such as marble, wood, and lapis lazuli. Visitors are often most impressed by the Nathaniel Russell House's magnificent "flying" spiral staircase, a work of such sublime carpentry and engineering that it needs no external support, twisting upward of its own volition.

When you visit, keep in mind that you're in the epicenter of not only Charleston's historic preservation movement but perhaps the nation's as well. In 1955, the Nathaniel Russell House was the first major project of the Historic Charleston Foundation, which raised $65,000 to purchase it. Two years later, admission fees from the house would support Historic Charleston's groundbreaking revolving fund for preservation, the prototype for many such successful programs. For an extra $6, you can gain admission to the Aiken-Rhett House farther uptown, also administered by the Historic Charleston Foundation.

MAP 1: 51 Meeting St., 843/724-8481, www.historiccharleston.org; Mon.-Sat. 10am-5pm, Sun. 2pm-5pm, last tour begins 4:30pm; $12 adults, $5 children

Calhoun Mansion

The single largest of Charleston's surviving grand homes, the 1876 Calhoun Mansion boasts 35 opulent rooms (with 23 fireplaces!) in a striking Italianate design taking up a whopping 24,000 square feet. The grounds feature some charming garden spaces. A 90-minute "grand tour" is available for $50 per person; call for an appointment. Though the interiors at this privately run house are packed with antiques and furnishings, not all of them are accurate for the period.

MAP 1: 16 Meeting St., 843/722-8205, www.calhounmansion.net; tours daily 11am-5pm; $15

Miles Brewton House

A short distance from the Nathaniel Russell House but much less viewed by visitors, the circa-1769 Miles Brewton House, now a private residence, is maybe the best example of Georgian-Palladian architecture in the world. The almost medieval wrought-iron fencing, or *chevaux-de-frise*, was added in 1822 after rumors of a slave uprising spread through town. This imposing double house was the site of not one but two headquarters of occupying armies, that of British general Henry Clinton in the Revolution and the federal garrison after the end of the Civil War. The great Susan Pringle Frost, principal founder of the Preservation Society of Charleston and a Brewton descendant, grew up here.

MAP 1: 27 King St.

Heyward-Washington House

The Heyward-Washington House takes the regional practice of naming a historic home for the two most significant names in its pedigree to its logical extreme. Built in 1772 by the father of Declaration of Independence signer Thomas Heyward Jr., the house also hosted George Washington during the president's visit to Charleston in 1791. It's now owned and operated by the Charleston Museum. The main attraction at the Heyward-Washington House is its masterful woodwork, exemplified by the cabinetry of legendary Charleston carpenter Thomas Elfe. You'll see his work all over the house, from the mantles to a Chippendale chair. Look for his signature, a figure eight with four diamonds.

MAP 1: 87 Church St., 843/722-0354, www.charlestonmuseum.org; Mon.-Sat. 10am-5pm, Sun. 1pm-5pm; $10 adults, $5 children, combo tickets to Charleston Museum and Manigault House available

Cabbage Row

You know the addresses that make up Cabbage Row better as "Catfish Row" in Gershwin's opera *Porgy and Bess* (itself based on the book *Porgy* by the great Charleston author DuBose Heyward, who lived at 76 Church St.). Today this complex—which once housed 10 families—next to the Heyward-Washington House is certainly upgraded from years past, but the row still has the humble appeal of the tenement housing it once was, primarily for freed African American slaves after the Civil War. The house nearby at 94 Church Street was where John C. Calhoun and others drew up the infamous Nullification Acts that eventually led to the South's secession.

MAP 1: 89-91 Church St.

St. Michael's Episcopal Church

The oldest church in South Carolina, St. Michael's Episcopal Church is actually the second sanctuary on this spot. The first church here was made out of black cypress and was called St. Philip's, or "the English Church," which was later rebuilt on Church Street. Although the designer is not known, we do know that work on this sanctuary in the style of Christopher Wren began in 1752 as a response to the overflowing congregation at the rebuilt St. Philip's, and it didn't finish until 1761. Other than a small addition on the southeast corner in 1883, the St. Michael's you see today is virtually unchanged, including the massive pulpit, outsized in the style of the time.

Services here over the years hosted such luminaries as the Marquis de Lafayette, George Washington, and Robert E. Lee, the latter two of whom are known to have sat in the "governor's pew." Two signers of the U.S.

Clockwise from top left: garden of the Nathaniel Russell House; monument at the Battery; Rainbow Row.

Constitution, John Rutledge and Charles Cotesworth Pinckney, are buried in the sanctuary. The 186-foot steeple, painted black during the Revolution in a futile effort to disguise it from British guns, actually sank eight inches after the earthquake of 1886. Inside the tower, the famous "bells of St. Michael's" have an interesting story to tell, having made seven transatlantic voyages for a variety of reasons. They were forged in London's Whitechapel Foundry and sent over in 1764, only to be brought back as a war prize during the Revolution, after which they were returned to the church. Damaged during the Civil War, they were sent back to the foundry of their birth to be recast and returned to Charleston. In 1989 they were damaged by Hurricane Hugo, sent back to Whitechapel yet again, and returned to St. Michael's in 1993. Throughout the life span of the bells, the clock tower has continued to tell time, although the minute hand wasn't added until 1849.

St. Michael's offers informal, free guided tours to visitors after Sunday services; contact the greeter for more information.

MAP 1: 71 Broad St., 843/723-0603; services Sun. 8am and 10:30am, tours available after services

Four Corners of Law

No guidebook is complete without a mention of the famous intersection of Broad and Meeting Streets, nicknamed "Four Corners of Law" for its confluence of federal law (the Post Office building), state law (the state courthouse), municipal law (City Hall), and God's law (St. Michael's Episcopal Church). The phrase "Four Corners of Law" was actually popularized by *Ripley's Believe It or Not!* Still, there's no doubt that this intersection has been key to Charleston from the beginning. Meeting Street was laid out around 1672 and takes its name from the White Meeting House of early Dissenters, meaning non-Anglicans. Broad Street was also referred to as Cooper Street in the early days. Right in the middle of the street once stood the very first statue in the United States, a figure of William Pitt erected in 1766.

MAP 1: Broad St. and Meeting St.

Waterfront

Map 1

The Old Exchange and Provost Dungeon

The Old Exchange and Provost Dungeon at the intersection of East Bay and Meeting Streets is absolutely brimming with history. The last building erected by the British before the American Revolution, it's also one of the three most historically significant colonial buildings in the United States, along with Philadelphia's Independence Hall and Boston's Faneuil Hall.

This is actually the former Royal Exchange and Custom House, the cellar of which served as a British prison. The complex was built in 1771 over a portion of the original 1698 seawall, a portion of which you can see today during the short but fascinating tour of the "dungeon" (actually built

The Great Charleston Earthquake

The Charleston peninsula is bordered by three faults: the Woodstock Fault above North Charleston, the Charleston Fault running along the east bank of the Cooper River, and the Ashley Fault to the west of the Ashley River. On August 31, 1886, one of them buckled, causing one of the most damaging earthquakes ever to hit the United States.

The earthquake of 1886 was signaled by foreshocks earlier that week. Residents of Summerville, 20 miles up the Ashley River, felt a small earthquake after midnight on Friday, August 27. Most slept through it. But soon after dawn a larger shock came, complete with a loud bang, causing many to run outside their houses. That Saturday afternoon another tremor hit Summerville, breaking windows and throwing a bed against a wall in one home. Still, Charlestonians remained unconcerned. Then, that Tuesday at 9:50pm came the big one. With an epicenter somewhere near the Middleton Place Plantation, the Charleston earthquake is estimated to have measured about 7 on the Richter scale. Tremors were felt across half the country, with the ground shaking in Chicago and a church damaged in Indianapolis. A dam 120 miles away in Aiken gave way, washing a train off the tracks. Cracks opened up parallel to the Ashley River, with part of the riverbank falling into the water. Thousands of chimneys all over the state fell or were rendered useless. A Charleston minister at his summer home in Asheville, North Carolina, described a noise like the sound of wheels driving straight up the mountain, followed by the sound of many railroad cars going by. A moment later, one corner of his house lifted off the ground and slammed back down again. The quake brought a series of "sand blows," a phenomenon where craters open and spew sand and water into the air. In Charleston's case, some of the craters were 20 feet wide, shooting debris another 20 feet into the air. The whole event lasted less than a minute.

In crowded Charleston, the damage was horrific: over 2,000 buildings destroyed, a quarter of the city's value gone, 27 killed immediately and almost 100 more to die from injuries and disease. Because of the large numbers of newly homeless, tent cities sprang up in every available park and green space. The American Red Cross's first field mission soon brought some relief, but the scarcity of food, and especially fresh water, made life difficult.

Almost every surviving building had experienced structural damage, in some cases severe. This led to the widespread use of the "earthquake bolt" now seen throughout older Charleston homes. Essentially acting as a very long screw with a washer on each end, the idea of the earthquake bolt is simple: Poke a long iron rod through two walls that need stabilizing, and cap the ends. Charleston being Charleston, the caps were often decorated with a pattern or symbol.

The seismic activity of Charleston's earthquake was so intense that more than 300 aftershocks occurred in the 35 years after the event. Geologists think that most seismic events measured in the region today—including a large event in December 2008, centered near Summerville—are probably also aftershocks.

as a warehouse). Three of Charleston's four signers of the Declaration of Independence did time downstairs for sedition against the crown. Later, happier times were experienced in the ballroom upstairs, as it was here that the state selected its delegates to the Continental Congress and ratified the U.S. Constitution; it's also where George Washington took a spin on the dance floor during his raucous "Farewell Tour" in 1791. While the highlight for most is the basement dungeon, or provost, where the infamous "gentleman pirate" Stede Bonnet was imprisoned in 1718 before being hanged, visitors shouldn't miss the sunny upstairs ballroom and its selection of Washington-oriented history.

MAP 1: 122 E. Bay St., 843/727-2165, www.oldexchange.com; daily 9am-5pm; $10 adults, $5 children and students

Waterfront Park

Dubbing it "this generation's gift to the future," Mayor Joe Riley made this eight-acre project another part of his downtown renovation. Situated on Concord Street roughly between Exchange Street and Vendue Range, Waterfront Park was, like many waterfront locales in Charleston, built on what used to be marsh and water. This particularly massive chunk of "made land" juts about a football field's length farther out than the old waterline. Visitors and locals alike enjoy the relaxing vista of Charleston Harbor, often from the many swinging benches arranged in an unusual front-to-back, single-file pattern all down the pier. On the end you can find viewing binoculars to see the various sights out on the Cooper River, chief among them the USS *Yorktown* at Patriots Point and the big bridge to Mount Pleasant. Children will enjoy the large "Vendue" wading fountain at the park's entrance off Vendue Range, while a bit farther south is the large and quite artful Pineapple Fountain with its surrounding wading pool. Contemporary art lovers of all ages will appreciate the nearby **Waterfront Park City Gallery** (34 Prioleau St., www.citygalleryatwaterfrontpark.com, Mon.-Fri. noon-5pm, free).

MAP 1: Concord St., 843/724-7327; daily dawn-dusk; free

South Carolina Aquarium

If you've been to the more expansive aquariums in Monterey or Boston, you might be disappointed at the breadth of offerings at the South Carolina Aquarium. But nonetheless, it's clean and well done and is a great place for the whole family to have some fun while getting educated about the rich aquatic life off the coast and throughout this small but ecologically diverse state.

When you enter you're greeted with the 15,000-gallon Carolina Seas tank, with placid nurse sharks and vicious-looking moray eels. Other exhibits highlight the five key South Carolina ecosystems: beach, salt marsh, coastal plain, piedmont, and mountain forest. Another neat display is the Touch Tank, a hands-on collection of invertebrates found along the coast, such as sea urchins and horseshoe crabs. The pièce de résistance, however, is

Mayor Joe's Legacy

Few cities anywhere have been as greatly influenced by one mayor as Charleston has by Joseph P. "Joe" Riley, reelected in November 2011 to his 10th four-year term (he swears this will be his last). "Mayor Joe," or just "Joe," as he's usually called, is not only responsible for the majority of redevelopment in the city, he continues to set the bar for its award-winning tourism industry.

Riley won his first mayoral race at the age of 32, the second Irish American mayor of the city. The lawyer, Citadel grad, and former member of the state legislature had a clear vision for his administration: to bring unprecedented numbers of women and minorities into city government, rejuvenate then-seedy King Street, and enlarge the city's tax base by annexing surrounding areas (during Riley's tenure the city has grown from 16.7 square miles to over 100).

Here's only a partial list of the major projects and events Mayor Joe has made happen in Charleston:

- Charleston Maritime Center
- Charleston Place
- Children's Museum of the Lowcountry
- Hampton Park rehabilitation
- King Street-Market Street retail district
- Mayor Joseph P. Riley Ballpark (named after the mayor at the insistence of city council, over his objections)
- MOJA Arts Festival
- Piccolo Spoleto
- South Carolina Aquarium
- Spoleto USA
- Waterfront Park
- West Ashley Bikeway & Greenway

certainly the three-story Great Ocean Tank with its hundreds of deeper-water marine creatures, including sharks, puffer fish, and sea turtles. Speaking of sea turtles: A key part of the aquarium's research and outreach efforts is the Turtle Hospital, which attempts to rehabilitate and save sick and injured specimens. The hospital has so far saved 20 sea turtles, the first one being a 270-pound female affectionately known as "Edisto Mama."

MAP 1: 100 Aquarium Wharf, 843/720-1990, www.scaquarium.org; Mar.-Aug. daily 9am-5pm, Sept.-Feb. daily 9am-4pm; $24.95 adults, $17.95 children, 4D film extra, combo tickets with Fort Sumter tour available

★ Fort Sumter National Monument

This is it: the place that brought about the beginning of the Civil War, a Troy for modern times. Though many historians insist the war would have happened regardless of President Lincoln's decision to keep Fort Sumter in federal hands, nonetheless the stated casus belli was Major Robert Anderson's refusal to surrender the fort when requested to do so in the early morning hours of April 12, 1861. A few hours later came the first shot of the war, fired from Fort Johnson by Confederate captain George James. That 10-inch mortar shell, a signal for the general bombardment to begin, exploded above Fort Sumter, and nothing in Charleston, or the South, or the United States, would ever be the same again. Notorious secessionist Edmund Ruffin gets credit for firing the first shot in anger, only moments after James's signal shell, from a battery at Cummings Point. Ruffin's 64-pound projectile scored a direct hit, smashing into the fort's southwest corner. The first return shot from Fort Sumter was fired by none other than Captain Abner Doubleday, the man once credited as the father of baseball. The first death of the Civil War also happened at Fort Sumter—not during the Confederate bombardment, but on the day after. U.S. Army private Daniel Hough died when the cannon he was loading, to be fired as part of a 100-gun surrender salute to the Stars and Stripes, exploded prematurely. Today the battered but still-standing Fort Sumter remains astride the entrance to Charleston Harbor on an artificial 70,000-ton sandbar. Sumter was part of the so-called Third System of fortifications ordered after the War of 1812. Interestingly, the fort was still not quite finished when the Confederate guns opened up on it 50 years later, and it never enjoyed its intended full complement of 135 big guns.

As you might expect, you can only visit by boat, specifically those run by the approved concessionaire **Fort Sumter Tours** (843/881-7337, www.fortsumtertours.com, $18 adults, $11 ages 6-11, $16 seniors). Once at the fort, there's no charge for admission. Ferries leave from Liberty Square at Aquarium Wharf on the peninsula three times a day during the high season (Apr.-Oct.); call or check the website for times. Make sure to arrive about 30 minutes before the ferry departs. You can also get to Fort Sumter by ferry from Patriots Point at Mount Pleasant through the same concessionaire.

Budget at least 2.5 hours for the whole trip, including an hour at Fort Sumter. At Liberty Square on the peninsula is the **Fort Sumter Visitor Education Center** (340 Concord St., www.nps.gov/fosu, daily 8:30am-5pm, free), so you can learn more about where you're about to go. Once at the fort, you can be enlightened by the regular ranger talks on the fort's history and construction (generally at 11am and 2:30pm), take in the interpretive exhibits throughout the site, and enjoy the view of the spires of the Holy City from afar. For many, though, the highlight is the boat trip itself, with beautiful views of Charleston Harbor and the islands of the Cooper River estuary. If you want to skip Sumter, you can still take an enjoyable 90-minute ferry ride around the harbor and past the fort on the affiliated **Spiritline Cruises** (800/789-3678, www.spiritlinecruises.com, $20 adults, $12 ages 6-11). Ferries depart from Liberty Square at Aquarium Wharf on the peninsula. Purchase tickets at the visitors center.

Some visitors are disappointed to find many of the fort's gun embrasures bricked over. This was done during the Spanish-American War, when the old fort was turned into an earthwork and the newer Battery Huger (Huge-EE) was built on top of it.

MAP 1: 843/883-3123, www.nps.gov/fosu; hours seasonal; free

Circular Congregational Church

The historic Circular Congregational Church has one of the most interesting pedigrees of any house of worship in Charleston, which is saying a lot. Services were originally held on the site of the "White Meeting House," for which Meeting Street is named; they were moved here beginning in 1681 and catered to a polyglot mix of Congregationalists, Presbyterians, and Huguenots. For that reason it was often called the Church of Dissenters (*Dissenter* being the common term at the time for anyone not an Anglican). As with many structures in town, the 1886 earthquake necessitated a rebuild, and the current edifice dates from 1891. Ironically, in this municipality called "the Holy City" for its many high spires, the Circular Church has no steeple, and instead stays low to the ground in an almost medieval fashion. Look for the adjacent meetinghouse; a green-friendly addition houses the congregation's Christian outreach, has geothermal heating and cooling, and boasts Charleston's only vegetative roof.

MAP 1: 150 Meeting St., 843/577-6400, www.circularchurch.org; services fall-spring Sun. 11am, summer Sun. 10:15am, tours Mon.-Fri. 10:30am

Dock Street Theatre

Fresh from an extensive renovation, the Dock Street Theatre, right down the street from the Huguenot Church, is where any thespian or lover of the stage must pay homage to this incarnation of the first theater built in North America. In a distressingly familiar Charleston story, the original 1736 Dock Street Theatre burned down. A second theater opened on the same site in 1754. That building was in turn demolished for a grander edifice in 1773, which, you guessed it, also burned down. The current building dates from 1809, when the Planter's Hotel was built near the site of the original Dock Street Theatre. (So why is the theatre not actually on Dock Street? Because that street on the theater's north side was renamed Queen Street, the name it bears today.) To mark the theater's centennial, the hotel added a stage facility in 1835, and it's that building you see now. For the theater's second centennial, the Works Progress Administration completely refurbished Dock Street back into a working theater in time to distract Charlestonians from the pains of the Great Depression. In addition to a very active and well-regarded annual season from the resident Charleston Stage Company, the 464-seat venue has hosted umpteen events of the Spoleto Festival over the past three decades and since its renovation continues to do so.

MAP 1: 135 Church St., 843/720-3968

French Huguenot Church

One of the oldest congregations in town, the French Huguenot Church also has the distinction of being the only remaining independent Huguenot Church in the country. Founded around 1681 by French Calvinists, the

Clockwise from top left: St. Philip's Episcopal Church; Dock Street Theatre; Circular Congregational Church.

church had about 450 congregants by 1700. While they were refugees from religious persecution, they weren't destitute, as they had to pay for their passage to America. As is the case with so many historic churches in the area, the building you see isn't the original sanctuary. The first church was built on this site in 1687, and became known as the "Church of Tides" because at that time the Cooper River lapped at its property line. This sanctuary was deliberately destroyed as a firebreak during the great conflagration of 1796. The church was replaced in 1800, but that building was in turn demolished in favor of the picturesque, stucco-coated Gothic Revival sanctuary you see today, which was completed in 1845 and subsequently survived Union shelling and the 1886 earthquake. Does the church look kind of Dutch to you? There's a good reason for that. In their diaspora, French Huguenots spent a lot of time in Holland and became influenced by the tidy sensibilities of the Dutch people. The history of the circa-1845 organ is interesting as well. A rare "tracker" organ, so named for its ultrafast linkage between the keys and the pipe valves, it was built by famed organ builder Henry Erben. After the fall of Charleston in 1865, Union troops had begun dismantling the instrument for shipment to New York when the church organist, T. P. O'Neale, successfully pleaded with them to let it stay.

Sunday services are conducted in English now, but a single annual service in French is still celebrated in April. The unique Huguenot Cross of Languedoc, which you'll occasionally see ornamenting the church, is essentially a Maltese Cross, its eight points representing the eight beatitudes. Between the four arms of the cross are four fleurs-de-lis, the age-old French symbol of purity.

MAP 1: 44 Queen St., 843/722-4385, www.frenchhuguenotchurch.org; liturgy Sun. 10:30am

Old Powder Magazine

The Old Powder Magazine may be small, but the building is quite historically significant. The 1713 edifice is the oldest public building in South Carolina and also the only one remaining from the days of the Lords Proprietors. As the name indicates, this was where the city's gunpowder was stored during the Revolution. The magazine is designed to implode rather than explode in the event of a direct hit. This is another labor of love of the Historic Charleston Foundation, which has leased the building—which from a distance looks curiously like an ancient Byzantine church—from The Colonial Dames since 1993. It was opened to the public as an attraction in 1997. Now directly across the street from a huge parking garage, the site has continuing funding issues, so occasionally the hours for tours can be erratic. Inside, you'll see displays, a section of the original brick, and an exposed earthquake rod. Next door is the privately owned, circa-1709 **Trott's Cottage**, the first brick dwelling in Charleston.

MAP 1: 79 Cumberland St., 843/722-9350, www.powdermag.org; Mon.-Sat. 10am-4pm, Sun. 1pm-4pm; $5 adults, $2 children

French Huguenots

A visitor can't spend a few hours in Charleston without coming across many French-sounding names. Some are common surnames, such as Ravenel, Manigault (MAN-i-go), Gaillard, Laurens, or Huger (huge-EE). Some are street or place names, such as Mazyck or Legare (Le-GREE). The Gallic influence in Charleston was of the Calvinist Protestant variety. Known as Huguenots, these French immigrants—refugees from an increasingly intolerant Catholic regime in France—were numerous enough in the settlement by the 1690s that they were granted full citizenship and property rights if they swore allegiance to the British crown.

the French Huguenot Church

Unlike other colonies, Carolina never put much of a premium on religious conformity, a trait that exists to this day despite the area's overall conservatism. And unlike many who fled European monarchies to come to the New World, the French Huguenots were far from poverty-stricken. Most arrived already well educated and skilled in one or more useful trades. In Charleston's early days, they were mostly farmers or tar burners (makers of tar and pitch for maritime use). Their pragmatism and work ethic would lead them to higher positions in local society, such as lawyers, judges, and politicians. One of the wealthiest Charlestonians, the merchant Gabriel Manigault, was by some accounts the richest person in the American colonies during the early 1700s. South Carolina's most famous French Huguenot was Francis Marion, the "Swamp Fox" of Revolutionary War fame. Born on the Santee River, Marion grew up in Georgetown and is now interred near Moncks Corner.

The library of the **Huguenot Society of Carolina** (138 Logan St., 843/723-3235, www.huguenotsociety.org, Mon.-Fri. 9am-2pm) is a great research tool for anyone interested in French Protestant history and genealogy.

To this day, the spiritual home of Charleston's Huguenots is the same as always: the French Huguenot Church on Church Street, one of the earliest congregations in the city. The church still holds a liturgy every April in French.

Old Slave Mart Museum

Slave auctions became big business in the South after 1808, when the United States banned the importation of slaves, thus increasing both price and demand. The auctions generally took place in public buildings where everyone could watch the wrenching spectacle. In the 1850s, public auctions in Charleston were put to a stop when city leaders discovered that visitors from European nations—all of which had banned slavery years before—were horrified at the practice. The slave trade was moved indoors to "marts" near the waterfront where sales could be conducted out of the public eye. The last remaining such structure is the Old Slave Mart Museum. Built in 1859, and originally known as Ryan's Mart after the builder, it was only in service a short time before the outbreak of the Civil War. The last auction was held in November 1863. After the war, the Slave Mart became a tenement, and then in 1938 an African American history museum. The city of Charleston acquired the building in the 1980s and reopened it as a museum in late 2007. There are two main areas: the orientation area, where visitors learn about the transatlantic slave trade and the architectural history of the building itself, and the main exhibit area, where visitors can see documents, tools, and displays recreating what happened inside during this sordid chapter in local history and celebrating the resilience of the area's African American population.

MAP 1: 6 Chalmers St., 843/958-6467, www.charlestoncity.info; Mon.-Sat. 9am-5pm; $7 adults, $5 children, free under age 6

★ St. Philip's Episcopal Church

With a pedigree dating back to the colony's fledgling years, St. Philip's Episcopal Church is the oldest Anglican congregation south of Virginia. That pedigree gets a little complicated and downright tragic at times, but any connoisseur of Charleston history needs to be clear on the fine points: The first St. Philip's was built in 1680 at the corner of Meeting Street and Broad Street, the present site of St. Michael's Episcopal Church. That first St. Philip's was badly damaged by a hurricane in 1710, and the city fathers approved the building of a new sanctuary dedicated to the saint on Church Street. However, that building was nearly destroyed by yet another hurricane during construction. Fighting with local Native Americans further delayed rebuilding in 1721. Alas, the second St. Philip's burned to the ground in 1835—a distressingly common fate for so many old buildings in this area. Construction immediately began on a replacement, and it's that building you see today. Heavily damaged by Hurricane Hugo in 1989, a $4.5 million renovation kept the church usable. So, to recap: St. Philip's was originally on the site of the present St. Michael's. And while St. Philip's is the oldest congregation in South Carolina, St. Michael's has the oldest physical church building in the state. Are we clear?

South Carolina's great statesman John C. Calhoun—who ironically despised Charlestonians for what he saw as their loose morals—was originally buried across Church Street in the former "stranger's churchyard," or West Cemetery, after his death in 1850. (Charles Pinckney and Edward Rutledge are two other notable South Carolinians buried here.) But near the end of the Civil War, Calhoun's body was moved to an unmarked grave closer to the sanctuary in an attempt to hide its location from Union troops, who it was feared would go out of their way to wreak vengeance on the tomb of one of slavery's staunchest advocates and the man who invented the doctrine of nullification. In 1880, with Reconstruction in full swing, the state legislature directed and funded the building of the large memorial to Calhoun in the West Cemetery.

MAP 1: 142 Church St., 843/722-7734, www.stphilipschurchsc.org; sanctuary Mon.-Fri. 10am-noon and 2pm-4pm, services Sun. 8:15am

Confederate Museum

Located on the second floor of City Market's iconic main building, Market Hall on Meeting Street, the small but spirited Confederate Museum hosts an interesting collection of Civil War memorabilia, with an emphasis on the military side, and is also the local headquarters of the United Daughters of the Confederacy. Perhaps its best contribution, however, is its research library.

MAP 1: 188 Meeting St., 843/723-1541; Tues.-Sat. 11am-3:30pm; $5 adults, $3 children, cash only

Gibbes Museum of Art

The Gibbes Museum of Art is one of those rare Southern museums that manages a good blend of the modern and the traditional, the local and the international. Begun in 1905 as the Gibbes Art Gallery—the final wish of James Shoolbred Gibbes, who willed $100,000 for its construction—the complex has grown through the years in size and influence. The key addition to the original beaux arts building came in 1978 with the addition of the modern wing in the rear, which effectively doubled the museum's display space. Shortly thereafter the permanent collection and temporary exhibit space was also expanded. Serendipitously, these renovations enabled the Gibbes to become the key visual arts venue for the Spoleto Festival, begun about the same time. The influential Gibbes Art School in the early 20th century formed a close association with the Woodstock School in New York, bringing important ties and prestige to the fledgling institution. Georgia O'Keeffe, who taught college for a time in Columbia, brought an exhibit here in 1955. The first solo show by an African American artist came here in 1974 with an exhibit of the work of William H. Johnson. Don't miss the nice little garden and its centerpiece, the 1972 fountain and sculpture of Persephone by Marshall Fredericks.

MAP 1: 135 Meeting St., 843/722-2706, www.gibbesmuseum.org; Tues.-Sat. 10am-5pm, Sun. 1pm-5pm; $9 adults, $7 students, $5 ages 6-12

Kahal Kadosh Beth Elohim Reform Temple

The birthplace of Reform Judaism in the United States and the oldest continuously active synagogue in the nation is Kahal Kadosh Beth Elohim Reform Temple. The congregation—Kahal Kadosh means "holy community" in Hebrew—was founded in 1749, with the current temple dating from 1840 and built in the Greek Revival style so popular at the time. The temple's Reform roots came about indirectly because of the great fire of 1838. In rebuilding, some congregants wanted to introduce musical instruments into the temple—previously a no-no—in the form of an organ. The Orthodox contingent lost the debate, and so the new building became the first home of Reform Judaism in the country, a fitting testament to Charleston's long-standing ecumenical spirit of religious tolerance and inclusiveness. Technically speaking, because all Reform temples in Europe were destroyed during the Holocaust, this is actually the oldest existing Reform synagogue in the world.

MAP 1: 90 Hasell St., 843/723-1090, www.kkbe.org; services Sat. 11am, tours Mon.-Fri. 10am-noon, Sun. 10am-4pm

The New Charleston Green

Most people know "Charleston green" as a unique local color, the result of adding a few drops of yellow to post-Civil War surplus black paint. But these days the phrase also refers to environmentally friendly development in Charleston.

The most obvious example is the ambitious Navy Yard redevelopment, which seeks to repurpose the closed-down facility. That project is part of a larger civic vision for the 3,000-acre historic Noisette community of North Charleston, with an accompanying wetlands protection conservancy. From its inception in 1902 at the command of President Theodore Roosevelt through the end of the Cold War, the Charleston Navy Yard was one of the city's biggest employers. Though the yard was closed in 1995, a 340-acre section now hosts an intriguing mix of green-friendly design firms, small nonprofits, and commercial maritime companies. But the largest Navy Yard development is still to come. Clemson University—with the help of a massive federal grant, the largest in the school's history—will oversee one of the world's largest wind turbine research facilities, to be constructed in Building 69.

Also in North Charleston, local retail chain Half Moon Outfitters has a green-friendly warehouse facility in an old grocery store. The first LEED (Leadership in Energy and Environmental Design) Platinum-certified building in South Carolina, the warehouse features solar panels, rainwater reservoirs, and locally harvested or salvaged interiors. There's also the LEED-certified North Charleston Elementary School as well as North Charleston's adoption of a "dark skies" ordinance to cut down on light pollution. On the peninsula, the historic meetinghouse of the Circular Congregational Church has a green addition with geothermal heating and cooling, rainwater cisterns, and Charleston's first vegetative roof.

East of the Cooper, in addition to walking the historic byways of the Old Village of Mount Pleasant, architecture and design buffs might also want to check out the 243-acre I'On Village (www.ionvillage.com) planned community, a successful model for this type of pedestrian-friendly New Urbanist development. On adjacent Daniel Island, the 4,000-acre planned residential community has been certified as an "Audubon Cooperative Sanctuary" for using wildlife-friendly techniques on its golf course and recreational grounds. Even ultra-upscale Kiawah Island has gone green—the fabled Kiawah bobcats are making a comeback, thanks to the efforts of the Kiawah Conservancy.

For many Charlestonians, the green movement manifests in simpler things: the pedestrian and bike lanes on the Ravenel Bridge, the thriving city recycling program, or the Sustainable Seafood Initiative, a partnership of local restaurants, universities, and conservation groups that brings the freshest, most environmentally responsible dishes to your table when you dine out in Charleston.

If you made a movie called *Dracula Meets the Lord of the Rings,* the Old City Jail might make a great set. Built in 1802 on a lot set aside for public use since 1680, the edifice was the indeed the Charleston County lockup until 1939. It was once even more imposing, but the top story and a large octagonal tower fell victim to the 1886 earthquake. Its history is also the stuff from which movies are made. Some of the last pirates were jailed here in 1822 while awaiting hanging, as was slave rebellion leader Denmark Vesey. (As a response to the aborted Vesey uprising, Charleston for a while required that all African sailors in port be detained at the jail.) During the Civil War, prisoners of both armies were held here at various times.

The Old City Jail currently houses the American College of the Building Arts. Unless you're a student there, the only way to tour the Old Jail is through **Bulldog Tours** (18 Anson St., 843/722-8687, www.bulldogtours. com). Their Haunted Jail Tour ($20 adults, $10 children) starts daily at 7pm, 8pm, 9pm, and 10pm; all tours are paid for at 40 North Market Street a short walking distance away, with jail tours starting at the jail itself.
MAP 1: 21 Magazine St., 843/577-5245

Old City Market

Part kitschy tourist trap, part glimpse into the old South, part community gathering place, Old City Market remains Charleston's most reliable, if perhaps least flashy, attraction. It is certainly the practical center of the city's tourist trade, not least because so many tours originate nearby. Originally built on Daniel's Creek—claimed from the marsh in the early 1800s after the city's first marketplace at Broad and Meeting Streets burned in 1796—one of City Market's early features was a colony of vultures who hung around the many butcher stalls. Sensing that the carrion eaters would keep the area cleaner than any human could, officials not only allowed the buzzards to hang around, they were protected by law, becoming known as "Charleston eagles" in tongue-in-cheek local jargon. No matter what anyone tries to tell you, Charleston's City Market never hosted a single slave auction. Indeed, when the Pinckney family donated this land to the city for a "Publick Market," one stipulation was that no slaves were ever to be sold here—or else the property would immediately revert to the family's descendants. A recent multimillion-dollar renovation has prettified the bulk of City Market into more of a big-city air-conditioned pedestrian shopping mall. It's not as shabbily charming as it once was, but certainly offers a more comfortable stroll during the warmer months.
MAP 1: Meeting St. and Market St., 843/973-7236; daily 6am-11:30pm

Philip Simmons Garden

Charleston's most beloved artisan is the late Philip Simmons. Born on nearby Daniel Island in 1912, Simmons went through an apprenticeship to become one of the most sought-after decorative ironworkers in the United States. In 1982 the National Endowment for the Arts awarded him

Clockwise from top left: the deliberately overgrown Unitarian Church cemetery; Joseph Manigault House; Old City Market.

its National Heritage Fellowship. His work is on display at the Smithsonian Institution and the Museum of International Folk Art in Santa Fe, New Mexico, among many other places. In 1989, the congregation at Simmons's **St. John's Reformed Episcopal Church** voted to make the church garden a commemoration of the life and work of this legendary African American artisan, who died in 2009 at age 97. Completed in two phases, the Bell Garden and the Heart Garden, the project is a delightful blend of Simmons's signature graceful, sinuous style and fragrant flowers.

MAP 1: 91 Anson St., 843/722-4241, http://philipsimmons.us

St. Mary of the Annunciation Church

The oldest Roman Catholic church in the Carolinas, St. Mary of the Annunciation traces its roots to 1789, when the Irish priest Father Matthew Ryan was sent to begin the first Catholic parish in the colony. The original church was destroyed in the great Charleston fire of 1838, and the present sanctuary dates from immediately thereafter. While it did receive a direct hit from a Union shell during the siege of Charleston in the Civil War—taking out the organ—the handsome Greek Revival edifice has survived in fine form the 1886 earthquake, the great hurricane of 1893, and 1989's Hurricane Hugo. You can tour the interior most weekdays 9:30am-3:30pm.

MAP 1: 89 Hasell St., 843/722-7696, www.catholic-doc.org/saintmarys; mass Sun. 9:30am

Unitarian Church

In a town filled with cool old church cemeteries, the coolest belongs to the Unitarian Church. As a nod to the beauty and power of nature, vegetation and shrubbery in the cemetery have been allowed to take their natural course (walkways excepted). Virginia creeper wraps around 200-year-old grave markers, honeybees feed on wildflowers, and tree roots threaten to engulf entire headstones. The whole effect is oddly relaxing, making it one of my favorite places in Charleston. The church itself—the second-oldest such edifice in Charleston and the oldest Unitarian sanctuary in the South—is pretty nice too. Begun in 1776 because of overcrowding at the Circular Congregational Church, the brand-new building saw rough usage by British troops during the Revolution. In 1787 the church was repaired, though it was not officially chartered as a Unitarian church until 1839. An extensive modernization happened in 1852. The church was spared in the fire of 1861, which destroyed the old Circular Church but stopped at the Unitarian Church's property line. Sadly, it was not so lucky during the 1886 earthquake, which toppled the original tower. The version you see today is a subsequent and less grand design.

Directly next door is **St. John's Lutheran Church** (5 Clifford St., 843/723-2426, www.stjohnscharleston.org, worship Sun. 8:30am and 11am), which had its origin in 1742 when Dr. Henry Melchior Muhlenberg stopped in town for a couple of days on his way to minister to the burgeoning Salzburger colony in Ebenezer, Georgia. He would later be known as the father of the Lutheran Church in America. To see the sanctuary at times other than Sunday mornings, go by the office next door Monday-Friday 9am-2pm and they'll let you take a walk through the interior.

MAP 1: 4 Archdale St., 843/723-4617, www.charlestonuu.org; services Sun. 11am, free tours Sat. 10am-1pm

William Rhett House

The oldest standing residence in Charleston is the circa-1713 William Rhett House, which once belonged to the colonel who captured the pirate Stede Bonnet. It's now a private residence, but you can admire this excellent prototypical example of a Charleston single house easily from the street and read the nearby historical marker.

MAP 1: 54 Hasell St.

Upper King   Map 2

Marion Square

While The Citadel moved lock, stock, and barrel almost a century ago, the college's old home, the South Carolina State Arsenal, still overlooks 6.5-acre Marion Square, a reminder of the former glory days when this was the institute's parade ground, the "Citadel Green" (the old Citadel is now a hotel). Seemingly refusing to give up on tradition—or perhaps just attracted by the many female College of Charleston students—uniformed cadets from The Citadel are still chockablock in Marion Square on any given weekend, a bit of local flavor that reminds you that you're definitely in Charleston. Marion Square is named for the "Swamp Fox" himself, Revolutionary War hero and father of modern guerrilla warfare Francis Marion, for whom the hotel at the square's southwest corner is also named. The square's newest feature is the Holocaust Memorial on Calhoun Street. However, the dominant monument is the towering memorial to John C. Calhoun. Its 1858 cornerstone includes one of the more interesting time capsules you'll encounter: $100 in Continental money, a lock of John Calhoun's hair, and a cannonball from the Fort Moultrie battle. Marion Square hosts many events, including the Farmers Market every Saturday mid-April-late December, the Food and Wine Festival, and, of course, some Spoleto events.

MAP 2: between King St. and Meeting St. at Calhoun St., 843/965-4104; daily dawn-dusk

College of Charleston

The oldest college in South Carolina and the first municipal college in the country, the College of Charleston boasts a fair share of history in addition to the way its 12,000-plus students bring a modern, youthful touch to so much of the city's public activities. Its services are no longer free, and despite its moniker the college is now a full-blown, state-supported university. Though the college has its share of modernistic buildings, a stroll around the gorgeous campus will uncover some historic gems. The oldest building

...use

...y the nearby Charleston Museum, the Joseph ...etimes called the "Huguenot House." Its splendor ...e fact that the French Protestants were far from ...e so many groups who came to America fleeing ...1-1803 National Historic Landmark was designed ...Gabriel Manigault for his brother, Joseph, a rice ... (Gabriel, quite the crackerjack dilettante architect, ...ston City Hall.) The three-story brick town house is a great example of Adams, or Federal, architecture. The furnishings are top-notch examples of 19th-century handiwork, and the rooms have been restored as accurately as possible. The foundations of various out-buildings, including a privy and slaves' quarters, are clustered around the picturesque little Gate Temple to the rear of the main house in the large enclosed garden. Each December, the Manigault House offers visitors a special treat, as the Garden Club of Charleston decorates it in period seasonal fashion, using only flowers that would have been used in the 19th century.

MAP 2: 350 Meeting St., 843/723-2926, www.charlestonmuseum.org; Mon.-Sat. 10am-5pm, Sun. 1pm-5pm, last tour 4:30pm; $10 adults, $5 children, combo tickets to Charleston Museum and Heyward-Washington House available

★ Aiken-Rhett House

One of my favorite spots in all of Charleston and a comparatively recent acquisition of the Historic Charleston Foundation, the poignant Aiken-Rhett House shows another side of that organization's mission. Whereas the Historic Charleston-run Nathaniel Russell House seeks to re-create a specific point in time, work at the Aiken-Rhett House emphasizes conservation and research. Built in 1818 and expanded by South Carolina governor William Aiken Jr., after whom we know the house today, parts of this rambling, almost Dickensian house remained sealed from 1918 until 1975 when the family relinquished the property to the Charleston Museum. As you walk the halls, staircases, and rooms—seeing the remains of original wallpaper and the various fixtures added through the years—you can really feel the impact of the people who lived within these walls and get a great sense of the full sweep of Charleston history. While the docents are friendly and helpful, the main way to enjoy the Aiken-Rhett House is by way of a self-guided MP3 player audio tour, which is unique in Charleston. While you might think this isolates you from the others in your party, it's actually part of the fun—you can synchronize your players and move as a unit if you'd like.

MAP 2: 48 Elizabeth St., 843/723-1159, www.historiccharleston.org; Mon.-Sat. 10am-5pm, Sun. 2pm-5pm, last tour 4:15pm; $12 adults, $5 children

Children's Museum of the Lowcountry

Yet another example of Charleston's savvy regarding the tourist industry is the Children's Museum of the Lowcountry. Recognizing that historic homes and Civil War memorabilia aren't enough to keep a family with young children in town for long, the city established this museum in 2005 specifically to give families with kids aged 3 months to 12 years a reason to spend more time (and money) downtown. A wide variety of hands-on activities—such as a 30-foot shrimp boat replica and a medieval castle—stretch the definition of *museum* to its limit. In truth, this is just as much an indoor playground as a museum, but no need to quibble. The Children's Museum has been getting rave reviews since it opened, and visiting parents and their children seem happy with the city's investment.

MAP 2: 25 Ann St., 843/853-8962, www.explorecml.org; Tues. and Fri. 9am-7pm, Wed.-Thurs. and Sat. 9am-5pm, Sun. noon-5pm; $10

Old Bethel United Methodist Church

The history of the Old Bethel United Methodist Church, the third-oldest church building in Charleston, is a little confusing. Completed in 1807, the church once stood across Calhoun Street, until a schism formed in the church community over whether black parishioners should be limited to sitting in the galleries (in those days in the South, all races attended church together far more frequently than during the Jim Crow era). The entire African American congregation wanted out, so in 1852 the original building was moved aside for the construction of a new church for Caucasians, and then entirely across the street in 1880. Look across the street and sure enough you'll see the circa-1853 **Bethel Methodist Church** (57 Pitt St., 843/723-4587, worship Sun. 9am and 11:15am).

MAP 2: 222 Calhoun St., 843/722-3470

Hampton Park

Map 2

The Citadel

Although for many its spiritual and historic center will always be at the Old State Arsenal in Marion Square, The Citadel has been at this 300-acre site farther up the peninsula along the Ashley River since 1922 and shows no signs of leaving. Getting there is a little tricky, in that the entrance to the college is situated behind beautiful Hampton Park off Rutledge Avenue, a main north-south artery on the western portion of the peninsula. The Citadel (technically its full name is The Citadel, The Military College of South Carolina) has entered popular consciousness through the works of graduate Pat Conroy, especially his novel *Lords of Discipline,* starring a thinly disguised "Carolina Military Institute." Other famous Bulldog alumni include construction magnate Charles Daniel (for whom the school library is named); Ernest "Fritz" Hollings, South Carolina governor and longtime U.S. senator; and current Charleston mayor Joe Riley. You'll see

SIGHTS HAMPTON PARK

The Citadel's living legacy all over Charleston in the person of the ubiquitous cadet, whose gray-and-white uniform, ramrod posture, and impeccable manners all hark back to the days of the Confederacy. But to best experience The Citadel, you should go to the campus itself.

There's lots for visitors to see, including **The Citadel Museum** (843/953-6779, daily noon-5pm, free), on your right just as you enter campus; the "Citadel Murals" in the Daniel Library; "Indian Hill," the highest point in Charleston and former site of an Indian trader's home; and the grave of U.S. general Mark Clark of World War II fame, who was Citadel president from 1954 to 1966. Ringing vast Summerall Field—the huge open space where you enter campus—are the many castle-like cadet barracks.

The most interesting single experience for visitors to The Citadel is the colorful Friday afternoon dress parade on Summerall Field, in which cadets pass for review in full dress uniform (the fabled "long gray line") accompanied by a marching band and pipers. Often called "the best free show in Charleston," the parade happens almost every Friday at 3:45pm during the school year; you might want to consult the website before your visit to confirm. Arrive well in advance to avoid parking problems.

The institute was born out of panic over the threat of a slave rebellion organized in 1822 by Denmark Vesey. The state legislature passed an act establishing the school to educate the strapping young men picked to protect Charleston from a slave revolt. Citadel folks will proudly tell you they actually fired the first shots of the Civil War, when on January 9, 1861, two cadets fired from a battery on Morris Island at the U.S. steamer *Star of the West* to keep it from supplying Fort Sumter. After slavery ended—and with it the school's original raison d'être—The Citadel continued, taking its current name in 1910 and moving to the Ashley River site in 1922. While The Citadel is rightly famous for its pomp and circumstance—as well as its now-defunct no-lock "honor system," done away with after the Virginia Tech shootings—the little-known truth is that to be one of the 2,000 or so currently enrolled Citadel Bulldogs, you don't have to go through all that, or the infamous "Hell Week" either. You can just sign up for one of their many evening graduate school programs.

MAP 2: 171 Moultrie St., 843/953-3294, www.citadel.edu; grounds daily 8am-6pm

West Ashley

Map 3

Charles Towne Landing

Any look at West Ashley must start where everything began, with the 600-acre historic site Charles Towne Landing. This is where Charleston's original settlers first arrived and camped in 1670, remaining only a few years before eventually moving to the more defensible peninsula where the Holy City now resides. For many years the site was in disrepair and borderline

of "damn the torpedoes" fame; (2) General
was in love with one of the Drayton women; and (3)
ytons, a doctor, craftily posted smallpox warning flags at
rts of the property. Of the three scenarios, the last is considered
likely.

Visitors expecting the more typical approach to house museums, i.e., subjective renovation with period furnishings that may or may not have any connection with the actual house, might be disappointed. But for others the experience at Drayton Hall is quietly exhilarating, almost in a Zen-like way. Planes are routed around the house so that no rattles will endanger its structural integrity. There's no furniture to speak of, only bare rooms, decorated with original paint, no matter how little remains. It can be jarring at first, but after you get into it, you might wonder why anyone does things any differently.

Another way the experience is different is in the professionalism of the National Trust for Historic Preservation, which has owned and administered Drayton Hall since 1974. The guides hold degrees in the field, and a tour of the house, which starts on the half-hour, takes every bit of 50 minutes. A separate 45-minute program called "Connections: From Africa to America," chronicles the diaspora of the slaves who originally worked this plantation, from their capture to their eventual freedom. "Connections" is presented at 11:15am, 1:15pm, and 3:15pm.

The site comprises not only the main house but two self-guided walking trails, one along the peaceful Ashley River and another along the marsh. Note also the foundations of the two "flankers," or guest wings, at each side of the main house. They survived the Yankees only for one to fall victim to the 1886 earthquake and the other to the 1893 hurricane. Also on-site is an African American cemetery with at least 33 known graves. It's kept deliberately untended and unlandscaped to honor the final wish of Richmond Bowens (1908-1998), the seventh-generation descendant of some of Drayton Hall's original slaves.

MAP 3: 3380 Ashley River Rd., 843/769-2600, www.draytonhall.org; Mon.-Sat. 9am-3:30pm, Sun. 11am-3:30pm, tours on the half-hour; $20 adults, $10 ages 12-18, $6 ages 6-11, grounds only $10

Magnolia Plantation and Gardens

A different legacy of the Drayton family is Magnolia Plantation and Gardens. It claims not only the first garden in the United States, dating back to the 1680s, but also the first public garden, dating to 1872. Magnolia's history spans back two full centuries before that, however, when Thomas Drayton Jr.—scion of Norman aristocracy, son of a wealthy Barbadian planter—came from the Caribbean to build his own fortune. He immediately married the daughter of Stephen Fox, who began this plantation in 1676. Through wars, fevers, depressions, earthquakes, and hurricanes,

Magnolia has stayed in the possession of an unbroken line scendants to this very day.

As a privately run attraction, Magnolia has little of the academ of other plantation sites in the area, most of which have long passed private hands. There's a slightly kitschy feel here, the opposite of the qui dignity of Drayton Hall. And unlike Middleton Place a few miles down the road, the gardens here are anything but manicured, with a wild, almost playful feel. That said, Magnolia can claim fame to being one of the earliest bona fide tourist attractions in the United States and the beginning of Charleston's now-booming tourist industry. It happened after the Civil War, when John Grimke Drayton, reduced to near-poverty, sold off most of his property, including the original Magnolia Plantation, just to stay afloat. (In a common practice at the time, as a condition of inheriting the plantation, Mr. Grimke, who married into the family, was required to legally change his name to Drayton.)

The original plantation home was burned during the war—either by Union troops or freed slaves—so Drayton barged a colonial-era summer house from Summerville down the Ashley River to this site and built the modern Magnolia Plantation around it specifically as an attraction. Before long, tourists regularly came here by crowded boat from Charleston (a wreck of one such ferry is still on-site). Magnolia's reputation became so exalted that at one point Baedecker's listed it as one of the three main attractions in North America, alongside the Grand Canyon and Niagara Falls. The family took things to the next level in the 1970s, when John Drayton Hastie bought out his brother and set about marketing Magnolia Plantation and Gardens as a modern tourist destination. While spring remains the best—and also the most crowded—time to come, a huge variety of camellias blooms in early winter, a time marked by a yearly Winter Camellia Festival.

Today Magnolia is a place to bring the whole family, picnic under the massive old live oaks, and wander the lush, almost overgrown grounds. Children will enjoy finding their way through "The Maze" of manicured camellia and holly bushes, complete with a viewing stand to look within the giant puzzle. Plant lovers will enjoy the themed gardens such as the Biblical Garden, the Barbados Tropical Garden, and the Audubon Swamp Garden, complete with alligators and named after John James Audubon, who visited here in 1851. House tours, the 45-minute Nature Train tour, the 45-minute Nature Boat tour, and a visit to the Audubon Swamp Garden run about $8 pp extra for each offering.

Of particular interest is the poignant old Drayton Tomb, along the Ashley River. Look closely at the nose of one of the cherubs on the tomb; it was shot off by a vengeful Union soldier. Nearby you'll find a nice walking and biking trail along the Ashley among the old paddy fields.

MAP 3: 3550 Ashley River Rd., 843/571-1266, www.magnoliaplantation.com; Mar.-Oct. daily 8am-4:30pm, Nov.-Feb. daily 9am-4:30pm; $15 adults, $10 children, free under age 6

Clockwise from top left: Drayton Hall; Middleton Place; Charles Towne Landing.

gardens. "Meandering" is not the right word to describe them, since they're systematically laid out. "Intricate" is the descriptor I prefer, and that sums up the attention to detail that characterizes all the garden's portions, each with a distinct personality and landscape design template. To get a real feel for how things used to be here, for an extra $15 pp you can take a 45-minute carriage ride through the bamboo forest to an abandoned rice field. Rides start around 10am and run every hour or so, weather permitting.

The 53-room **Inn at Middleton Place** (www.theinnatmiddletonplace. com), besides being a wholly gratifying lodging experience, is also a quite self-conscious and largely successful experiment. Its bold Frank Lloyd Wright-influenced modern design, comprising four units joined by walkways, is modern. But both inside and outside it manages to blend quite well with the surrounding fields, trees, and riverbanks. The inn also offers kayak tours and instruction—a particularly nice way to enjoy the grounds from the waters of the Ashley—and features its own organic garden and labyrinth, intriguing modern counterpoints to the formal gardens of the plantation itself.

They still grow the exquisite Carolina Gold rice in a field at Middleton Place, harvested in the old style each September. You can sample some of it in many dishes at the **Middleton Place Restaurant** (843/556-6020, www. middletonplace.org, lunch daily 11am-3pm, dinner Tues.-Thurs. 6pm-8pm, Fri.-Sat. 6pm-9pm, Sun. 6pm-8pm, $15-25). You can tour the gardens for free if you arrive for a dinner reservation at 5:30pm or later.

MAP 3: 4300 Ashley River Rd., 843/556-6020, www.middletonplace.org; daily 9am-5pm; $28 adults, $15 students, $10 children, guided house tour $15 extra

The Coburg Cow

The entire stretch of U.S. 17 (Savannah Hwy.) heading into Charleston from the west is redolent of a particularly Southern brand of retro Americana. The chief example is the famous Coburg Cow, a large, rotating dairy cow accompanied by a bottle of chocolate milk. The current installation dates from 1959, though a version of it was on this site as far back as the early 1930s when this area was open countryside. During Hurricane Hugo the Coburg Cow was moved to a safe location. In 2001 the attached dairy closed down, and the city threatened to have the cow moved or demolished. But community outcry preserved the delightful landmark, which is visible today on the south side of U.S. 17 in the 900 block. You can't miss it—it's a big cow on the side of the road!

MAP 3: 900 block of U.S. 17

Caw Caw Interpretive Center

About 10 minutes west of Charleston on U.S. 17 you'll find the unique Caw Caw Interpretive Center, a treasure trove for history buffs and naturalists wanting to learn more about the old rice culture of the South. With a particular emphasis on the expertise of those who worked on the rice plantations using techniques they brought with them from Africa, the county-run facility comprises 650 acres of land on an actual former rice plantation built on a cypress swamp, eight miles of interpretive trails, an educational center with exhibits, and a wildlife sanctuary with seven different habitats. Most Wednesday and Saturday mornings, guided bird walks are held at 8:30am ($5 pp). You can put in your own canoe for $10 October-April on Saturdays and Sundays. Bikes and dogs aren't allowed on the grounds.

MAP 3: 5200 Savannah Hwy., Ravenel, 843/889-8898, www.ccprc.com; Tues.-Sun. 9am-5pm; $1

North Charleston   Map 3

Magnolia Cemetery

Although not technically in North Charleston, historic Magnolia Cemetery is on the way, well north of the downtown tourist district in the area called "the Neck." This historic burial ground, while not quite the aesthetic equal of Savannah's famed Bonaventure Cemetery, is still a stirring site for its natural beauty and ornate memorials as well as for its historic aspects. Here are buried the crewmen who died aboard the CSS *Hunley,* reinterred after their retrieval from Charleston Harbor. In all, over 2,000 Civil War dead are buried here, including five Confederate generals and 84 rebels who fell at Gettysburg and were moved here.

MAP 3: Cunnington Ave. at Huguenin Ave., 843/722-8638; Sept.-May daily 8am-5pm, June-Aug. daily 8am-6pm

Charleston Navy Yard

A vast postindustrial wasteland to some and a fascinating outdoor museum to others, the Charleston Navy Yard is in the baby steps of rehabilitation from one of the Cold War era's major military centers to the largest single urban redevelopment project in the United States. The U.S. Navy's gone now, forced off the site during a phase of base realignment in the mid-1990s. But a 340-acre section, the **Navy Yard at Noisette** (1360 Truxtun Ave., 843/302-2100, daily 24 hours), now hosts an intriguing mix of homes, green design firms, nonprofits, and commercial maritime companies and was named the country's sixth-greenest neighborhood by *Natural Home* magazine in 2008. It has even played host to some scenes of the Lifetime TV series *Army Wives.* Enter on Spruill Avenue and you'll find yourself on wide streets lined with huge, boarded-up warehouse facilities, old machine shops, and dormant power stations. A notable project is the restoration of **10 Storehouse Row** (2120 Noisette Blvd., 843/302-2100, Mon.-Fri. 9am-5pm), which now hosts design firms, galleries, and a small café. Nearby, Clemson University will soon be administering one of the world's largest wind turbine research facilities. At the north end lies the new **Riverfront Park** (843/745-1087, daily dawn-dusk) in the old Chicora Gardens military

Clockwise from top left: Warren Lasch Conservation Center, home of the CSS *Hunley*; Magnolia Cemetery; Riverfront Park.

residential area. There's a nifty little fishing pier on the Cooper River, an excellent naval-themed band shell, and many sleekly designed modernist sculptures paying tribute to the sailors and ships that made history here. From Charleston you get to the Navy Yard by taking I-26 north to exit 216B (you can reach the I-26 junction by just going north on Meeting Street). After exiting, take a left onto Spruill Avenue and a right onto McMillan Avenue, which takes you straight in.

MAP 3: west bank of Cooper River, south of Riverfront Park

★ CSS *Hunley*

For the longest time, the only glimpse of the ill-fated Confederate submarine afforded to visitors was a not-quite-accurate replica outside the Charleston Museum. But after maritime novelist and adventurer Clive Cussler and his team finally found the CSS *Hunley* in 1995 off Sullivan's Island, the tantalizing dream became a reality: We'd finally find out what it looked like, and perhaps even be lucky enough to bring it to the surface. That moment came on August 8, 2000, when a team comprising the non-profit **Friends of the *Hunley*** (Warren Lasch Conservation Center, 1250 Supply St., Bldg. 255, 866/866-9938, www.hunley.org, Sat. 10am-5pm, Sun. noon-5pm, $12, free under age 5), the federal government, and private partners successfully implemented a plan to safely raise the vessel. It was recently moved to its new home on the grounds of the old Navy Yard, named after Warren Lasch, chairman of the Friends of the Hunley. You can now view the sub, see the life-size model from the TNT movie *The Hunley,* and look at artifacts such as the "lucky" gold piece of the commander. You can even see facial reconstructions of some of the eight sailors who died on board the sub that fateful February day in 1864, when it mysteriously sank right after successfully destroying the USS *Housatonic* with the torpedo attached to its bow. So that research and conservation can be performed during the week, tours only happen on Saturday-Sunday. Because of this limited window of opportunity and the popularity of the site, reserve tickets ahead of time. (The remains of the crew lie in Magnolia Cemetery, where they were buried in 2004 with full military honors.) To get to the Warren Lasch Center from Charleston, take I-26 north to exit 216B. Take a left onto Spruill Avenue and a right onto McMillan Avenue. Once in the Navy Yard, take a right on Hobson Avenue, and after about one mile take a left onto Supply Street. The Lasch Center is the low white building on the left.

MAP 3: Warren Lasch Conservation Center, 1250 Supply St., Bldg. 255, 866/866-9938, www.hunley.org; Sat. 10am-5pm, Sun. noon-5pm; $12, free under age 5

Park Circle

The focus of restoration in North Charleston is the old Park Circle neighborhood. The adjacent **Olde North Charleston** development has a number of quality shops, bars, and restaurants.

It's got a mouthful of a name, but the North Charleston and American LaFrance Fire Museum and Educational Center, right next to the huge Tanger Outlet Mall, does what it does with a lot of chutzpah—which is fitting considering that it pays tribute to firefighters and the tools of their dangerous trade. The museum, which opened in 2007 and shares a huge 25,000-square-foot space with the North Charleston Convention and

Raising the *Hunley*

The raising of the Confederate submarine CSS *Hunley* from the muck of Charleston Harbor sounds like the plot of an adventure novel—which makes sense considering that the major player is an adventure novelist. For 15 years, undersea diver and best-selling author Clive Cussler looked for the final resting place of the *Hunley*. The sub was mysteriously lost at sea after sinking the USS *Housatonic* on February 17, 1864, with the high-explosive "torpedo" mounted on a long spar on its bow. It marked the first time a sub ever sank a ship in battle.

For over a century before Cussler, treasure-seekers had searched for the sub, with P. T. Barnum even offering $100,000 to the first person to find it. But on May 3, 1995, a magnetometer operated by Cussler and his group, the National Underwater Marine Agency, discovered the *Hunley*'s final resting place—in 30 feet of water and under three feet of sediment about four miles off Sullivan's Island at the mouth of the harbor. A 19-person dive crew and a team of archaeologists began a process that would result in raising the vessel on August 8, 2000. But first, a dilemma had to be solved. For 136 years saltwater had permeated its metallic skin. Exposure to air would rapidly disintegrate the entire thing. So the conservation team, with input from the U.S. Navy, came up with a plan to keep the vessel intact at the specially constructed

Warren Lasch Conservation Center (1250 Supply St., Bldg. 255, 866/866-9938, www.hunley.org, Sat. 10am-5pm, Sun. noon-5pm, $12, free under age 5) in the old Navy Yard while research and conservation were performed on it piece by piece.

Upon seeing the tiny, cramped vessel—much smaller than most experts imagined it would be—visitors are often visibly moved at the bravery and sacrifice of the nine-man Confederate crew, who would have known that the *Hunley*'s two previous crews had drowned at sea in training accidents.

The Lasch Center is only open to the public on weekends. Archaeology continues apace during the week—inch by painstaking inch, muck and tiny artifacts removed millimeter by millimeter. The process is so thorough that archaeologists have even identified an individual eyelash from one of the crewmembers. Other interesting artifacts include a threefold wallet with a leather strap; seven canteens, and a wooden cask in one of the ballast tanks.

The very first order of business once the sub was brought up was properly burying the sailors. In 2004, Charleston came to a stop as a ceremonial funeral procession took the remains of the nine to historic Magnolia Cemetery, where they were buried with full military honors.

Visitors Bureau, is primarily dedicated to maintaining and increasing its collection of antique American LaFrance firefighting vehicles and equipment. The 18 fire engines here date from 1857 to 1969. The museum's exhibits have taken on greater poignancy in the wake of the tragic loss of nine Charleston firefighters killed trying to extinguish a warehouse blaze on U.S. 17 in summer 2007—second only to the 9/11 attacks as the largest single loss of life for a U.S. firefighting department.

MAP 3: 4975 Centre Pointe Dr., North Charleston, 843/740-5550, www.legacyofheroes. org; Mon.-Sat. 10am-5pm, Sun. 1pm-5pm, last ticket 4pm; $6 adults, free under age 14

Summerville
Map 3

The Dorchester County town of Summerville, population 30,000, is a friendly, scenic, and upscale suburb north of Charleston. Founded as Pineland Village in 1785, Summerville made its reputation as a place for plantation owners and their families to escape the insects and heat of the swampier areas of the Lowcountry. Summerville got a second wind at the turn of the 20th century, when it was recommended by doctors all over the world as a great place to recover from tuberculosis (supposedly all the turpentine fumes in the air from the pine trees were a big help).

Summerville boasts a whopping 700 buildings on the National Register of Historic Places. For a walking tour of the historic district, download the map at www.visitsummerville.com or pick up a hard copy at the **Summerville Visitors Center** (402 N. Main St., 843/873-8535, Mon.-Fri. 9am-5pm, Sat. 10am-3pm, Sun. 1pm-4pm). Alas, the grand old Pine Forest Inn, perhaps the greatest of all Summerville landmarks and the "winter White House" for presidents William Taft and Theodore Roosevelt, was torn down after World War II, a victim of the Florida vacation craze. Summerville is about 30 minutes from downtown Charleston; take I-26 north.

Azalea Park

Much visitor activity in Summerville centers on Azalea Park, rather obviously named for its most scenic inhabitants. Several fun yearly events take place here, most notably the **Flowertown Festival** (www.flowertown-festival.com, free) each April, a three-day affair heralding the coming of spring and the blooming of the flowers. One of the biggest festivals in South Carolina, 250,000 people usually attend. Another event, **Sculpture in the South** (www.sculptureinthesouth.com) in May, takes advantage of the extensive public sculpture in the park.

MAP 3: S. Main St. and W. 5th St. S.; daily dusk-dawn; free

Just south of Summerville on the way back to Charleston is the interesting Colonial Dorchester State Historic Site, chronicling a virtually unknown segment of Carolina history. A contingent of Massachusetts Puritans ("Congregationalists" in the parlance of the time) were given special dispensation in 1697 to form a settlement of their own specifically to enhance commercial activity on the Ashley River. Today little is left of old Dorchester but the tabby walls of the 1757 fort overlooking the Ashley. Don't miss the unspectacular but still historically vital remains of the wooden wharf on the walking trail along the river, once the epicenter of a thriving port. The most-photographed thing on-site is the bell tower of the Anglican church of St. George—which actually wasn't where the original settlers worshipped and was in fact quite resented by them since they were forced to pay for its construction. The dispute with the Anglican Church became tense enough to cause many Congregationalists to leave and settle little Midway, Georgia, where many became key figures in the movement for American independence. The resulting Revolutionary War would be the downfall of Dorchester itself, abandoned during the upheaval.

MAP 3: 300 County Road S-18-373, 843/873-1740, www.southcarolinaparks.com; daily 9am-6pm; $2 adults, free under age 16

Summerville-Dorchester Museum

To learn more about Summerville's interesting history, go just off Main Street to the Summerville-Dorchester Museum. Located in the former town police station, the museum has a wealth of good exhibits. The museum opened in 1992 thanks to a group of Summerville citizens that wanted to preserve the region's history.

MAP 3: 100 E. Doty Ave., 843/875-9666, www.summervilledorchestermuseum.org; Mon.-Sat. 9am-2pm; donations accepted

Mount Pleasant and East Cooper

Map 4

Patriots Point Naval and Maritime Museum

Directly across Charleston Harbor from the old city lies the Patriots Point Naval and Maritime Museum complex, one of the first chapters in Charleston's tourism renaissance. The project began in 1975 with what is still its main attraction, the World War II aircraft carrier **USS *Yorktown*,** named in honor of the carrier lost at the Battle of Midway. Much of "The Fighting Lady" is open to the public, and kids and nautical buffs will thrill to walk the decks and explore the many stations below deck on this massive 900-foot vessel, a veritable floating city. You can even have a full meal in the CPO Mess Hall just like the crew once did (except you'll have to pay $8.50

pp). And if you really want to get up close and personal, try the Navy Flight Simulator for a small additional fee. Speaking of planes, aviation buffs will be overjoyed to see that the *Yorktown* flight deck (the top of the ship) and the hangar deck (right below) are packed with authentic warplanes, not only from World War II but from subsequent conflicts the ship participated in.

Other ships moored beside the *Yorktown* and open for tours are the Coast Guard cutter USCG *Ingham*, the submarine USS *Clamagore*, and the destroyer USS *Laffey*, which survived being hit by three Japanese bombs and five kamikaze attacks—all within an hour.

A big plus is the free 90-minute guided tour. If you really want to make a family history day out of it, you can hop on the ferry from Patriots Point to Fort Sumter and back.

MAP 4: 40 Patriots Point Rd., 843/884-2727, www.patriotspoint.org; daily 9am-6:30pm; $20 adults, $12 ages 6-11, free for active-duty military

Old Village

It won't blow you away if you've seen Charleston or Beaufort, but Mount Pleasant's old town has its share of fine colonial and antebellum homes and historic churches. Indeed, Mount Pleasant's history is almost as old as Charleston's. First settled for farming in 1680, it soon acquired cachet as a great place for planters to spend the hot summers away from the mosquitoes inland. The main drag is Pitt Street, where you can shop and meander among plenty of stores and restaurants (try an ice cream soda at the historic Pitt Street Pharmacy). The huge meeting hall on the waterfront, Alhambra Hall, was the old ferry terminal.

MAP 4: West of Royall Ave. to the waterfront, Mount Pleasant

Boone Hall Plantation

Visitors who've also been to Savannah's Wormsloe Plantation will see the similarity in the majestic, live oak-lined entrance avenue to Boone Hall Plantation. But this site is about half a century older, dating back to a grant to Major John Boone in the 1680s (the oaks of the entranceway were planted in 1743). Unusual for this area, where fortunes were originally made mostly on rice, Boone Hall's main claim to fame was as a cotton plantation as well as a noted brick-making plant. Boone Hall takes the phrase "living history" to its extreme; it's not only an active agricultural facility, it also lets visitors go on "u-pick" walks through its fields, which boast succulent strawberries, peaches, tomatoes, and even pumpkins in October—as well as free hayrides. Currently owned by the McRae family, which first opened it to the public in 1959, Boone Hall is called "the most photographed plantation in America." And photogenic it is, with natural beauty to spare in its scenic location on the Wando River and its adorable Butterfly Garden. But as you're clicking away with your camera, keep in mind that the plantation's "big house" is not original; it's a 1935 reconstruction. While Boone Hall's most genuine historic buildings include the big Cotton Gin House (1853) and the 1750

Smokehouse, to me the most poignant and educational structures by far are the nine humble brick slave cabins from the 1790s, expertly restored and most fitted with interpretive displays. The cabins are the center of Boone Hall's educational programs, including an exploration of Gullah culture at the outdoor "Gullah Theatre." Summers see some serious Civil War re-enacting going on. In all, three different tours are available: a 30-minute house tour, a tour of Slave Street, and a garden tour.

MAP 4: 1235 Long Point Rd., 843/884-4371, www.boonehallplantation.com; mid-Mar.-Labor Day, Mon.-Sat. 8:30am-6:30pm, Sun. noon-5pm, Labor Day-Nov. Mon.-Sat. 9am-5pm, Sun. 1pm-4pm, Dec.-mid-Mar. Mon.-Sat. 9am-5pm, Sun. noon-5pm; $20 adults, $10 children

Charles Pinckney National Historic Site

This is one of my favorite sights in Charleston, for its uplifting, well-explored subject matter as well as its tastefully maintained house and grounds. Though "Constitution Charlie's" old Snee Farm is down to only 28 acres from its original magnificent 700, the Charles Pinckney National Historic Site that encompasses it is still an important repository of local and national history. Sometimes called "the forgotten founder," Charles Pinckney was not only a hero of the American Revolution and a notable early abolitionist but one of the main authors of the U.S. Constitution. His great aunt Eliza Lucas Pinckney was the first woman agriculturalist in the United States, responsible for opening up the indigo trade. Her son Charles Cotesworth Pinckney was one of the signers of the Constitution. The current main house, doubling as the visitors center, dates from 1828, 11 years after Pinckney sold Snee Farm to pay off debts. That said, it's still a great example of Lowcountry architecture. It replaces Pinckney's original home, where President George Washington slept and had breakfast under a nearby oak tree in 1791 while touring the South. Another highlight at this National Park Service-administered site is the 0.5-mile self-guided walk around the grounds, some of it on boardwalks over the marsh. No matter what anyone tells you, no one is buried underneath the tombstone in the grove of oak trees bearing the name of Constitution Charlie's father, Colonel Charles Pinckney. The marker incorrectly states the elder Pinckney's age; it was put here only as a monument. Another memorial to the colonel is in the churchyard of the 1840s-era Christ Church about one mile down Long Point Road.

MAP 4: 1240 Long Point Rd., 843/881-5516, www.nps.gov/chpi; daily 9am-5pm; free

Isle of Palms

This primarily residential area of about 5,000 people received the state's first "Blue Wave" designation from the Clean Beaches Council for its well-managed and preserved beaches. Like adjacent Sullivan's Island, there are pockets of great wealth here, but also a laid-back, windswept beach-town vibe. You get here from Mount Pleasant by taking the Isle of Palms

Aside from just enjoying the whole scene, the main self-contained attraction here is **Isle of Palms County Park** (14th Ave., 843/886-3863, www.ccprc.com, May-Labor Day daily 9am-7pm, Mar.-Apr. and Sept.-Oct. daily 10am-6pm, Nov.-Feb. daily 10am-5pm, $7 per vehicle, free for pedestrians and cyclists), with its oceanfront beach, complete with umbrella rental, a volleyball court, a playground, and lifeguards. Get here from the Isle of Palms Connector by going through the light at Palm Boulevard and taking the next left at the gate. The island's other claim to fame is the excellent (and surprisingly affordable) **Wild Dunes Resort** (5757 Palm Blvd., 888/778-1876, www.wilddunes.com), with its two Fazio golf courses and 17 clay tennis courts. Breach Inlet, between Isle of Palms and Sullivan's Island, is where the Confederate sub *Hunley* sortied to do battle with the USS *Housatonic*. During 1989's Hurricane Hugo, the entire island was submerged.

MAP 4: off U.S. 17, via Hwy. 517

Sullivan's Island

Part funky beach town, part ritzy getaway, Sullivan's Island has a certain timeless quality. While much of it was rebuilt after Hurricane Hugo's devastation, plenty of local character remains, as evidenced by some cool little bars in its tiny "business district" on the main drag of Middle Street. There's a ton of history on Sullivan's, but you can also just while the day away on the quiet, windswept beach on the Atlantic or ride a bike all over the island and back. Unless you have a boat, you can only get here from Mount Pleasant. From U.S. 17, follow the signs for Highway 703 and Sullivan's Island. Cross the Ben Sawyer Bridge, and then turn right onto Middle Street; continue for about 1.5 miles.

Fort Moultrie

While Fort Sumter gets the vast bulk of the attention, the older Fort Moultrie on Sullivan's Island actually has a much more sweeping history. Furthering the irony, Major Robert Anderson's detachment at Fort Sumter at the opening of the Civil War was actually the Fort Moultrie garrison, reassigned to Sumter because Moultrie was thought too vulnerable from the landward side. Indeed, Moultrie's first incarnation, a perimeter of felled palm trees, didn't even have a name when it was unsuccessfully attacked by the British in the summer of 1776, the first victory by the colonists in the Revolution. The redcoat cannonballs bounced off those flexible trunks, and thus was born South Carolina's nickname, "The Palmetto State." The hero of the battle, Sergeant William Jasper, would gain immortality for putting the blue-and-white regimental banner—forerunner to the modern blue-and-white state flag—on a makeshift staff after the first one was shot away. Subsequently named for the commander at the time, William Moultrie, the fort was captured by the British in a later engagement. That first fort fell into decay and a new one was built over it in 1798 but was soon destroyed by a hurricane.

In 1809 a brick fort was built here; it soon gained notoriety as the place where the great chief Osceola was detained soon after his capture, and where he posed for the famous portrait by George Catlin. His captors got more than they bargained for when they jokingly asked the old guerrilla soldier for a rendition of the Seminole battle cry. According to accounts, Osceola's realistic performance scared some bystanders half to death. The chief died here in 1838, and his modest grave site is still on-site, in front of the fort on the landward side.

Other famous people to have trod on Sullivan's Island include Edgar Allan Poe, who was inspired by Sullivan's lonely, evocative environment to write *The Gold Bug* and other works. There's a Gold Bug Avenue and a Poe Avenue here today, and the local library is named after him as well. A young Lieutenant William Tecumseh Sherman was also stationed here during his Charleston stint in the 1830s before his encounter with history in the Civil War.

Moultrie's main Civil War role was as a target for Union shot during the long siege of Charleston. It was pounded so hard and for so long that its walls fell below a nearby sand hill and were finally unable to be hit anymore. A full military upgrade happened in the late 1800s, extending over most of Sullivan's Island (some private owners have even bought some of the old batteries and converted them into homes). It's the series of later forts that you'll visit on your trip to the Moultrie site, which is technically part of the Fort Sumter National Monument and administered by the National Park Service.

Most of the outdoor tours are self-guided, but ranger programs typically happen Memorial Day-Labor Day daily at 11am and 2:30pm There's a bookstore and visitors center across the street, offering a 20-minute video on the hour and half-hour 9am-4:30pm. Keep in mind there's no regular ferry to Fort Sumter from Fort Moultrie; the closest ferry to Sumter leaves from Patriots Point on Mount Pleasant.

MAP 4: 1214 Middle St., 843/883-3123, www.nps.gov/fosu; daily 9am-5pm; $3 adults, free under age 16

Bench by the Road

Scholars say that about half of all African Americans alive today had an ancestor who once set foot on Sullivan's Island. As the first point of entry for at least half of all slaves imported to the United States, the island's "pest houses" acted as quarantine areas so slaves could be checked for communicable diseases before going to auction in Charleston proper. But few people seem to know this. In a 1989 magazine interview, African American author and Nobel laureate Toni Morrison said about historic sites concerning slavery, "There is no suitable memorial, or plaque, or wreath or wall, or park or skyscraper lobby. There's no 300-foot tower, there's no small bench by the road." In 2008, that last item became a reality, as the first of several planned "benches by the road" was installed on Sullivan's Island to mark the sacrifice of enslaved African Americans. It's a simple black steel bench, with an attached marker and a nearby plaque. The Bench by the Road is at the Fort Moultrie visitors center.

MAP 4: Fort Moultrie visitors center, 1214 Middle St.

Awendaw and Points North

This area just north of Charleston along U.S. 17—named for the Sewee Indian village originally located here and known to the world chiefly as the place where Hurricane Hugo made landfall in 1989—is seeing some new growth, but still hews to its primarily rural, nature-loving roots.

Cape Romain National Wildlife Refuge

One of the best natural experiences in the area is about a 30-minute drive north of Charleston at Cape Romain National Wildlife Refuge. Essentially comprising four barrier islands, the 66,000-acre refuge—almost all of which is marsh—provides a lot of great paddling opportunities, chief among them **Bulls Island** (no overnight camping). A fairly lengthy trek from where you put in lies famous Boneyard Beach, where hundreds of downed trees lie on the sand, bleached by sun and salt. Slightly to the south within the refuge, **Capers Island Heritage Preserve** (843/953-9300, www. dnr.sc.gov, daily dawn-dusk, free) is still a popular camping locale despite heavy damage from 1989's Hurricane Hugo. Get permits in advance by calling the South Carolina Department of Natural Resources. You can kayak to the refuge yourself or take the only approved ferry service from **Coastal Expeditions** (514-B Mill St., Mount Pleasant, 843/881-4582, www.coastalexpeditions.com, $40 adults, $20 children, 30 minutes). **Barrier Island Eco Tours** (50 41st Ave., Isle of Palms, 843/886-5000, www.nature-tours. com, 3.5-hour boat excursions $38 adults, $28 children) on Isle of Palms also runs trips to the area.

MAP 4: 5801 U.S. 17 N., 843/928-3264, www.fws.gov/caperomain; daily dawn-dusk

Sewee Visitor and Environmental Education Center

Twenty miles north of Charleston you'll find the Sewee Visitor and Environmental Education Center. Besides being a gateway of sorts for the almost entirely aquatic Cape Romain National Wildlife Refuge, Sewee is primarily known for housing several rare red wolves, who were part of a unique release program on nearby Bull Island begun in the late 1970s. They're kept at the center to maintain the genetic integrity of the species.

MAP 4: 5821 U.S. 17, 843/928-3368, www.fws.gov/seweecenter; Tues.-Sat. 9am-5pm; free

Folly Beach and the Southwest Islands

Map 5

Folly Beach

A large percentage of the town of Folly Beach was destroyed by Hurricane Hugo in 1989, and erosion since then has increased and hit the beach itself pretty hard. All that said, enough of Folly's funky charm is left to make it worth visiting. Called "The Edge of America" during its heyday as a swinging resort getaway from the 1930s through the 1950s, Folly Beach is now a slightly beaten but enjoyable little getaway on this barrier island. As with all areas of Charleston, the cost of living here is rapidly increasing, but Folly Beach still reminds locals of a time that once was: a time of soda fountains, poodle skirts, stylish one-piece bathing suits, and growling hot rods. Folly's main claim to larger historic fame is playing host to George Gershwin, who stayed at a cottage on West Arctic Avenue to write the score for *Porgy and Bess,* set across the harbor in downtown Charleston. (Ironically, Gershwin's opera couldn't be performed in its original setting until 1970 because of segregationist Jim Crow laws.) Original *Porgy* author DuBose Heyward stayed around the corner at a summer cottage on West Ashley Avenue that he dubbed "Follywood."

Called Folly Road until it gets to the beach, Center Street is the main drag here, dividing the beach into east and west. In this area you'll find the **Folly Beach Fishing Pier** (101 E. Arctic Ave., 843/588-3474, Apr.-Oct. daily 6am-11pm, Nov. and Mar. daily 7am-7pm, Dec.-Feb. daily 8am-5pm, $5-7 parking, $8 fishing fee), which replaced the grand old wooden pier-and-pavilion structure that tragically burned down in 1960.

Back in the day, restaurants, bars, and amusement areas with rides lined the way up to the old pavilion. As the premier musical venue in the region, the pavilion hosted legends like Tommy and Jimmy Dorsey, Benny Goodman, and Count Basie. The new fishing pier, while not as grand as the old one, is worth visiting—a massive, well-built edifice jutting over 1,000 feet into the Atlantic with a large diamond-shaped pavilion at the end. Fishing-rod holders and cleaning stations line the entire thing. Out on the "front beach," daytime activities once included boxing matches and extralegal drag races. In the old days, the "Washout" section on the far west end was where you went to go crabbing or fly-fishing or maybe even steal a kiss from your sweetie. Today, though, the Washout is known as the prime surfing area in the Carolinas, with a dedicated group of diehards.

To get to Folly Beach from Charleston, go west on Calhoun Street and take the James Island Connector. Take a left on Folly Road (Hwy. 171), which becomes Center Street on into Folly Beach.

At the far east end of Folly Island, about 300 yards offshore, you'll see the **Morris Island Lighthouse,** an 1876 beacon that was once surrounded by lush green landscape, now completely surrounded by water as the land has eroded around it. Now privately owned, there's an extensive effort to save and preserve the lighthouse (www.savethelight.org). There's also an effort to keep high-dollar condo development off of beautiful bird-friendly Morris Island itself (www.morrisisland.org). To get there while there's still something left to enjoy, take East Ashley Street until it dead-ends. Park in the lot and take a 0.25-mile walk to the beach.

MAP 5: south of Charleston via Hwy. 30 and Hwy. 171

Kiawah Island and Seabrook Island

This beautiful island with a beautiful beach to match—about 45 minutes away from downtown Charleston—has as its main attraction the sumptuous **Kiawah Island Golf Resort** (12 Kiawah Beach Dr., 800/654-2924, www.kiawahgolf.com, $600-800), a key location for PGA tournaments. But even if you don't play golf, the resort is an amazing stay. The main component is **The Sanctuary,** an upscale hotel featuring an opulent lobby complete with grand staircases, a large pool area overlooking the beach, tasteful Spanish Colonial-style architecture, and 255 smallish but excellently appointed guest rooms.

Several smaller private, family-friendly resorts also exist on Kiawah, with fully furnished homes and villas and every amenity you could ask for. Go to www.explorekiawah.com for a full range of options or call 800/877-0837.

Through the efforts of the **Kiawah Island Conservancy** (23 Beachwalker Dr., 843/768-2029, www.kiawahconservancy.org), over 300 acres of the island have been kept as an undeveloped nature preserve. The island's famous bobcat population has made quite a comeback, with somewhere between 24 and 36 animals currently active. The bobcats are vital to the island ecosystem, since as top predator they help cull what would otherwise become untenably large populations of deer and rabbit.

The beach at Kiawah is a particular delight, set as it is on such a comparatively undeveloped island. No matter where you stay on Kiawah, a great thing about the island is the notable lack of light pollution—don't forget to look up at night and enjoy the stars!

Like its neighbor Kiawah, **Seabrook Island** is also a private resort-dominated island. In addition to offering miles of beautiful beaches, on its 2,200 acres are a wide variety of golfing, tennis, equestrian, and swimming facilities as well as extensive dining and shopping options. There are also a lot of kids' activities as well. For information on lodging options and packages, go to www.seabrook.com or call 866/249-9934. Seabrook Island is about 45 minutes from Charleston. From downtown, take SC 30 West to Maybank Highway, then a left onto Cherry Point Road.

Kiawah Island Beachwalker Park

Only one facility for the general public exists on Kiawah Island, the Kiawah Island Beachwalker Park. Get here from downtown Charleston by taking Lockwood Drive onto the Highway 30 Connector bridge over the Ashley River. Turn right onto Folly Road, then left onto Maybank Highway. After about 20 minutes, take a left onto Bohicket Road, which leads to Kiawah in 14 miles. Turn left from Bohicket Road onto the Kiawah Island Parkway. Just before the security gate, turn right on Beachwalker Drive and follow the signs to the park.

MAP 5: Kiawah Island, 843/768-2395, www.ccprc.com; Mar.-Apr. and Sept. daily 10am-6pm, May-Labor Day daily 9am-7pm, Oct. Mon.-Fri. 9am-5pm, Sat.-Sun. 10am-6pm, Nov.-Feb. daily 10am-5pm; $7 per vehicle, free for pedestrians and cyclists

Johns Island
Angel Oak Park
The outlying community of Johns Island is where you'll find the inspiring Angel Oak Park, home of a massive live oak, 65 feet in circumference, that's over 1,000 years old and commonly considered the oldest tree east of the Mississippi River. As is the case with all live oaks, don't expect impressive height—when oaks age they spread *out*, not up. The sprawling, picturesque tree and the park containing it are owned by the city of Charleston, and the scenic grounds are often used for weddings and special events. Angel Oak Park is about 30 minutes from Charleston. Take U.S. 17 over the Ashley River, then Highway 171 to Maybank Highway. Take a left onto Bohicket Road, and then look for signs on the right.

MAP 5: 3688 Angel Oak Rd.; Mon.-Sat. 9am-5pm, Sun. 1pm-5pm; free

Legare Farms
Legare Farms is open to the public for various activities, including its annual pumpkin patch in October, its "sweet corn" festival in June, and bird walks (Sat. 8:30am, $6 adults, $3 children) in fall. To make the 20-minute drive from downtown Charleston, take SC 30 West to Maybank Highway, then a left onto River Road and a right onto Jenkins Farm Road.

MAP 5: 2620 Hanscombe Point Rd., 843/559-0763, www.legarefarms.com; hours vary

Wadmalaw Island
Charleston Tea Plantation
Currently owned by the R. C. Bigelow Tea corporation, the Charleston Tea Plantation is no cute living-history exhibit: It's a big, working tea plantation—the only one in the U.S.—with acre after acre of *Camellia sinensis* being worked by modern farm machinery. Visitors get to see a sample of how the tea is made, "from the field to the cup." Factory tours are free, and a trolley tour of the "Back 40" is $10. And, of course, there's a gift shop where you can sample and buy all types of teas and tea-related products. Growing season is April-October. The tea bushes, direct descendants of plants brought over in the 1800s from India and China, "flush up" 2-3 inches every few weeks during growing season. Charleston Tea Plantation is about 30 minutes from Charleston. Take the Ashley River Bridge, stay left to Folly Road (Hwy. 171), turn right onto Maybank Highway for 18 miles, and look for the sign on the left.

MAP 5: 6617 Maybank Hwy., 843/559-0383, www.charlestonteaplantation.com; Mon.-Sat. 10am-4pm, Sun. noon-4pm; free

Clockwise from top left: Fort Moultrie; Folly Beach Pier; namesake of Angel Oak Park.

South Carolina has several good wineries, among them Wadmalaw's own Irvin House Vineyards, the Charleston area's only vineyard. Jim Irvin, a Kentucky boy, and his wife, Anne, a Johns Island native, make several varieties of muscadine wine here, with tastings and a gift shop. They also give free tours of the 50-acre grounds every Saturday at 2pm. There's a Grape-Stomping Festival at the end of each August ($5 per car). Also on the Irvin Vineyards grounds you'll find **Firefly Distillery** (6775 Bears Bluff Rd., 843/559-6867, www.fireflyvodka.com), home of their signature Firefly Sweet Tea Vodka. They offer tastings (Feb.-Dec. Wed.-Sat. 11am-5pm, $6 per tasting). To get here from Charleston, go west on Maybank Highway about 10 miles to Bears Bluff Road, veering right. The vineyard entrance is on the left after about eight miles.

MAP 5: 6775 Bears Bluff Rd., 843/559-6867, www.charlestonwine.com; Thurs.-Sat. 10am-5pm

Restaurants and Nightlife

Look for ★ to find
recommended restaurants and nightlife.

Highlights

★ **Greatest Food Adventure:** Sean Brock's flagship restaurant, **McCrady's** combines old-school attention to service and detail with a daring approach to cuisine (page 81).

★ **Most Scrumptious Breakfast:** It's not fancy, but **Dixie Supply Bakery & Café** offers hearty Southern takes on breakfast classics (page 83).

★ **Most Delightful Date Night:** The award-winning **FIG** offers incredible fine dining with friendly service in a classy but relaxed atmosphere (page 87).

★ **Most Muscular Mussels:** The best bowl of mussels you'll have outside France is at the bistro **39 Rue de Jean** (page 92).

★ **Best Dive Bar:** The humble **Recovery Room** on Upper King is the nation's second-biggest-selling bar for PBR (page 92).

★ **Most Ridiculous Ribs:** The smoky slabs at **Fiery Ron's Home Team BBQ** are so good you'll hardly be able to stand it, but try anyway (page 94).

★ **Freshest Comfort Food:** Charleston is full of great farm-to-table spots, but **Glass Onion** offers the most accessible Southern classics made from local produce (page 96).

★ **Best Bar for Burgers:** In West Ashley, **Gene's Haufbrau** combines an awesome beer selection with some of the best burgers in town (page 97).

★ **Best She-Crab Soup:** Just north of town on Highway 17 you'll find **SeeWee Restaurant,** known for its seafood (page 99).

★ **Closest Intersection of France and South Carolina:** On Johns Island is **Fat Hen,** where the specialties are Southern in origin and French in execution (page 102).

PRICE KEY
$ Entrées less than $10
$$ Entrées $10–20
$$$ Entrées more than $20

Charleston's long history of good taste and livability combines with an affluent and sophisticated population to attract some of the brightest chefs and restaurateurs in the country. Kitchens here eschew fickle trends, instead emphasizing quality, professionalism, and most of all, freshness of ingredients. Even Charleston's bars have great food, so don't assume you have to make reservations at a formal restaurant to fully enjoy the cuisine here.

Unlike the locals-versus-tourists divide you find so often in other destination cities, in Charleston it's nothing for a couple of visitors to find themselves at a table next to four or five college students enjoying themselves in true Charlestonian fashion: loudly and with lots of good food and strong drink nearby. Indeed, the Holy City is downright ecumenical in its partying. The smokiest dives also have some of the best brunches. Tourist hot spots written up in all the guidebooks also have their share of local regulars. But through it all, one constant remains: Charleston's finely honed ability to seek out and enjoy the good life.

Bars close in Charleston at 2am, though there is a movement afoot to make the closing time earlier in some areas of town. At the retail level, all hard-liquor sales stop at 7pm, with none at all on Sundays. You can buy beer and wine in grocery stores 24-7.

The Upper King neighborhood is the youngest and most vibrant nightlife area in Charleston. While it has plenty of good restaurants, by and large you'll find the more classic fine-dining spots farther south into downtown.

Charleston's live music scene is hit-or-miss. With the long-ago passing of the heyday of Hootie & the Blowfish, there's no distinct "Charleston sound" to speak of (though Hootie frontman-turned-country star Darius Rucker still plays frequently in the area), but they do a good job of bringing in well-regarded national and regional touring acts. The best place to find up-to-date music listings is the local free weekly *Charleston City Paper* (www.charlestoncitypaper.com).

South of Broad

Map 1

CLASSIC SOUTHERN
Carolina's ⑤⑤⑤

The only bona fide restaurant in the quiet old South of Broad area is also one of Charleston's best and oldest. Chef Jeremiah Bacon spent seven years honing his craft in New York City. His Lowcountry take on European classics includes grilled salmon with potato gnocchi, tagliatelle with Lowcountry prosciutto, and pan-roasted diver scallops, with as many fresh ingredients as possible from the nearby Kensington Plantation. A tried-and-true favorite that predates Bacon's tenure, however, is Perdita's *fruit de mer*—a recipe that goes back to the restaurant's 1950s predecessor, Perdita's, which is commonly regarded as Charleston's first fine-dining restaurant. A recent renovation of this Revolutionary War-era building—once the legendary Sailor's Tavern—hasn't negatively affected the romantic ambience of the three themed areas: Perdita's Room (the oldest dining area), the Sidewalk Room, and the Bar Room. Free valet parking is a nice plus.

MAP 1: 10 Exchange St., 843/724-3800; Sun.-Thurs. 5pm-10pm, Fri.-Sat. 5pm-11pm

Waterfront

Map 1

CLASSIC SOUTHERN
High Cotton ⑤⑤⑤

For many visitors to Charleston, there comes a point when they just get tired of stuffing themselves with seafood. If you find yourself in that situation, the perfect antidote is High Cotton, a meat-lover's paradise offering some of the best steaks in town as well as a creative menu of assorted lamb and pork dishes.

MAP 1: 199 E. Bay St., 843/724-3815, www.mavericksouthernkitchens.com; Mon.-Thurs. 5:30pm-10pm, Fri. 5:30pm-11pm, Sat. 11:30am-2:30pm and 5:30pm-11pm, Sun. 10am-2pm and 5:30pm-10pm

Cypress ⑤⑤⑤

While not as flashy as some other local chefs, Craig Deihl has, over the past decade, brought Cypress—which shares ownership with Magnolias—to the forefront of the local foodie movement. From aged beef sourced at a local farm to sustainably caught wreckfish, the menu reflects a deep commitment to locavore sensibilities. Any meat or seafood entrée is a can't-lose proposition here.

MAP 1: 167 E. Bay St., 843/727-0111, www.magnolias-blossom-cypress.com; Sun.-Thurs. 5:30pm-10pm, Fri.-Sat. 5:30pm-11pm

Magnolias ⑤⑤⑤

Magnolias began life as one of Charleston's first serious eating spots. A warm, wood interior highlights the renovation, and the menu remains as attractive as ever, with a delightful take on Southern classics like the lump crab cakes, the shellfish over grits, and a rainbow trout. The appetizers are particularly strong—start with the famous fried green tomatoes or maybe the boiled peanut hummus.

MAP 1: 185 E. Bay St., 843/577-7771, www.magnolias-blossom-cypress.com; Mon.-Sat. 11:30am-10pm, Sun. 3:45pm-10pm

★ McCrady's ⑤⑤⑤

Few restaurants in Charleston inspire such impassioned vocal advocates as McCrady's. Housed in one of Charleston's oldest tavern buildings (circa 1788), McCrady's is where you enjoy the prodigious talents of Chef Sean Brock, whose *sous vide,* or vacuum cooking, is spoken of in hushed tones by his clientele. McCrady's is not the place to gorge on usual Lowcountry fare. Portions here are small and dynamic, based on a rotating seasonal menu. Many diners find the seven-course Chef's Tasting ($90), in which you get whatever floats Chef Brock's boat that night, a near-religious experience. For an extra $75, master sommelier Clint Sloan provides paired wine selections. Or you can just go with a three-course ($45) or four-course ($60) dinner where you pick your courses. You may read complaints in online reviews about the prices at McCrady's. Let me set the record straight: (a) They're not high at all when you break them down per multiple course, and (b) the perfect blending of flavors you will enjoy with each and every dish on the menu is worth every penny and then some.

MAP 1: 2 Unity Alley, 843/577-0025, www.mccradysrestaurant.com; Sun.-Thurs. 5:30pm-10pm, Fri.-Sat. 5:30pm-11pm

Slightly North of Broad ⑤⑤⑤

Don't be put off by the initials of Slightly North of Broad. Its acronym, "SNOB," is an ironic play on the often pejorative reference to the insular South of Broad neighborhood. This hot spot, routinely voted best restaurant

Clockwise from top left: Husk; Slightly North of Broad; McCrady's.

in town in such contests, is anything but snobby. Hopping with happy foodies for lunch and dinner, the fun is enhanced by the long open kitchen with
its own counter area. The dynamic but comforting menu here is practi-
cally a bible of the new wave of Lowcountry cuisine, with dishes like beef
tenderloin, jumbo lump crab cakes, grilled barbecue tuna—and of course
the pan-seared flounder. An interesting twist at SNOB is the selection of
"medium plates," i.e., dishes a little more generous than an appetizer but
with the same adventurous spirit.

MAP 1: 192 E. Bay St., 843/723-3424, www.mavericksouthernkitchens.com; Mon.-Fri.
11:30am-3pm and 5:30pm-11pm, Sat.-Sun. 5:30pm-11pm

LOUNGES
Rooftop Bar and Restaurant
The aptly named Rooftop Bar and Restaurant at newly restored The Vendue
is a very popular waterfront happy-hour spot from which to enjoy the sunset over the Charleston skyline.

MAP 1: 23 Vendue Range, 843/723-0485; Tues.-Sat. 6pm-2am

PUBS AND BARS
Social Wine Bar
The action gets going late at Social Wine Bar, near the French Quarter.
While the hot and cold tapas are tasty, the real action here, as you'd expect, is the wine. They offer at least 50 wines by the glass and literally hundreds by the bottle. My favorite thing to do here is partake of the popular
"flights," triple tastes of kindred spirits.

MAP 1: 188 E. Bay St., 843/577-5665; daily 4pm-2am

French Quarter   Map 1

BREAKFAST AND BRUNCH
★ Dixie Supply Bakery & Café $
You can sit inside the crowded, noisy diner, or outside literally in the parking lot of a strip mall; either way you're doing the right thing at Dixie Supply
Bakery & Café. Dixie Supply has a certain amount of cachet after an appear-
ance on *Diners, Drive-ins and Dives,* but don't let the trendiness keep you
away. A case could be made that their signature Tomato Pie—melted cheese
over a perfect tomato slice with a delicious crust on the bottom, served with
a hunk of sweet potato corn bread—is the single best dish in Charleston.
You place your order at the front counter, the cook's a few feet away. When
your plate is ready, they call you, and you just come up and get your food
and take it back to your table. It can get crowded, but just brave the lines
and go. And while they do take plastic, they appreciate cash.

MAP 1: 62 State St., 843/722-5650, www.dixiecafecharleston.com; daily 8am-2:30pm

PUBS AND BARS

Blind Tiger

Because of its commercial nature, Broad Street can get quiet when the sun goes down and the office workers disperse back to the burbs. But a warm little oasis can be found a few steps off Broad Street in the Blind Tiger, which takes its name from the local Prohibition-era nickname for a speakeasy.

MAP 1: 36-38 Broad St., 843/577-0088; daily 11:30am-2am

Tommy Condon's Irish Pub

The Guinness flows freely at touristy Tommy Condon's Irish Pub—after the obligatory and traditional slow-pour, that is—as do the patriotic Irish songs performed live most nights.

MAP 1: 160 Church St., 843/577-3818, www.tommycondons.com; Sun.-Thurs. 11am-2am, Fri.-Sat. 11am-2am

North of Broad

Map 1

CLASSIC SOUTHERN

Husk $$$

Executive chef Sean Brock of McCrady's fame already has a healthy reputation as one of Charleston's—indeed, the country's—leading purveyors of the farm-to-table fine-dining aesthetic. He cemented that reputation with Husk, voted "Best New Restaurant in the U.S." by *Bon Appétit* magazine soon after its 2011 opening. The spare, focused menu—"If it doesn't come from the South, it's not coming through the door," Brock says of his ingredients—is constantly changing with the seasons. On a recent lunch visit my party enjoyed two types of catfish (a fried catfish BLT on Texas toast and a lightly cornmeal-dusted broiled catfish with local vegetables), Husk's signature cheeseburger, and—wait for it—lamb barbecue. Another visit brought a wonderful appetizer of teriyaki pig's ears in lettuce wraps! Husk is literally right next door to Poogan's Porch, and as with Poogan's, reservations are recommended.

MAP 1: 76 Queen St., 843/577-2500, www.huskrestaurant.com; Mon.-Thurs. 11:30am-2pm and 5:30pm-10pm, Fri.-Sat. 11:30am-2pm and 5:30pm-11pm, Sun. 10am-2:30pm and 5:30pm-10pm

Jestine's Kitchen $$

The long lines at Wentworth and Meeting Streets across from the fire station are waiting to follow Rachael Ray's lead and get into Jestine's Kitchen to enjoy a simple, Southern take on such meat-and-three comfort food classics as meat loaf, pecan-fried fish, and fried green tomatoes. Most of the recipes are handed down from the restaurant's namesake, Jestine Matthews, the African American woman who raised owner Dana Berlin.

MAP 1: 251 Meeting St., 843/722-7224; Tues.-Thurs. 11am-9:30pm, Fri.-Sat. 11am-10pm

Peninsula Grill ⑤⑤⑤

Walk through the gaslit courtyard of the Planter's Inn at Market and Meeting Streets into the intimate dining room of the Peninsula Grill and begin an epicurean journey you'll not soon forget. Known far and wide for impeccable service as well as the mastery of Chef Robert Carter, Peninsula Grill is perhaps Charleston's quintessential purveyor of high-style Lowcountry cuisine. From the lobster skillet cake and crab cake appetizer to the bourbon-grilled jumbo shrimp to the benne-crusted rack of lamb to sides like wild mushroom grits and hoppin' John, the menu reads like a "greatest hits" of regional cooking. You'll almost certainly want to start with the sampler trio of soups and finish with Carter's legendary coconut cake. Choose from 20 wines by the glass or from over 300 bottles. Four stars from the Mobil Travel Club, four diamonds from AAA, and countless other accolades have come this restaurant's way. Reservations are strongly recommended.

MAP 1: 112 N. Market St., 843/723-0700, www.peninsulagrill.com; daily from 5:30pm

Poogan's Porch ⑤⑤

Named for a now-deceased beloved dog who once greeted guests, Poogan's Porch is the prototype of a classic Charleston restaurant: lovingly restored old home, professional but unpretentious service, great fried green tomatoes, and rich, calorie-laden Lowcountry classics. I can't decide which entrée I like best, the crab cakes or the shrimp and grits. Some swear that even the biscuits at Poogan's—flaky, fresh-baked, and moist—are better than some entrées around town, although that's a stretch. Brunch is the big thing here, a bustling affair with big portions, Bloody Marys, mimosas, and soft sunlight.

MAP 1: 72 Queen St., 843/577-2337, www.poogansporch.com; Mon.-Fri. 11:30am-2:30pm and 5pm-9:30pm, Sat.-Sun. 9am-3pm and 5pm-9:30pm

COFFEE, TEA, AND SWEETS

City Lights Coffeehouse ⑤

If you find yourself needing a quick pick-me-up while shopping on King Street, avoid the lines at the two Starbucks on the avenue and instead turn east on Market Street and duck inside City Lights Coffeehouse. The sweet goodies are delectable in this cozy little Euro-style place, and the Counter Culture organic coffee is to die for. If you're really lucky, they'll have some of their Ethiopian Sidamo brewed.

MAP 1: 141 Market St., 843/853-7067; Mon.-Thurs. 7am-9pm, Fri.-Sat. 7am-10pm, Sun. 8am-6pm

Kaminsky's 💲

Routinely voted as having the best desserts in the city, the cakes alone at Kaminsky's are worth the trip to the City Market area. The fresh fruit torte, the red velvet, and the "Mountain of Chocolate" are the three best sellers. There's also a Mount Pleasant location (1028 Johnnie Dodds Blvd., 843/971-7437).

MAP 1: 78 N. Market St., 843/853-8270; daily noon-2am

FRENCH

Gaulart & Maliclet 💲💲

On the north side of Broad Street itself you'll find Gaulart & Maliclet, subtitled "Fast and French." This is a gourmet bistro with a strong take-out component. Prices are especially reasonable for this area of town, with great lunch specials under $10 and Thursday-night "fondue for two" coming in at just over $20.

MAP 1: 98 Broad St., 843/577-9797, www.fastandfrench.org; Mon. 8am-4pm, Tues.-Thurs. 8am-10pm, Fri.-Sat. 8am-10:30pm

Queen Street Grocery 💲

If you find yourself in lodging near the Broad Street area—or if you just love crepes—you will want to acquaint yourself with the Queen Street Grocery. The kind of place frequented almost exclusively by locals, this corner store is where you can load up on some of the tastiest made-to-order crepes this side of France—as well as light groceries, beer, wine, and cigarettes.

MAP 1: 133 Queen St., 843/723-4121, www.queenstreetgrocerycafe.com; kitchen Mon.-Sat. 10am-5pm, Sun. 11am-3pm, store Mon.-Sat. 8am-8:30pm

MEDITERRANEAN

Il Cortile del Re 💲💲💲

One of the most romantic restaurants in Charleston—which is saying a lot—Il Cortile del Re is amid the antiques stores on Lower King. Thankfully the Italian owners don't overdo the old country sentimentality. Portions here manage to be simultaneously large and light, as in the overtopped mussel plate in a delightfully thin and spicy tomato sauce, or the big spinach salad with goat cheese croutons sprinkled with a subtle vinaigrette. The entrées emphasize the Tuscan countryside, focusing both on slow-roasted meats and sublime takes on traditional pasta dishes.

MAP 1: 193A King St., 843/853-1888; Mon.-Sat. 5pm-10:30pm

Fulton Five 💲💲💲

Literally right around the corner from Il Cortile del Re is the other in Charleston's one-two Italian punch, Fulton Five. The cuisine of northern Italy comes alive in this bustling, dimly lit room, from the *bresaola* salad of spinach and thin dried beef to the caper-encrusted tuna on a bed of sweet pea risotto. It's not cheap, and the portions aren't necessarily the largest, but with these tasty, non-tomato-based dishes and this romantic, gusto-filled atmosphere, you'll be satiated with life itself.

MAP 1: 5 Fulton St., 843/853-5555; Mon.-Sat. 5:30pm-close

NEW SOUTHERN

Charleston Grill $$$

Inside the plush Charleston Place Hotel you'll find Charleston Grill, one of the city's favorite (and priciest) fine-dining spots for locals and visitors alike. Veteran executive chef Bob Waggoner was recently replaced by his longtime sous chef Michelle Weaver, but the menu still specializes in French-influenced Lowcountry cuisine like a niçoise vegetable tart. There are a lot of great fusion dishes as well, such as the tuna and *hamachi* sashimi topped with pomegranate molasses and lemongrass oil. Reservations are a must.

MAP 1: 224 King St., 843/577-4522, www.charlestongrill.com; dinner daily from 6pm

Circa 1886 $$$

Focusing on purely seasonal offerings that never stay on the menu longer than three months, Circa 1886 combines the best old-world tradition of Charleston with the vibrancy of its more adventurous kitchens. The restaurant—surprisingly little-known despite its four-star Mobil rating—is located in the former carriage house of the grand Wentworth Mansion B&B just west of the main College of Charleston campus. It is now the playground of Chef Marc Collins, who delivers entrées like a robust beef au poivre and a shrimp-and-crab stuffed flounder, to name two recent offerings. Be sure to check the daily prix fixe offerings; those can be some great deals.

MAP 1: 149 Wentworth St., 843/853-7828, www.circa1886.com; Mon.-Sat. 5:30pm-9:30pm

Cru Café $$$

Cru Café boasts an adventurous menu within a traditional-looking Charleston single house just around the corner from the main stable for the city's carriage tours, with a choice of interior or exterior seating. Sample entrées include poblano and mozzarella fried chicken and seared maple leaf duck breast.

MAP 1: 18 Pinckney St., 843/534-2434; Tues.-Thurs. 11am-3pm and 5pm-10pm, Fri.-Sat. 11am-3pm and 5pm-11pm

★ FIG $$$

Just across the street from Hyman's Seafood is that establishment's diametrical opposite, the intimate bistro and stylish bar FIG—but the two do share one key thing: a passion for fresh, simple ingredients. While Hyman's packs in the tourists, FIG—short for "Food Is Good"—attracts young professional scenesters as well as the die-hard foodies. Chef Mike Lata won

James Beard's Best Chef of the Southeast award in 2009. FIG is one of Charleston's great champions of the Sustainable Seafood Initiative, and the kitchen staff strives to work as closely as possible with local farmers and anglers in determining its seasonal menu.

MAP 1: 232 Meeting St., 843/805-5900, www.eatatfig.com; Mon.-Thurs. 6pm-11pm, Fri.-Sat. 6pm-midnight

SEAFOOD
Hyman's Seafood $$

Hyman's Seafood is thought by many locals to border on a tourist trap, and it's mostly tourists who line up for hours to get in. To keep things manageable, Hyman's offers the same menu and prices for both lunch and dinner. After asking for some complimentary fresh boiled peanuts in lieu of bread, start with the Carolina Delight, a delicious appetizer (also available as an entrée) involving a lightly fried cake of grits topped with your choice of delectable seafood, or maybe a half dozen oysters from the Half Shell oyster bar. Definitely try the she-crab soup, some of the best you'll find anywhere. As for entrées, the ubiquitous Lowcountry crispy scored flounder is always a good bet.

MAP 1: 215 Meeting St., 843/723-6000, www.hymanseafood.com; Mon.-Thurs. 11am-9pm, Fri.-Sun. 11am-11pm

PUBS AND BARS
Vickery's Bar and Grill

If it's a nice day out, a good place to relax and enjoy happy hour outside is Vickery's Bar and Grill, actually part of a small regional chain based in Atlanta. Start with the oyster bisque, and maybe try the turkey and brie sandwich or crab cakes for your entrée.

Though Vickery's Bar and Grill does not market itself as a gay and lesbian establishment, it has nonetheless become quite popular with that population—not least because of the good reputation its parent tavern in Atlanta has with that city's large and influential gay community.

MAP 1: 15 Beaufain St., 843/577-5300, www.vickerysbarandgrill.com; Mon.-Sat. 11:30am-2am, Sun. 11am-1am

Upper King

Map 2

ASIAN
Basil $$

There's usually a long wait to get a table at the great Thai place Basil on Upper King, since they don't take reservations. But Basil also has one of the hippest, most happening bar scenes in the area, so you won't necessarily mind. Revelers enjoy fresh, succulent takes on Thai classics like cashew

Lowcountry Locavores

Charleston has merged its own indigenous and abiding culinary tradition with the "new" idea that you should grow your food as naturally as possible and purchase it as close to home as you can. From bacon and snapper to sweet potatoes, the typical Charleston dish of today harkens back to its soulful Southern roots, before the days of factory food..

Spurred in part by an influx of trained chefs after the establishment of the Spoleto Festival in the 1970s, the locavore movement in Charleston came from the efforts of epicureans committed to sustainability and the principles of community-supported agriculture (CSA). Spearheaded by visionaries like the James Beard Award-winning Mike Lata of the bistro FIG and Sean Brock of McCrady's, sustainable food initiatives have sprung up in Charleston and the Lowcountry, such as the South Carolina Aquarium's Sustainable Seafood Initiative (http://scaquarium.org), partnering with local restaurants to assure a sustainable wild-caught harvest; Certified South Carolina (www.certifiedsc.com), guaranteeing that the food you eat was grown in the Palmetto State; a local chapter of the Slow Food Movement (http://slowfoodcharleston.org); and Cypress Artisan Meat Share (www.magnolias-blossom-cypress.com), in which a group of highly regarded restaurants makes their fine locally sourced meats available to the public.

The list of Holy City restaurants relying almost exclusively on local and sustainable sources is long, but here are a few notable examples:

- **Husk** (76 Queen St., 843/577-2500, www.huskrestaurant.com)
- **McCrady's** (2 Unity Alley, 843/577-0025, www.mccradysrestaurant.com)
- **Cypress** (167 E. Bay St., 843/727-0111, www.magnolias-blossom-cypress.com)
- **Charleston Grill** (224 King St., 843/577-4522, www.charlestongrill.com)
- **High Cotton** (199 E. Bay St., 843/724-3815, www.mavericksouthernkitchens.com)
- **FIG** (232 Meeting St., 843/805-5900, www.eatatfig.com)
- **Al Di La** (25 Magnolia Rd., 843/571-2321)
- **Queen Street Grocery** (133 Queen St., 843/723-4121)
- **Carolina's** (10 Exchange St., 843/724-3800)
- **Middleton Place Restaurant** (4300 Ashley River Rd., 843/556-6020, www.middletonplace.org)
- **Circa 1886** (149 Wentworth St., 843/853-7828, www.circa1886.com)
- **COAST Bar and Grill** (39D John St., 843/722-8838, www.coastbarandgrill.com)
- **Cru Café** (18 Pinckney St., 843/534-2434, www.crucafe.com)
- **Hominy Grill** (207 Rutledge Ave., 912/937-0930, www.hominygrill.com)
- **Il Cortile del Re** (193A King St., 843/853-1888, www.ilcortiledelre.com)
- **Peninsula Grill** (112 N. Market St., 843/723-0700, www.peninsulagrill.com)
- **Tristan** (55 Market St., 843/534-2155, www.tristandining.com)

Top: Hyman's Seafood. **Bottom:** salad at Circa 1886.

chicken and pad thai, all cooked by Asian chefs. The signature dish, as you might imagine, is the basil duck.

MAP 2: 460 King St., 843/724-3490, www.basilthairestaurant.com; Mon.-Thurs. 11:30am-2:30pm and 5pm-10:30pm, Fri.-Sat. 5pm-11pm, Sun. 5pm-10pm

COFFEE, TEA, AND SWEETS
Kudu Coffee $

By common consensus, the best java joint in Charleston is Kudu Coffee in the Upper King area. A kudu is an African antelope, and the Africa theme extends to the beans, which all have an African pedigree. Poetry readings and occasional live music add to the mix. A lot of green-friendly, left-of-center community activism goes on here as well.

MAP 2: 4 Vanderhorst St., 843/853-7186; Mon.-Sat. 6:30am-7pm, Sun. 9am-6pm

ITALIAN
Indaco $$$

Upper King's newest "it" restaurant, Indaco features a small but well-curated menu of antipasti, custom wood-fired gourmet pizza, and delicious Italian specialties like black pepper tagliatelle. Yes, there's brussel sprouts pizza, and it's quite delicious! Indaco is set in a stylish, bustling, restored warehouse environment that draws some of Charleston's most beautiful foodies.

MAP 2: 525 King St., 843/727-1218, www.indacocharleston.com; Sun.-Thurs. 5pm-10pm, Fri.-Sat. 5pm-midnight

MEXICAN
Juanita Greenberg's Nacho Royale $

The quesadillas at Juanita Greenberg's Nacho Royale are perfectly packed with jack cheese but not overly so, full of spicy sausage, and finished with a delightful *pico de gallo*. This modest Mexican joint on Upper King caters primarily to a college crowd, as you can tell from the reasonable prices, the large patio out back, the extensive tequila list, and the bar that stays open until 2am on weekends.

MAP 2: 439 King St., 843/723-6224, www.juanitagreenbergs.com; daily 11am-11pm

SEAFOOD
COAST Bar and Grill $$$

Near 39 Rue de Jean you'll find the affiliated COAST Bar and Grill makes the most of its loud, hip former warehouse setting. The raw bar is satisfying, with a particularly nice take on and selection of ceviche. COAST is a strong local advocate of the Sustainable Seafood Initiative, whereby restaurants work directly with the local fishing industry.

MAP 2: 39D John St., 843/722-8838, www.coastbarandgrill.com; daily 5:30pm-close

★ **39 Rue de Jean** $$$

The best mussels I've ever had were at 39 Rue de Jean. But anything off the bistro-style menu is unbelievably tasty, from the foie gras to the comfit to the coq au vin to the steak frites. There are incredible Prohibition-style cocktails to go along with the extensive wine list.

MAP 2: 39 John St., 843/722-8881; Mon.-Thurs. 11:30am-11pm, Fri.-Sat. 11:30am-1am, Sun. 10am-11pm

BARS AND PUBS

★ **The Recovery Room**

The hottest hipster dive bar is currently The Recovery Room on bustling Upper King. The drinks are cheap and stiff, and the bar food is addictively tasty (two words: Tater Tots!).

MAP 2: 685 King St., 843/727-0999; Mon.-Fri. 4pm-2am, Sat. 3pm-2am, Sun. noon-2am

DANCE CLUBS

Trio Club

The Trio Club, right off Marion Square, is a favorite place to make the scene. There's a relaxing outdoor area with piped-in music, an intimate sofa-filled upstairs bar for dancing and chilling, and the dark candlelit downstairs with frequent live music.

MAP 2: 139 Calhoun St., 843/965-5333; Thurs.-Sat. 9pm-2am

GAY AND LESBIAN

Club Pantheon

Charleston's hottest and hippest dance spot of any type, gay or straight, is Club Pantheon on Upper King on the lower level of the parking garage across from the Visitors Center (375 Meeting St.). Pantheon is not cheap—cover charges are routinely well over $10—but it's worth it for the great DJs, the dancing, and the people-watching, not to mention the drag cabaret on Friday and Sunday nights.

MAP 2: 28 Ann St., 843/577-2582; Fri.-Sun. 10pm-2am

Dudley's

Just down the street from Club Pantheon—and owned by the same people—is a totally different kind of gay bar, Dudley's. Mellower and more appropriate for conversation or a friendly game of pool, Dudley's is a nice contrast to the thumping Pantheon a few doors down.

MAP 2: 42 Ann St., 843/577-6779; daily 4pm-2am

LIVE MUSIC

Music Farm

The venerable Music Farm on Upper King isn't much to look at from the outside, but inside the cavernous space has played host to all sorts of bands over the past two decades. Recent concerts have included Fitz and the Tantrums, the Dropkick Murphys, and the Drive-By Truckers.

MAP 2: 32 Ann St., 843/722-8904, www.musicfarm.com

Doin' the Charleston

It has been called the biggest song and dance craze of the 20th century. It first entered the American public consciousness via New York City in a 1923 Harlem musical called *Runnin' Wild,* but the roots of the dance soon to be known as the Charleston were indeed in the Holy City. No one is quite sure of the day and date, but local lore assures us that members of Charleston's legendary Jenkins Orphanage Band were the first to start dancing that crazy "Geechie step," a development that soon became part of the band's act. The Jenkins Orphanage was started in 1891 by the African American Baptist minister Reverend D. J. Jenkins and was originally housed in the Old Marine Hospital at 20 Franklin Street (which you can see today, although it's not open to the public). To raise money, Reverend Jenkins acquired donated instruments and started a band comprising talented orphans from the house. The orphans traveled as far away as London, where they were a hit with the locals but not with the constabulary, who unceremoni-ously fined them for stopping traffic. A Charleston attorney who happened to be in London at the time, Augustine Smyth, paid their way back home, becoming a lifelong supporter of the orphanage in the process.

From then on, playing in donated old Citadel uniforms, the Jenkins Orphanage Band frequently took its act on the road. They played at the St. Louis and Buffalo expositions, and even at President Taft's inauguration. They also frequently played in New York, and it was there that African American pianist and composer James P. Johnson heard the Charlestonians play and dance to their Gullah rhythms, considered exotic at the time. Johnson would incorporate what he heard into the tune "Charleston," one of many songs in the revue *Runnin' Wild.* The catchy song and its accompanying loose-limbed dance seemed tailor-made for the Roaring '20s and its liberated, hedonistic spirit. Before long the Charleston had swept the nation, becoming a staple of jazz clubs and speakeasies across the country, and indeed, the world.

Hampton Park

Map 2

CLASSIC SOUTHERN
Hominy Grill $ $

With a motto like "Grits are good for you," you know what you're in store for at Hominy Grill, set in a renovated barbershop at Rutledge Avenue and Cannon Street near the Medical University of South Carolina. Primarily revered for his Sunday brunch, Chef Robert Stehling has fun—almost mischievously so—breathing new life into American and Southern classics. Because this is largely a locals' place, you can impress your friends back home by saying you had the rare pleasure of the Hominy's sautéed shad roe with bacon and mushrooms—when the shad are running, that is.

MAP 2: 207 Rutledge Ave., 912/937-0930; Mon.-Fri. 7:30am-8:30pm, Sat.-Sun. 9am-8:30pm

Moe's Crosstown Tavern ⑤⑤

Moe's Crosstown Tavern is not only one of the classic Southern dives but also has one of the best kitchens on this side of town, known for hand-cut fries, great wings, and, most of all, excellent burgers. On Tuesdays, the burgers are half price at happy hour—one of Charleston's best deals.

MAP 2: 714 Rutledge Ave., 843/722-3287; Mon.-Sat. 11am-midnight

ITALIAN
Trattoria Lucca ⑤⑤⑤

A new rave of Charleston foodies is the Tuscan-inspired fare of Chef Ken Vedrinski at Trattoria Lucca. The menu is simple but perfectly focused, featuring handmade pasta and signature items like the pork chop or the fresh cheese plate. You'll be surprised at how much food your money gets you here. Sunday evenings see a family-style prix fixe communal dinner.

MAP 2: 41 Bogard St., 843/973-3323, www.trattorialuccadining.com; Tues.-Thurs. 6pm-10pm, Fri.-Sat. 6pm-11pm, Sun. 5pm-8pm

PUBS AND BARS
Moe's Crosstown Tavern

One of Charleston's favorite neighborhood spots is Moe's Crosstown Tavern at Rutledge and Francis in the Wagener Terrace/Hampton Square area. A newer location, **Moe's Downtown Tavern** (5 Cumberland St., 843/577-8500, daily 11am-2am) offers a similar vibe and menu, but the original, and best, Moe's experience is at the Crosstown.

MAP 2: 714 Rutledge Ave., 843/722-3287; daily 11am-2am

West Ashley

Map 3

AMERICAN
Gene's Haufbrau ⑤

The kitchen at Gene's Haufbrau complements its fairly typical bar-food menu with some good wraps. Start with the "Drunken Trio" (beer-battered cheese sticks, mushrooms, and onion rings) and follow with a portobello wrap or a good old-fashioned crawfish po'boy. One of the best meals for the money in town is Gene's rotating $6.95 blue plate special, offered Monday-Friday 11:30am-4:30pm. The late-night kitchen hours, until 1am, are a big plus.

MAP 3: 17 Savannah Hwy., 843/225-4363, www.geneshaufbrau.com; daily 11:30am-1am

BARBECUE
★ Fiery Ron's Home Team BBQ ⑤⑤

My favorite barbecue joint anywhere, the rowdy and always hopping Fiery Ron's Home Team BBQ has pulled pork and ribs that rank with the best

Clockwise from top left: EVO Pizza; Hominy Grill; Fiery Ron's Home Team BBQ.

I've had anywhere in the country. Even the sides are amazing here, including perfect collards and tasty mac-and-cheese. Chef Madison Ruckel provides an array of table-side sauces, including hot sauce, indigenous South Carolina mustard sauce, and his own "Alabama white," a light and delicious mayonnaise-based sauce. As if that weren't enough, the owners' close ties to the regional jam-band community mean there's great live blues and indie rock after 10pm most nights (Thursday is bluegrass night) to spice up the bar action, which goes until 2am.

MAP 3: 1205 Ashley River Rd., 843/225-7427, www.hometeambbq.com; Mon.-Sat. 11am-9pm, Sun. 11:30am-9pm

CLASSIC SOUTHERN
Middleton Place Restaurant $$

Tucked away on the grounds of the Middleton Place Plantation is the romantic Middleton Place Restaurant. Theirs is a respectful take on traditional plantation fare like hoppin' John, gumbo, she-crab soup, and collards. The special annual Thanksgiving buffet is a real treat. Reservations are required for dinner. A nice plus is being able to wander the gorgeous landscaped gardens before dusk if you arrive at 5:30pm or later with a dinner reservation.

MAP 3: 4300 Ashley River Rd., 843/556-6020, www.middletonplace.org; Tues.-Thurs. and Sun. 11am-3pm and 6pm-8pm, Fri.-Sat. 11am-3pm and 6pm-9pm

MEDITERRANEAN
Al Di La $$

Anything on this northern Italian-themed menu is good, but the risotto—a legacy of original chef John Marshall—is the specialty dish at Al Di La, a very popular West Ashley fine-dining spot. Reservations are recommended.

MAP 3: 25 Magnolia Rd., 843/571-2321, www.aldilarestaurant.com; Tues.-Sat. 6pm-10pm

NEW SOUTHERN
★ Glass Onion $$

One of the more unassuming advocates of farm-to-table dining, Glass Onion is also in an unassuming location on U.S. 17 (Savannah Hwy.) on the western approach to town. That said, their food is right in the thick of the sustainable food movement and also incredibly tasty to boot (not to mention that there is more parking than downtown). The interior says "diner," and indeed the emphasis here is on Southern soul and comfort food classics. A recent trip saw a duck leg with pork belly as a special entrée, and a chicken and andouille gumbo that was zesty without being overspiced, thick without being pasty. There are occasional "all-you-can-eat quail" nights, and every Tuesday is Fried Chicken Dinner night, with what many insist is the best fried chicken in Charleston. The Glass Onion also boasts a good variety of specialty craft brews to wash it all down with. Another plus: In this town full of Sunday brunches, Glass Onion's specialty is a Saturday brunch!

MAP 3: 1219 Savannah Hwy., 843/225-1717, www.ilovetheglassonion.com; Mon.-Thurs. 11am-9pm, Fri. 11am-10pm, Sat. 10am-3pm and 4pm-10pm

LOUNGES

Voodoo Lounge

Across the street from Gene's Haufbrau, the retro-chic Voodoo Lounge is another very popular West Ashley hangout. It has a wide selection of trendy cocktails and killer gourmet tacos.

MAP 3: 15 Magnolia Rd., 843/769-0228; Mon.-Fri. 4pm-2am, Sat.-Sun. 5:30pm-2am, kitchen until 1am

PUBS AND BARS

★ Gene's Haufbrau

Located not too far over the Ashley River on U.S. 17, Charleston institution Gene's Haufbrau is worth making a special trip into West Ashley. Boasting the largest beer selection in Charleston—from the Butte Creek Organic Ale from California to a can of PBR—Gene's also claims to be the oldest bar in town, established in 1952.

MAP 3: 17 Savannah Hwy., 843/225-4363, www.geneshaufbrau.com; daily 11:30am-2am

North Charleston Map 3

PIZZA

EVO Pizzeria ⑤⑤

If you have a hankering for pizza in North Charleston, don't miss EVO Pizzeria in the Olde North Charleston area at Park Circle. They specialize in a small but rich menu of unusual gourmet pizza toppings, like pistachio pesto.

MAP 3: 1075 E. Montague Ave., 843/225-1796, www.evopizza.com; Tues.-Fri. 11am-2:30pm and 5pm-10pm, Sat. 6pm-10pm

PUBS AND BARS

Madra Rua Irish Pub

If you find yourself up in North Charleston, by all means stop by Madra Rua Irish Pub, an authentic watering hole with a better-than-average pub food menu that's also a great place to watch a soccer game.

MAP 3: 1034 E. Montague Ave., 843/554-2522; daily 11am-1am

AMERICAN
Alex's Restaurant ⑤

For a down-home-style pancakes-and-sandwich place that's popular with the locals at all hours of the day, try Alex's Restaurant.

MAP 3: 120 E. 5th N. St., 843/871-3202; daily 24 hours

Guerin's Pharmacy ⑤

A popular local landmark is Guerin's Pharmacy, which claims to be the state's oldest pharmacy. Complete with an old-fashioned soda fountain, they offer malted milkshakes and lemonade.

MAP 3: 140 S. Main St., 843/873-2531; Mon.-Fri. 9am-6pm, Sat. 9am-5pm

Mount Pleasant and East Cooper
Map 4

In Mount Pleasant, most restaurant action centers on the picturesque shrimping village of Shem Creek, which is dotted on both banks with bars and restaurants, most dealing in fresh local seafood. As with Murrells Inlet up the coast, some spots on Shem Creek border on tourist traps. Don't be afraid to go where the lines aren't.

AMERICAN
Poe's Tavern ⑤⑤

For a burger and an adult beverage or two, go straight to friendly Poe's Tavern, a nod to Edgar Allan Poe's stint at nearby Fort Moultrie.

MAP 4: 2210 Middle St., 843/883-0083, www.poestavern.com; daily 11am-10pm

SEAFOOD
Red Drum Gastropub ⑤⑤

If you find yourself thirsty and hungry in Mount Pleasant after dark, you might want to stop in the Red Drum Gastropub, so named because the food here is just as important as the drink. While you're likely to need reservations for the dining room, where you can enjoy Lowcountry-Tex-Mex fusion-style cuisine with a typically Mount Pleasant-like emphasis on seafood, the bar scene is very hopping and fun, with live music every Wednesday-Thursday night.

MAP 4: 803 Coleman Blvd., 843/849-0313, www.reddrumrestaurant.com; Mon.-Tues. 5:30pm-9pm, Wed.-Sat. 5:30pm-10pm

Farmers Markets

A fun and favorite local fixture April-mid-December, the **Charleston Farmers Market** (843/724-7309, www.charlestoncity.info, Sat. 8am-2pm) rings beautiful Marion Square with stalls of local produce, street eats, local arts and crafts, and kids' activities.

Running April-October, East Cooper has its own version in the **Mount Pleasant Farmers Market** (843/884-8517, http://townofmount-pleasant.com, Tues. 3pm-dark) at the Moultrie Middle School on Coleman Boulevard.

★ SeeWee Restaurant 💲💲

A must-stop roadside diner in the Awendaw area is SeeWee Restaurant, about 20 minutes' drive north of Charleston in a humble former general store on the west side of U.S. 17 (the restrooms are still outside). Folks come from Charleston and as far away as Myrtle Beach to enjoy signature menu items like the grouper and the unreal she-crab soup, considered by some epicures to be the best in the world; you can't miss with any of their seafood entrées. Occasionally the crowds can get thick, but rest assured it's worth any wait.

MAP 4: 4808 U.S. 17 N., 843/928-3609; Mon.-Thurs. 11am-8:30pm, Fri.-Sat. 11am-9:30pm, Sun. 11am-8pm

Vickery's Shem Creek Bar and Grill 💲💲

A popular spot, especially for the younger crowd, is Vickery's Shem Creek Bar and Grill. With a similar menu to its partner location on the peninsula, this Vickery's has the pleasant added bonus of a beautiful view overlooking the creek. You'll get more of the Vickery's Cuban flair here, with a great black bean soup and an awesome Cuban sandwich.

MAP 4: 1313 Shrimp Boat Ln., 843/884-4440; daily 11:30am-1am

Water's Edge 💲💲💲

A well-regarded spot on Shem Creek is Water's Edge, which consistently takes home a *Wine Spectator* Award of Excellence for its great selection of vintages. Native Charlestonian Jimmy Purcell concentrates on fresh seafood with a slightly more upscale flair than many Shem Creek places.

MAP 4: 1407 Shrimp Boat Ln., 843/884-4074; daily 11am-11pm

VEGETARIAN

Mustard Seed 💲💲

For a vegetarian-friendly change of pace from seafood, go to the Mustard Seed. The pad thai is probably the best thing on New York-trained chef Sal Parco's creative and dynamic menu, but you might also get a kick out of the sweet potato ravioli.

MAP 4: 1026 Chuck Dawley Blvd., 843/849-0050; Mon.-Sat. 11am-2:30pm and 5pm-9:30pm

The Sprout Cafe ⑤

For a real change of pace, try The Sprout Cafe on U.S. 17. Dealing totally in raw foods, the restaurant emphasizes healthy and fresh ingredients. You might be surprised at the inventiveness of their breakfast-through-dinner seasonal menu—memorably described by the staff as "grab and go"—which might include a tasty crepe topped with a pear-and-nut puree and maple syrup, or a raw squash and zucchini "pasta" dish topped with walnut "meatballs."

MAP 4: 629 Johnnie Dodds Blvd., 843/849-8554, www.thehealthysprout.com; Mon.-Fri. 6am-8pm, Sat. 9am-3pm, Sun. 11am-3pm

PUBS AND BARS

Dunleavy's Pub

Though Sullivan's Island has a lot of high-dollar homes, it still has friendly watering holes like Dunleavy's Pub. Inside is a great bar festooned with memorabilia, or you can enjoy a patio table.

MAP 4: 2213-B Middle St., 843/883-9646; Sun.-Thurs. 11:30am-1am, Fri.-Sat. 11:30am-2am

Poe's Tavern

The other Sullivan's watering hole of note is Poe's Tavern across the street, a nod to Edgar Allan Poe and his service on the island as a clerk in the U.S. Army. It's a lively, mostly locals scene, set within a fun but suitably dark interior (though you might opt for one of the outdoor tables on the raised patio). Simply put, no trip to Sullivan's is complete without a stop at one (or possibly both) of these two local landmarks, which are within a stone's throw of each other.

MAP 4: 2210 Middle St., 843/883-0083; www.poestavern.com; daily 11am-2am

Folly Beach and the Southwest Islands   Map 5

BARBECUE

JB's Smokeshack ⑤

If barbecue is your thing, head straight to JB's Smokeshack, one of the best 'cue joints in the Lowcountry. They offer a buffet for $8.88 pp ($5 under age 11), or you can opt for a barbecue plate, including hash, rice, and two sides. In a nice twist, the plates include a three-meat option: pork, chicken, ribs, or brisket.

MAP 5: 3406 Maybank Hwy., 843/557-0426, www.jbssmokeshack.com; Wed.-Sat. 11am-8:30pm

Top: BLU Restaurant and Bar. **Bottom:** Fat Hen.

BREAKFAST AND BRUNCH
Lost Dog Café ⑤

The closest thing to a taste of old Folly is the Lost Dog Café, so named for its bulletin board stacked with alerts about lost pets, pets for adoption, and new pups and kittens for sale or giveaway. They open early, the better to offer a tasty, healthy breakfast to the surfing crowd. It's a great place to pick up a quick, inexpensive, and tasty meal while you're near the beach.
MAP 5: 106 W. Huron Ave., 843/588-9669; daily 6:30am-3pm

Sunrise Bistro ⑤

For a hearty and delicious breakfast, go to Sunrise Bistro, one of those unassuming diners that always seems to have an eager crowd. Everything, from the omelets to the pancakes down to the simplest bagel with coffee, is spot-on, and a great value to boot. The best offerings here are during the day.
MAP 5: 1797 Main Rd., 843/718-1858, www.sunrise-bistro.com; Tues.-Thurs. 7am-2:30pm, Fri.-Sat. 7am-2:30pm and 5pm-9pm, Sun. 9am-1pm

FRENCH
★ Fat Hen ⑤⑤

Fat Hen is a self-styled "country French bistro" begun by a couple of old Charleston restaurant hands. The fried oysters are a particular specialty. There's also a bar menu for late-night hours (10pm-2am).
MAP 5: 3140 Maybank Hwy., 843/559-9090; Tues.-Sat. 11:30am-3pm and 5:30pm-10pm, Sun. 10am-3pm

MEXICAN
Taco Boy ⑤

Taco Boy is a fun place to get a fish taco, have a margarita, and take a walk on the nearby beach afterward. Though no one is under any illusions that this is an authentic Mexican restaurant, the fresh guacamole is particularly rave-worthy, and there's a good selection of tequilas and beers *hecho en México,* with the bar staying open until 2am on weekends.
MAP 5: 15 Center St., 843/588-9761; Sun.-Thurs. 11am-10pm, Fri.-Sat. 11am-11pm

SEAFOOD
Bowens Island Restaurant ⑤

Fans of the legendary Bowens Island Restaurant, on James Island just before you get to Folly, went into mourning when it burned to the ground in 2006. But you can't keep a good oysterman down, and owner Robert Barber rebuilt. A universe removed from the Lexus-and-khaki scene downtown, Bowens Island isn't the place for the uptight. This is the spot to go when you want shovels of oysters literally thrown onto your table, freshly steamed and delicious and all-you-can-eat. The fried shrimp, flounder, and hush puppies are incredible too. To get there from the peninsula, take Calhoun Street west onto the James Island Connector (Hwy. 30). Take exit 3 onto Highway 171 south and look for Bowens Island Road on the right. The restaurant will be on the left in a short while, after passing by several ritzy McMansions that in no way resemble the restaurant you're about to experience.

MAP 5: 1870 Bowens Island Rd., 843/795-2757; Tues.-Sat. 5-10pm; cash only

LIVE MUSIC
The Pour House
The hippest music spot in town is out on James Island at The Pour House, where the local characters are sometimes just as entertaining as the acts onstage.

MAP 5: 1977 Maybank Hwy., 843/571-4343, www.charlestonpourhouse.com; 9pm-2am on nights with music scheduled

PUBS AND BARS
BLU Restaurant and Bar
If you're in Folly Beach, enjoy the great views and the great cocktails at BLU Restaurant and Bar inside the Holiday Inn Folly Beach Oceanfront. There's nothing like a Spiked Lemonade on a hot Charleston day at the beach.

MAP 5: 1 Center St., 843/588-6658, www.blufollybeach.com; daily 7am-10pm

Sand Dollar Social Club
Another notable Folly Beach watering hole is the Sand Dollar Social Club, the kind of cash-only, mostly local dive you often find in little beach towns. You have to pony up for a "membership" to this private club, but it's only a buck. There's a catch, though: You can't get in until your 24-hour "waiting period" is over.

MAP 5: 7 Center St., 843/588-9498; Sun.-Fri. noon-1am, Sat. noon-2am

Arts and Culture

U nlike the (literally) more puritanical colonies farther up the North American coast, Charleston was an arts-friendly settlement from the beginning. The first theatrical production on the continent happened in Charleston in January 1735, when a nomadic troupe rented a space at Church and Broad

Streets to perform Thomas Otway's *The Orphan*. The play's success led to the building of the Dock Street Theatre on what is now Queen Street. Notable thespians performing in town included Edwin Booth, Junius Booth Jr. (brothers of Lincoln's assassin John Wilkes), and Edgar Allan Poe's mother Eliza.

While not considered a visual arts mecca, since native son Joseph Allen Smith began one of the country's first art collections in Charleston in the late 1700s, the Holy City has been fertile ground for visual artists. For most visitors, the center of gallery activity is in the French Quarter between South Market and Tradd Streets.

Shopping in Charleston centers on King Street, unique not only for the fact that so many national-name stores are lined up so close to each other but because there are so many great restaurants of so many different types scattered in and among the retail outlets, ideally positioned for when you need to take a break to rest and refuel.

King Street has three distinct areas with three distinct types of merchandise: **Lower King** is primarily top-of-the-line antiques stores (most are closed Sundays, so plan your trip accordingly); **Middle King** is where you'll find upscale name-brand outlets such as Banana Republic and American

Previous: historic King Street; Robert Lange Studios.

Look for ★ to find
recommended arts and culture listings.

Highlights

★ **Closest Brush with History:** The professional **Charleston Stage** company performs in the restored Dock Street Theatre, where North America's first theater productions were held (page 109).

★ **Most Laughs Per Capita:** Theatre 99 is home to **The Have Nots!,** a top-quality improv comedy troupe (page 111).

★ **Victorious Vintage:** Funk, fun, and frivolity meet at **The Trunk Show** on Meeting Street, the place for vintage duds and high-end costume wear (page 112).

★ **Most Precious Place for Precious Metals:** One of Charleston's oldest, quirkiest, and most respected jewelry stores is **Croghan's Jewel Box,** in business on Lower King for over a century and through 11 generations (page 114).

★ **Greatest Gallery:** The nonprofit **Redux Contemporary Art Center** on Upper King brings a taste of counterculture and cutting-edge art to this often conservative town (page 116).

★ **Bibliophiles Welcome:** Charming **Blue Bicycle Books** on Upper King is the place to go for local and regional authors (page 117).

★ **Best Antiquing Adventure:** Rambling **Page's Thieves Market** in Mount Pleasant has a surprise around every unpredictable corner (page 119).

Apparel as well as some excellent shoe stores; and **Upper King,** north of Calhoun Street, is where you'll find funky housewares shops, generally locally owned.

South of Broad Map 1

ART GALLERIES
Charleston Renaissance Gallery
Charleston Renaissance Gallery specializes in 19th- and 20th-century oils and sculpture and features artists from the American South, including some splendid pieces from the Charleston Renaissance.

MAP 1: 103 Church St., 843/723-0025, www.fineartsouth.com; Mon.-Sat. 10am-5pm

Helena Fox Fine Art
Helena Fox Fine Art deals in 20th-century representational art.

MAP 1: 106-A Church St., 843/723-0073, www.helenafoxfineart.com; Mon.-Sat. 10am-5pm

Waterfront Map 1

ART GALLERIES
City Gallery at Waterfront
The City Gallery at Waterfront is funded by the city, with exhibits focusing on local and regional culture and folkways.

MAP 1: 34 Prioleau St., 843/958-6484; Tues.-Fri. 11am-6pm, Sat.-Sun. noon-5pm

SHOPS
Home Goods
Charleston Cooks!
Affiliated with the hip local restaurant chain Maverick Kitchens, Charleston Cooks! has an almost overwhelming array of gourmet items and kitchenware, and even offers cooking classes.

MAP 1: 194 E. Bay St., 843/722-1212, www.charlestoncooks.com; Mon.-Sat. 10am-9pm, Sun. 11am-6pm

Indigo
Indigo, a favorite home accessories store, has plenty of one-of-a-kind pieces, many of them by regional artists and rustic in flavor, almost like outsider art.

MAP 1: 4 Vendue Range, 800/549-2513; Sun.-Thurs. 10am-6pm, Fri.-Sat. 10am-7pm

ART GALLERIES
Anne Worsham Richardson Birds Eye View Gallery
The Anne Worsham Richardson Birds Eye View Gallery is the home of
South Carolina's official painter of the state flower and state bird.
MAP 1: 119-A Church St., 843/723-1276, www.anneworshamrichardson.com; Mon.-Sat.
10am-5pm

Pink House Gallery
The Pink House Gallery is in the oldest tavern building in the South, built
circa 1694. The exhibits here offer a glimpse into old Charleston, including
exclusive antique prints.
MAP 1: 17 Chalmers St., 843/723-3608, http://pinkhousegallery.tripod.com; Mon.-Sat.
10am-5pm

Robert Lange Studios
In the heart of the French Quarter, Robert Lange Studios is oriented toward
modern art. It hosts not only the work of its owners, Robert and Megan
Lange, but also a slate of up-and-coming regional artists.
MAP 1: 2 Queen St., 843/805-8052, www.robertlangestudios.com; daily 11am-5pm

PERFORMING ARTS
Music
Charleston Symphony Orchestra
The Charleston Symphony Orchestra (CSO) performed for the first time on
December 28, 1936, at the Hibernian Hall on Meeting Street. During that
first season the CSO accompanied *The Recruiting Officer,* the inaugural show
at the renovated Dock Street Theatre. For seven decades, the CSO continued
to provide world-class orchestral music, gaining "Metropolitan" status in the
1970s, when they accompanied the first-ever local performance of *Porgy and
Bess,* which despite its Charleston setting couldn't be performed locally before then due to segregation laws. Check the website for upcoming concerts.
MAP 1: Dock Street Theatre, 135 Church St., 843/554-6060, www.charlestonsymphony.com

Art Walks

The best way to experience art
in Charleston's French Quarter is
to go on one of the popular and
free **French Quarter ArtWalks**
(843/724-3424, www.frenchquar-
terarts.com), held the first Friday of
March, May, October, and December
5pm-8pm and featuring lots of wine,
food, and, of course, art. You can
download a map at the website.

Chamber Music in Charleston

Chamber Music Charleston (various locations, 843/763-4941, www.chambermusiccharleston.org), which relies on many core Charleston Symphony Orchestra musicians, continues to perform around town, including at Piccolo Spoleto. They play a wide variety of picturesque historic venues, including the Old Exchange (120 E. Bay St.), the Calhoun Mansion (16 Meeting St.), and the Footlight Players Theatre (20 Queen St.). They can also be found at private house concerts, which sell out quickly.

Theater
★ Charleston Stage

Several high-quality troupes continue to keep Charleston's proud theater tradition alive, chief among them being Charleston Stage, the resident company of the Dock Street Theatre. In addition to its well-received regular season of classics and modern staples, Charleston Stage has debuted more than 30 original scripts over the years, most recently *Gershwin at Folly*, recounting the composer's time at Folly Beach working on *Porgy and Bess*.

MAP 1: Dock Street Theatre, 135 Church St., 843/577-7183, www.charlestonstage.com

The Footlight Players

The Footlight Players are the oldest continuously active company in town, founded in 1931. This community-based amateur company performs a mix of crowd-pleasers (*Who's Afraid of Virginia Woolf?*) and creative adaptations (*Miracle in Bedford Falls*, a musical based on *It's a Wonderful Life*) at their space at 20 Queen Street.

MAP 1: Footlight Players Theatre, 20 Queen St., 843/722-4487, www.footlightplayers.net

PURE Theatre

The players of PURE Theatre perform at the Circular Congregational Church's Lance Hall (150 Meeting St.). Their shows emphasize compelling, mature drama, beautifully performed. This is where to catch less glitzy, grittier productions like *Rabbit Hole*, *American Buffalo*, and *Cold Tectonics*, a hit at Piccolo Spoleto.

MAP 1: Lance Hall, 150 Meeting St., 843/723-4444, www.puretheatre.org

SHOPS
Books and Music
Shops of Historic Charleston Foundation

Along the same lines as the Preservation Society is the great Shops of Historic Charleston Foundation, with plenty of tasteful Charleston-themed gift ideas, from books to kitchenware, housed in a beautiful building.

MAP 1: 108 Meeting St., 843/724-8484, www.historiccharleston.org

ARTS AND CULTURE
FRENCH QUARTER

Top: Pure Theatre. **Bottom:** Ann Long Fine Art.

ART GALLERIES
Ann Long Fine Art
Right up the street from the Sylvan Gallery and incorporating works from
the estate of Charleston legend Elizabeth O'Neill Verner is Ann Long Fine
Art, which seeks to combine the painterly aesthetic of the Old World with
the edgy vision of the New.

MAP 1: 54 Broad St., 843/577-0447, www.annlongfineart.com; Mon.-Sat. 11am-5pm

Sylvan Gallery
For a more modern take from local artists, check out the Sylvan Gallery,
which specializes in 20th- and 21st-century art and sculpture.

MAP 1: 171 King St., 843/722-2172, www.thesylvangallery.com; Mon.-Fri. 9am-5pm, Sat.
10am-5pm, Sun. 11am-4pm

The Audubon Gallery
Farther up King and specializing in original Audubon prints and an-
tique botanical prints is The Audubon Gallery, the sister store of the Joel
Oppenheimer Gallery in Chicago.

MAP 1: 190 King St., 843/853-1100, www.audubonart.com; Mon.-Sat. 10am-5pm

PERFORMING ARTS
Theater
★ The Have Nots!
The city's most unusual players are The Have Nots!, with a total ensemble
of 35 comedians who typically perform their brand of edgy improv every
Friday night at Theatre 99.

MAP 1: Theatre 99, 280 Meeting St., 843/853-6687, www.theatre99.com; Wed. 8pm,
Fri.-Sat. 8pm and 10pm; $5-12.50

SHOPS
Antiques
Alexandra AD
A relatively new addition to Lower King's cluster of antiques shops,
Alexandra AD features great chandeliers, lamps, and fabrics.

MAP 1: 156 King St., 843/722-4897; Mon.-Sat. 10am-5pm

A'riga IV
On the 200 block of King Street, A'riga IV deals in a quirky mix of 19th-
century decorative arts, including rare apothecary items.

MAP 1: 204 King St., 843/577-3075; Mon.-Sat. 10:30am-4:30pm

George C. Birlant & Co.

Since 1929, George C. Birlant & Co. has been importing 18th- and 19th-century furniture, silver, china, and crystal, and also deals in the famous "Charleston Battery Bench."

MAP 1: 191 King St., 843/722-3842; Mon.-Sat. 9am-5:30pm

Books and Music
Pauline Books and Media

The charming Pauline Books and Media is run by the Daughters of Saint Paul and carries Christian books, Bibles, rosaries, and images from a Roman Catholic perspective.

MAP 1: 243 King St., 843/577-0175; Mon.-Sat. 10am-6pm

Preservation Society of Charleston Book and Gift Shop

It's easy to overlook at the far southern end of retail development on King, but the excellent Preservation Society of Charleston Book and Gift Shop is perhaps the best place in town to pick up books on Charleston lore and history as well as locally themed gift items.

MAP 1: 147 King St., 843/722-4630; Mon.-Sat. 10am-5pm

Clothes
Berlins Men's and Women's

A charmingly old-school and notable locally owned clothing store on King Street is the classy Berlins Men's and Women's, dating from 1883. It has survived both the Great Charleston Earthquake of 1886 and Hurricane Hugo in 1989. Despite the name, Berlins focuses on men's clothing, offering designs from Canali, Coppley, Jack Victor, and more.

MAP 1: 114-120 King St., 843/722-1665; Mon.-Sat. 9:30am-6pm

Oops!

Big companies' losses are your gain at Oops!, which buys factory mistakes and discontinued lines from major brands at a discount, passing along the savings to you. The range here tends toward colorful and preppy.

MAP 1: 326 King St., 843/722-7768; Mon.-Fri. 10am-6pm, Sat. 10am-7pm, Sun. noon-6pm

★ The Trunk Show

Women come from throughout the region to shop at the incredible consignment store The Trunk Show. You can find one-of-a-kind vintage and designer wear and accessories. Some finds are bargains, some not so much, but there's no denying the quality and breadth of the offerings.

MAP 1: 281 Meeting St., 843/722-0442; Mon.-Sat. 10am-6pm

Top: Preservation Society of Charleston Book and Gift Shop. **Bottom:** The Trunk Show.

Worthwhile

For a locally owned clothing shop, try the innovative Worthwhile, which has lots of organic fashions.

MAP 1: 268 King St., 843/723-4418, www.shopworthwhile.com; Mon.-Sat. 10am-6pm, Sun. noon-5pm

Health and Beauty

Stella Nova

The Euro-style window display of Stella Nova beckons at the corner of King and Society. Inside this locally owned cosmetics store and studio you'll find a wide selection of high-end makeup and beauty products. There's also a Stella Nova day spa (78 Society St., 843/723-0909, Mon.-Sat. 9am-6pm, Sun. noon-5pm).

MAP 1: 292 King St., 843/722-9797; Mon.-Sat. 10am-7pm, Sun. 1pm-5pm

Jewelry

Art Jewelry by Mikhail Smolkin

Art Jewelry by Mikhail Smolkin features one-of-a-kind pieces by this St. Petersburg, Russia, native.

MAP 1: 312 King St., 843/722-3634, www.fineartjewelry.com; Mon.-Sat. 10am-5pm

★ Croghan's Jewel Box

Since 1919, Croghan's Jewel Box has offered amazing locally crafted diamonds, silver, and designer pieces to generations of Charlestonians. An expansion in the late 1990s tripled the size of the historic location.

MAP 1: 308 King St., 843/723-3594, www.croghansjewelbox.com; Mon.-Fri. 9:30am-5:30pm, Sat. 10am-5pm

Joint Venture Estate Jewelers

Joint Venture Estate Jewelers specializes in antique, vintage, and modern estate jewelry as well as pre-owned watches, including Rolex, Patek Philippe, and Cartier, with a fairly unique consignment emphasis.

MAP 1: 185 King St., 843/722-6730, www.jventure.com; Mon.-Sat. 10am-5:30pm

Shoes

Bob Ellis Shoe Store

A famous locally owned place for footwear is Bob Ellis Shoe Store, which has served Charleston's elite with high-end shoes since 1950.

MAP 1: 332 King St., 843/722-2515, www.bobellisshoes.com; Mon.-Sat. 10am-6pm

Copper Penny Shooz

Copper Penny Shooz combines hip and upscale footwear for women, "curated with a Southern eye," as this Charleston-based regional chain's motto goes.

MAP 1: 317 King St., 843/723-3838; Mon.-Sat. 10am-7pm, Sun. noon-6pm

Phillips Shoes

Funky and fun Phillips Shoes deals in Dansko for men, women, and kids (don't miss the awesome painting above the register of Elvis fitting a customer).

MAP 1: 320 King St., 843/965-5270; Mon.-Sat. 10am-6pm

Rangoni of Florence

Rangoni of Florence imports the best women's shoes from Italy, with a few men's designs as well.

MAP 1: 270 King St., 843/577-9554; Mon.-Sat. 9:30am-6pm, Sun. 12:30pm-5:30pm

Shopping Centers and Malls
Belmond Charleston Place

Belmond Charleston Place, a combined retail-hotel development begun to much controversy in the late 1970s, was the first big downtown redevelopment project of Mayor Riley's tenure. While naysayers said people would never come downtown to shop for boutique items, Riley proved them wrong, and years later Belmond Charleston Place remains a big shopping draw for locals and visitors alike. Highlights inside the large, stylish space include Gucci, Talbots, Louis Vuitton, Yves Delorme, Everything But Water, and Godiva.

MAP 1: 205 Meeting St., 843/722-4900, www.charlestonplaceshops.com; Mon.-Wed. 10am-6pm, Thurs.-Sat. 10am-8pm, Sun. noon-5pm

City Market

For years dominated by a flea market vibe, City Market was recently upgraded and is now chockablock with boutique retail all along its lengthy interior. The more humble crafts tables are toward the back. If you must have one of the handcrafted sweetgrass baskets, try out your haggling skills—the prices have wiggle room built in. In addition to the myriad of tourist-oriented shops in the City Market itself, there are a few gems in the surrounding area that also appeal to locals.

MAP 1: Meeting St. and Market St., 843/973-7236; daily 9:30am-10:30pm

Sporting Goods
Half Moon Outfitters

With retail locations in Charleston and throughout South Carolina and Georgia and a new cutting-edge, green-friendly warehouse in North Charleston, Half Moon Outfitters is something of a local legend. Here you can find not only top-of-the-line camping and outdoor gear and good tips on local recreation but some really stylish outdoorsy apparel as well.

MAP 1: 280 King St., 843/853-0990, www.halfmoonoutfitters.com; Mon.-Sat. 10am-7pm, Sun. noon-6pm

ART GALLERIES
Gallery Chuma

In the Upper King area is Gallery Chuma, which specializes in the art of the Gullah people of the South Carolina coast. They put on lots of cultural and educational events about Gullah culture as well as display art on the subject.

MAP 2: 43 John St., 843/722-7568, www.gallerychuma.com; Mon.-Sat. 10am-6pm

★ Redux Contemporary Art Center

One of the most important single venues, the nonprofit Redux Contemporary Art Center features modernistic work in a variety of media, including illustration, video installation, blueprints, performance art, and graffiti. Outreach is hugely important to this venture and includes lecture series, classes, workshops, and internships.

MAP 2: 136 St. Philip St., 843/722-0697, www.reduxstudios.org; Tues.-Thurs. noon-8pm, Fri.-Sat. noon-5pm

SHOPS
Arts and Crafts
Artist & Craftsman Supply

Charleston's favorite art supply store is Artist & Craftsman Supply, part of a well-regarded Maine-based chain. They cater to the pro as well as the dabbler and have a fun children's art section as well.

MAP 2: 434 King St., 843/579-0077, www.artistcraftsman.com; Mon.-Sat. 10am-7pm, Sun. noon-5pm

Collegiate Music

The excellent music department at the College of Charleston sponsors the annual **Charleston Music Fest** (www.charlestonmusicfest.com), a series of chamber music concerts at various venues around the beautiful campus, featuring many faculty members of the college as well as visiting guest artists. Other college musical offerings include the **College of Charleston Concert Choir** (www.cofc.edu/music), which performs at various venues, usually churches, around town during the fall; the **College of Charleston Opera,** which performs at least one full-length production during the school year and often takes the stage at Piccolo Spoleto; and the popular **Yuletide Madrigal Singers,** who sing in early December at a series of concerts in historic Randolph Hall.

★ Blue Bicycle Books

Housed in an extremely long and narrow storefront on Upper King, Jonathan Sanchez's funky and friendly Blue Bicycle Books deals primarily in used books and has a particularly nice stock of local and regional books, art books, and fiction.

MAP 2: 420 King St., 843/722-2666, www.bluebicyclebooks.com; Mon.-Sat. 10am-6pm, Sun. 1pm-6pm

Health and Beauty
Allure Salon

For stylish haircuts and expert, cutting-edge color work, go to Allure on Upper King. They've styled some of Charleston's poshest weddings and are the founding hair care sponsor of Charleston Fashion Week.

MAP 2: 415 King St., 843/722-8689; Tues. and Thurs. 10am-7pm, Wed. and Fri. 9am-5pm, Sat. 10am-3pm

Spa Adagio

Inside the Francis Marion Hotel near Marion Square is Spa Adagio, offering massage, waxing, and skin and nail care.

MAP 2: 387 King St., 843/577-2444; Mon.-Sat. 10am-7pm, Sun. by appointment only

Home Goods
Charleston Gardens

A great home and garden store on Upper King, Charleston Gardens is the outlet for a locally originated national mail-order chain famous for furniture and accessories.

MAP 2: 650 King St., 866/469-0118, www.charlestongardens.com; Mon.-Sat. 9am-5pm

Haute Design Studio

Head to Haute Design Studio for upper-end furnishings with an edgy feel.

MAP 2: 489 King St., 843/577-9886, www.hautedesign.com; Mon.-Fri. 9am-5:30pm

Hampton Park

Map 2

SHOPS
Hats
Magar Hatworks

If hats are your thing, make sure you visit Magar Hatworks, where Leigh Magar makes and sells her whimsical, all-natural hats, some of which she designs for Barneys New York.

MAP 2: 57 Cannon St., 843/577-7740, www.magarhatworks.com; by appointment

SHOPS
Home Goods
ESD, Elizabeth Stuart Design

Probably Charleston's best-regarded home goods store is the nationally recognized ESD, Elizabeth Stuart Design, with a wide range of antique and new furnishings, art, lighting, jewelry, and more.

MAP 3: 422 Savannah Hwy./U.S. 17, 843/225-6282, www.esdcharleston.com; Mon.-Sat. 10am-6pm

North Charleston
Map 3

SHOPS
Music
The Guitar Center

The biggest music store in the region is The Guitar Center in North Charleston across from Northwood Mall. With just about everything a musician might want or need, it's part of a chain that has been around since the late 1950s, but the Charleston location is relatively new.

MAP 3: 7620 Rivers Ave., 843/572-9063; Mon.-Fri. 11am-7pm, Sat. 10am-7pm, Sun. noon-6pm

Shopping Centers
Tanger Outlet

North Charleston hosts the Tanger Outlet. Get factory-priced bargains from stores such as Adidas, Banana Republic, Brooks Brothers, CorningWare, Old Navy, Timberland, and more.

MAP 3: 4840 Tanger Outlet Blvd., 843/529-3095, www.tangeroutlet.com; Mon.-Sat. 10am-9pm, Sun. 11am-6pm

SHOPS
Antiques
★ Page's Thieves Market

Mount Pleasant boasts a fun antiques and auction spot, Page's Thieves Market. Its rambling interior has hosted bargain and vintage shoppers for 50 years, and it's routinely voted Charleston's Best Antiques Store.

MAP 4: 1460 Ben Sawyer Blvd., 843/884-9672, www.pagesthievesmarket.com; Mon.-Fri. 9am-5:30pm, Sat. 9am-5pm

Shopping Centers
Mount Pleasant Towne Center

The newest and most pleasant mall in the area is the retro-themed, pedestrian-friendly Mount Pleasant Towne Center, which opened in 1999 to serve the growing population of East Cooper residents tired of having to cross a bridge to get to a big mall. In addition to national chains you'll find a few cool local stores in here, like Stella Nova spa and day salon, Copper Penny Shooz, and the men's store Jos. A. Bank.

MAP 4: 1600 Palmetto Grande Dr., 843/216-9900, www.mtpleasanttownecentre.com; Mon.-Sat. 10am-9pm, Sun. noon-6pm

Folly Beach and
the Southwest Islands

Map 5

CINEMA
The Terrace

The most interesting art house and indie venue in town is The Terrace, and not only because they offer beer and wine, which you can enjoy at your seat. Shows before 5pm are $7. It's west of Charleston on James Island; get there by taking U.S. 17 west from Charleston and go south on Highway 171, then take a right on Maybank Highway (Hwy. 700).

MAP 5: 1956 Maybank Hwy., 843/762-9494, www.terracetheater.com

Sports and Activities

Because of the generally great weather in Charleston, encouraged by the steady, soft sea breeze, outdoor activities are always popular and available. Though it's not much of a spectator sports town, there are plenty of things to do on your own, such as golf, tennis, walking, hiking, boating, and fishing.

Offshore diving centers on a network of artificial reefs (see www.dnr.sc.gov for a list and locations), particularly the "Charleston 60" sunken barge and the popular "Train Wreck," comprising 50 deliberately sunk New York City subway cars. In addition to being fun dive sites, these artificial reefs have proven to be important feeding and spawning grounds for marine life.

The surfing at the famous **Washout** area on the east side of Folly Beach isn't what it used to be due to storm activity and beach erosion. But diehards still gather at this area when the swell hits. Check out the conditions yourself from the three views of the Folly Surfcam (www.follysurfcam.com).

The country's first golf course was constructed in Charleston in 1786, so as you'd expect, there's great golfing in the area, generally on the outlying islands. The folks at the nonprofit **Charleston Golf, Inc.** (423 King St., 843/958-3629, www.charlestongolfguide.com) are your best one-stop resource for tee times and packages.

Charleston-area beaches are perfect for a leisurely bike ride on the sand. Sullivan's Island is a particular favorite, and you might be surprised at how long you can ride in one direction on these beaches. Those desiring a more demanding use of their legs can walk or ride their bike in the dedicated

Previous: schooner sailing ship on the Cooper River; Kiawah Island Golf Resort.

Look for ★ to find
recommended activities.

Highlights

★ **Best Place to Meet Bill Murray:** The iconic actor and former SNL star is also part-owner of the **Charleston River Dogs** minor league baseball team and occasionally attends games (page 127).

★ **Most Fanatic Fans:** The South means college football. Though no one would say the **Citadel Bulldogs** play at the region's highest level, the fans who pack Johnson Hagood Stadium are among the most devout (page 127).

★ **Wildest Walk in the Woods:** The **I'on Swamp Trail** takes hikers through portions of the huge Francis Marion National Forest. Some of North America's best migratory bird-watching is in this area,

including occasional glimpses of the very rare Bachman's warbler (page 129).

★ **Most Excellent Ecotour:** Charleston's original outfitter, **Coastal Expeditions,** offers plenty of specialized kayak tours from Shem Creek, Folly Creek, and Isle of Palms. They're also the exclusive provider of guided boat tours to scenic Bulls Island within Cape Romain NWR (page 133).

★ **Loveliest Links:** You can't beat the windswept natural scenery of **Kiawah Island Golf Resort,** home of the famed Ocean Course. Even if you're not a golfer, there's plenty to enjoy at this sea island getaway (page 136).

Free Tennis, Anyone?

There are four free, public, city-funded facilities on the peninsula:

- **Moultrie Playground:** Broad St. and Ashley Ave., 843/769-8258, www.charlestoncity.info, six lighted hard courts

- **Jack Adams Tennis Center:** 290 Congress St., six lighted hard courts

- **Hazel Parker Playground:** 70 E. Bay St., on the Cooper River, one hard court

- **Corrine Jones Playground:** Marlowe St. and Peachtree St., two hard courts

TOURS
Kayaking Tours
★ Coastal Expeditions

An excellent outfit for guided kayak tours is Coastal Expeditions, which also runs the only approved ferry service to the Cape Romain National Wildlife Refuge. They'll rent you a kayak for roughly $50 per day. Coastal Expeditions also sells an outstanding kayaking, boating, and fishing map of the area (about $12).

MAP 4: 654 Serotina Ct., 843/881-4582, www.coastalexpeditions.com

Nature Adventures Outfitters

The best tour operator close to downtown is Nature Adventures Outfitters, which puts in on Shem Creek in Mount Pleasant for most of its 2-, 2.5-, 3-, and 3.5-hour and full-day guided trips, with prices from $40 to $85. They also offer blackwater tours out of landings at other locations; see the website for specific directions for those tours.

MAP 4: Shrimp Boat Ln., 843/568-3222, www.kayakcharlestonsc.com

Ecotours

This aspect of Charleston's tourism scene is very well represented. The best operators include: **Barrier Island Eco Tours** (50 41st Ave., 843/886-5000, www.nature-tours.com, from $38), taking you up to the Cape Romain Refuge out of Isle of Palms; **Coastal Expeditions** (514-B Mill St., 843/884-7684, www.coastalexpeditions.com, prices vary), with a base on Shem Creek in Mount Pleasant, offering several different-length sea kayak adventures; and **PaddleFish Kayaking** (843/330-9777, www.paddlefishkayaking.com, from $45), offering several kinds of kayaking tours (no experience necessary) from downtown, Kiawah Island, and Seabrook Island.

Folly Beach and the Southwest Islands

Map 5

BEACHES

Folly Beach County Park

In addition to the charming town of Folly Beach itself, there's the modest county-run Folly Beach County Park at the far west end of Folly Island. It has a picnic area, restrooms, outdoor showers, and beach chair and umbrella rentals. Get there by taking Highway 171 (Folly Rd.) until it turns into Center Street, and then take a right on West Ashley Avenue.

MAP 5: 1100 W. Ashley Ave., Folly Beach, 843/588-2426, www.ccprc.com; May-Feb. daily 10am-dark, Mar.-Apr. daily 9am-dark; $7 per vehicle, free for pedestrians and cyclists

Kiawah Island Beachwalker Park

On the west end of Kiawah Island to the south of Charleston is Kiawah Island Beachwalker Park, the only public facility on this mostly private resort island. It has restrooms, showers, a picnic area with grills, and beach chair and umbrella rentals. Get there from downtown by taking Lockwood Avenue onto the Highway 30 Connector bridge over the Ashley River. Turn right onto Folly Road, then take a left onto Maybank Highway. After about 20 minutes you'll take another left onto Bohicket Road, which leads you to Kiawah in 14 miles. Turn left from Bohicket Road onto the Kiawah Island Parkway. Just before the security gate, turn right on Beachwalker Drive and follow the signs to the park.

MAP 5: Kiawah Island, 843/768-2395, www.ccprc.com; Mar.-Apr. and Oct. Sat.-Sun. 10am-6pm, May-Aug. daily 9am-7pm, Sept. daily 10am-6pm; $7 per vehicle, free for pedestrians and cyclists

BIRD-WATCHING

Legare Farms

On Johns Island southwest of Charleston is Legare Farms, which holds migratory bird walks ($6 adults, $3 children) in the fall each Saturday at 8:30am.

MAP 5: 2620 Hanscombe Point Rd., Johns Island, 843/559-0788, www.legarefarms.com; farm hours vary

GOLF

Charleston Municipal Golf Course

The main public course is the 18-hole City of Charleston Golf Course, affectionately referred to as The Muni. To get there from the peninsula, take U.S. 17 south over the Ashley River, take Highway 171 (Folly Rd.) south, and then take a right onto Maybank Highway.

MAP 5: 2110 Maybank Hwy., 843/795-6517, www.charleston-sc.gov/golf; $22-24/18 holes

Clockwise from top left: tennis at Kiawah Island Golf Resort; surfing at Folly Beach; relaxing on Folly Beach.

Probably the most renowned area facilities are at the acclaimed Kiawah Island Golf Resort, about 20 miles from Charleston. The resort has five courses in all, the best known of which is the **Kiawah Island Ocean Course**, site of the famous "War by the Shore" 1991 Ryder Cup. This 2.5-mile course, which is walking-only until noon each day, hosted the Senior PGA Championship in 2007 and the PGA Championship in 2012. The resort offers a golf academy and private lessons galore. These are public courses, but be aware that tee times are limited for golfers who aren't guests at the resort.

MAP 5: 12 Kiawah Beach Dr., Kiawah Island, 800/654-2924, www.kiawahresort.com/golf; $150-350/18 holes, 25 percent discount for resort guests

SURFING AND KITEBOARDING

Folly Beach Shaka Surf School

Around since 2004, Folly Beach Shaka Surf School offers private and group surf lessons, including youth surf camps throughout summer, women-only weekend outings, and yoga classes geared toward surfers. Surf camps are located on the east end of Folly Beach.

MAP 5: 107 E. Indian Ave., Folly Beach, 843/607-9911, www.shakasurfschool.com

McKevlin's Surf Shop

The best local surf shop is undoubtedly the historic McKevlin's Surf Shop on Folly Beach, one of the first surf shops on the East Coast, dating to 1965. Check out an employee's "No Pop-Outs" blog at http://mckevlins.blogspot.com.

MAP 5: 8 Center St., Folly Beach, 843/588-2247, www.mckevlins.com; spring-summer daily 9am-6pm, fall-winter daily 10am-5:30pm

TENNIS

Kiawah Island Golf Resort

The best resort tennis activity is at the Kiawah Island Golf Resort. The resort's Roy Barth Tennis Center has nine clay and three hard courts, while the West Beach Tennis Club has 10 Har-Tru courts and 2 lighted hard courts.

MAP 5: 12 Kiawah Beach Dr., Kiawah Island, 800/654-2924, www.kiawahresort.com; $44/hour for nonguests

Hotels

Look for ★ to find
recommended hotels.

Highlights

★ **Closest Brush with the Declaration of Independence:** Before purchasing what is now the **Governor's House Inn** and being elected chief executive of South Carolina, Edward Rutledge was the youngest signer of the Declaration (page 140).

★ **Most Romantic Getaway:** Local legend has it that as a young naval officer, John F. Kennedy met one of his many paramours, an alleged German spy, at **Two Meeting Street Inn** (page 140).

★ **Best Rooftop Bar:** Enjoy views of the French Quarter and the Waterfront from the famous Rooftop Bar on top of **The Vendue** (page 141).

★ **Cozy in the City:** Though close to the City Market area's tourist bustle, the classy **Andrew Pinckney Inn** is quiet and calming (page 141).

★ **Most Comfortable Lap of Luxury:** The **Belmond Charleston Place** is smack downtown and offers the city's premier lodging and spa facilities, steps away from Charleston's prime shopping district (page 141).

★ **Closest Brush with the Constitution:** The only B&B in the United States which was once the home of a signer of the U.S. Constitution, the **John Rutledge House Inn** is one of the South's most sumptuous and highest-rated lodgings (page 143).

★ **Least Expensive Awesome Stay:** The charming **Not So Hostel** offers friendly and informal communal lodging a quick bike ride away from downtown (page 146).

★ **Most Calming Commune with Nature:** The sparsely modernist **Inn at Middleton Place** offers a relaxing, state-of-the-art getaway in the scenic and peaceful heart of the old Middleton Place Plantation grounds (page 146).

★ **Best Outdoor Pool:** The **Kiawah Island Golf Resort** not only offers first-class golf and accommodations on a beautifully preserved barrier island, it also has a huge resort-style pool just off the windswept beach (page 149).

A s one of the country's key national and inter-national destination cities, Charleston has a very well-developed infrastructure for housing visi-tors. It's a task made much easier by the city's long-standing tradition of hospitality and the high stan-dards it has set for itself over the decades.

Because the bar is set so high, few visitors experience a bad stay in town. Hotels and bed-and-breakfasts are well maintained and have a high level of service, ranging from very good to excellent. There's a 12.5 percent tax on hotel rooms in Charleston. No one can say lodging is inexpensive near the tourist areas of the city, but you almost always get what you pay for—and then some.

The real issue for most visitors boils down to two questions: How much do you want to spend, and in which part of town do you want to stay? Because the price differential is not that much between the peninsula and the outskirts, I recommend staying on the peninsula. You'll pay more, but not *that* much more, with the bonus of being able to walk to most places you want to see—which is the best way to enjoy the city.

The farther south you go on the peninsula, the quieter and more afflu-ent it tends to be. Folks looking for a more wild and woolly good time will be drawn to the Upper King area farther north.

Charleston County runs a family-friendly, fairly boisterous campground at **James Island County Park** (871 Riverland Dr., 843/795-7275, www.ccprc.com, $31 tent site, $37 pull-through site). A neat feature here is the $5-pp round-trip shuttle to the visitors center downtown, Folly Beach Pier, and Folly Beach County Park. The park also has 10 furnished cottages (843/795-4386, $138) for rental, sleeping up to eight people. Reservations are recommended. For more commercial camping in Mount Pleasant, try the **KOA of Mt. Pleasant** (3157 U.S. 17 N., 843/849-5177, www.koa.com, from $30 tent sites, from $50 pull-through sites).

South of Broad
Map 1

★ Governor's House Inn ⑤⑤⑤

On the south side of Broad Street is a great old Charleston lodging, Governor's House Inn. This circa-1760 building, a National Historic Landmark, is associated with Edward Rutledge, signer of the Declaration of Independence. Though most of its 11 guest rooms—all with four-poster beds, period furnishings, and high ceilings—go for around $300, some of the smaller guest rooms can be had for closer to $200 in the off-season.

MAP 1: 117 Broad St., 843/720-2070, www.governorshouse.com

★ Two Meeting Street Inn ⑤⑤

The nine guest rooms of Two Meeting Street Inn down by the Battery are individually appointed, with themes like "The Music Room" and the "The Spell Room." The decor in this 1892 Queen Anne bed-and-breakfast is very traditional, with lots of floral patterns and hunt club-style pieces and artwork. It's considered by many to be the most romantic lodging in town, and you won't soon forget the experience of sitting on the veranda enjoying the sights, sounds, and breezes. Three of the guest rooms—the Canton, Granite, and Roberts—can be had for not much over $200.

MAP 1: 2 Meeting St., 843/723-7322, www.twomeetingstreet.com

Waterfront
Map 1

Harbourview Inn ⑤⑤⑤

About as close to the Cooper River as a hotel gets, the Harbourview Inn comprises a "historic wing" and a larger, newer, but still tastefully done main building. For the best of those eponymous harbor views, try to get a room on the third floor or you might have some obstructions. It's the little touches that keep guests happy here, with wine, cheese, coffee, tea, and cookies galore and an emphasis on smiling, personalized service. The guest rooms are quite spacious, with big baths and 14-foot ceilings. You can take your complimentary breakfast—good but not great—in your room or eat it on the nice rooftop terrace.

MAP 1: 2 Vendue Range, 843/853-8439, www.harbourviewcharleston.com

★ **The Vendue** $$$

The guest rooms and the thoroughly hospitable service are the focus at nearby The Vendue, just off a $5 million renovation and expansion. All guest rooms are sumptuously appointed in that boutique style, with lots of warm, rich fabrics, unique pieces, and high-end bath amenities. That said, the public spaces are cool as well, the renovation being particularly focused on featuring quality art and essentially creating one huge exhibition space. The inn gets a lot of traffic in the evenings because of the popular and hopping Rooftop Bar, which has amazing views.

MAP 1: 19 Vendue Range, 800/845-7900, www.thevendue.com

French Quarter
Map 1

French Quarter Inn $$$

A great place in this part of town is the French Quarter Inn. The decor in the 50 surprisingly spacious guest rooms is suitably high-period French, with low-style noncanopied beds and crisp fresh linens. Many guest rooms feature fireplaces, whirlpool baths, and private balconies. One of Charleston's hottest restaurants, Tristan, is on the ground floor. You're treated to champagne on your arrival, and goodies are available all day, with wine and cheese served every night at 5pm.

MAP 1: 166 Church St., 843/722-1900, www.fqicharleston.com

North of Broad
Map 1

★ Andrew Pinckney Inn $$

It calls itself a boutique hotel, perhaps because each room is totally different and sumptuously appointed. But the charming Andrew Pinckney Inn is very nearly in a class by itself in Charleston not only for its great rates but for its casual West Indies-style decor, charming courtyard, gorgeous three-story atrium, and rooftop terrace on which you can enjoy your complimentary (and delicious) breakfast. For the money and the amenities, it's possibly the single best lodging package in town.

MAP 1: 199 Church St., 843/937-8800, www.andrewpinckneyinn.com

★ Belmond Charleston Place $$$

Considered Charleston's premier hotel, Charleston Place maintains a surprisingly high level of service and decor considering its massive 440-room size. Now owned by the London-based Orient-Express Hotels, Charleston Place is routinely rated as one of the best hotels in North America by *Condé Nast Traveler* and other publications. The guest rooms aren't especially

Clockwise from top left: The Vendue; French Quarter Inn; Harbourview Inn.

large, but they are well appointed, featuring Italian marble baths, high-speed Internet, and voice messaging—and, of course, there's a pool available. A series of suite offerings—Junior, Junior Executive, Parlor, and the 800-square-foot Senior—feature enlarged living areas and multiple TVs and phones. A Manager's Suite on the Private Club level up top comprises 1,200 square feet of total luxury that will set you back at least $1,600 per night. It's the additional offerings that make Charleston Place closer to a lifestyle decision than a lodging choice. The on-site spa (843/937-8522) offers all kinds of massages, including couples and "mommy to be" sessions. Diners and tipplers have three fine options to choose from: the famous **Charleston Grill** (843/577-4522, daily 6pm-close, $27-65) for fine dining; the breakfast, lunch, and brunch hot spot **Palmetto Cafe** (843/722-4900, daily 6:30am-3pm, $24-31); and the **Thoroughbred Club** (daily 11am-midnight) for cocktails and, for groups of 10 or more, afternoon tea.

MAP 1: 205 Meeting St., 843/722-4900, www.charlestonplace.com

Fulton Lane Inn ⑤⑤⑤

Affiliated with the Kings Courtyard—and right next door, in fact—is the smaller, cozier Fulton Lane Inn, with its lobby entrance on tiny Fulton Lane between the two inns. Small, simple guest rooms—some with fireplaces—have comfortable beds and spacious baths. This is the kind of place for active people who plan to spend most of their days out and about but want a cozy place to come back to at night. You mark down your continental breakfast order at night, leave it on your doorknob, and it shows up at the *exact* time you requested the next morning. Then when you're ready to shop and walk, just go down the stairs and take the exit right out onto busy King Street. Also nice is the $12-per-day parking with free in-and-out privileges.

MAP 1: 202 King St., 866/720-2940, www.fultonlaneinn.com

★ John Rutledge House Inn ⑤⑤⑤

On the north side of Broad Street, the magnificent John Rutledge House Inn is very close to the old South of Broad neighborhood not only in geography but in feel. Known as "America's most historic inn," the Rutledge House boasts a fine old pedigree indeed: Built for Constitution signer John Rutledge in 1763, it's one of only 15 homes belonging to the original signers to survive. George Washington breakfasted here with Mrs. Rutledge in 1791. The interior is stunning: Italian marble fireplaces, original plaster moldings, and masterful ironwork abound in the public spaces. The inn's 19 guest rooms are divided among the original mansion and two carriage houses. A friendly and knowledgeable concierge will give you all kinds of tips and make reservations for you.

MAP 1: 116 Broad St., 843/723-7999, www.johnrutledgehouseinn.com

Kings Courtyard Inn ⑤⑤⑤

If you plan on some serious shopping, you might want to stay right on the city's main shopping thoroughfare at the Kings Courtyard Inn. This 1853

Clockwise from top left: Kings Courtyard Inn; Andrew Pinckney Inn; Mills House Hotel.

Greek Revival building houses a lot more guest rooms—more than 40—than meets the eye, and it can get a little crowded at times. Still, its charming courtyard and awesome location on King Street are big bonuses, as is the convenient but cramped parking lot right next door (about $12 per day, a bargain for this part of town), with free in-and-out privileges.

MAP 1: 198 King St., 866/720-2949, www.kingscourtyardinn.com

Mills House Hotel ❸❸❸

Although it is a newer building by Charleston standards, the Mills House Hotel boasts an important pedigree and still tries hard to maintain the old tradition of impeccable Southern service at this historic location. An extensive round of renovations completed in 2007 has been well received. Dating to 1853, the first incarnation was a grand edifice that hosted luminaries such as Robert E. Lee. Through the years, fire and restoration wrought their changes, and the modern version basically dates from an extensive renovation in the 1970s. Because of its healthy banquet and event schedule—much of it centering on the very good restaurant and lounge inside—the Mills House isn't the place to go for peace and quiet. Rather, this Wyndham-affiliated property is where you go to feel the bustle of downtown Charleston and to be conveniently close to its main sightseeing and shopping attractions. Some of the upper floors of this seven-story building offer spectacular views. A particular delight is the courtyard complete with fountain, where you can enjoy a cocktail or coffee.

MAP 1: 115 Meeting St., 843/577-2400, www.millshouse.com

Upper King

Map 2

Ashley Inn ❸

Stretching the bounds of the "Upper King" definition, we come to the Ashley Inn well northwest of Marion Square, almost in the Citadel area. Although it's too far to walk from here to most any historic attraction in Charleston, the Ashley Inn does provide free bikes to its guests as well as free off-street parking, a particularly nice touch. It also deserves a special mention not only because of the romantic, well-appointed nature of its six guest rooms, suite, and carriage house but for its outstanding breakfasts. You get to pick a main dish, such as Carolina sausage pie, stuffed waffles, or cheese blintzes.

MAP 2: 201 Ashley Ave., 843/723-1848, www.charleston-sc-inns.com

Francis Marion Hotel ❸❸

In a renovated 1924 building overlooking beautiful Marion Square, the Francis Marion Hotel offers quality accommodations in the hippest, most bustling area of the peninsula—but be aware that it's quite a walk down to the Battery from here. The guest rooms are plush and big, though the baths can be cramped. The hotel's parking garage costs a reasonable $12 per day, with valet parking available until about 8pm. A Starbucks in the lobby pleases many guests on their way out or in. Most rooms hover around $300, but some are a real steal.

MAP 2: 387 King St., 843/722-0600, www.francismarioncharleston.com

Hampton Park Map 2

★ Not So Hostel ⑤

Charleston's least-expensive lodging is also its most unique: the Not So Hostel. The already-reasonable prices also include a make-your-own bagel breakfast, off-street parking, bikes, high-speed Internet access in the common room, and even an airport, train, and bus shuttle. The inn actually comprises three 1840s Charleston single houses, all with the obligatory piazzas. (However, unlike some hostels, there's air-conditioning in all the rooms.) Because the free bike usage makes up for its off-the-beaten-path location, a stay at the Not So Hostel is a fantastic way to enjoy the Holy City on a budget. One caveat: While they offer private rooms in addition to dorm-style accommodation, keep in mind this is still a hostel, despite the Charleston-style hospitality and perks. In other words, if there's a problem at 3am, you may not be able to get anyone to help you in a hurry.

MAP 2: 156 Spring St., 843/722-8383, www.notsohostel.com

West Ashley Map 3

★ The Inn at Middleton Place ⑤⑤

Looking like Frank Lloyd Wright parachuted into a 300-year-old plantation and got to work, The Inn at Middleton Place is one of Charleston's unique lodgings—and not only because it's on the grounds of the historic and beautiful Middleton Place Plantation. The four connected buildings, comprising over 50 guest rooms, are modern yet deliberately blend in with the forested, neutral-colored surroundings. The spacious guest rooms have that same woodsy minimalism, with excellent fireplaces, spacious Euro-style baths, and huge floor-to-ceiling windows overlooking the grounds and the river. Guests also have full access to the rest of the gorgeous Middleton grounds. The only downside is that you're a lengthy drive from the peninsula and all its attractions, restaurants, and nightlife. But don't worry about food—the excellent Middleton Place Restaurant is open for lunch and dinner.

MAP 3: 4290 Ashley River Rd., 843/556-0500, www.theinnatmiddletonplace.com

Top: John Rutledge House Inn. **Bottom:** Kiawah Island Golf Resort.

Woodlands Resort & Inn ⑤⑤⑤

The renowned Woodlands Resort & Inn is one of a handful of inns in United States with a five-star rating both for lodging and dining. Its 18 guest rooms within the 1906 great house are decorated in a mix of old-fashioned plantation high style and contemporary designer aesthetics, with modern, luxurious baths. There's also a freestanding guest cottage ($850) that seeks to replicate a hunting lodge type of vibe. As you'd expect, there's a full day spa on the premises; a one-hour massage, the most basic offering, will run you $110. The pool is outside, but it's heated for year-round enjoyment, at least theoretically. Woodlands is making a big play for the growing pet-friendly market and eagerly pampers your dog or cat while you stay. Within Woodlands is its award-winning world-class restaurant, simply called **The Dining Room** (Mon.-Sat. 11am-2pm and 6pm-9pm, brunch Sun. 11:30am-2pm, $25-40). It will come as no surprise to find out that the 900-entry wine list and sommelier are collectively awesome, as are the desserts. Jackets are required, and reservations are strongly advised.

MAP 3: 125 Parsons Rd., 843/875-2600, www.woodlandsmansion.com

Mount Pleasant and East Cooper
Map 4

Wild Dunes Resort ⑤⑤⑤

One of the more accessible and enjoyable resort-type stays in the Charleston area is on the Isle of Palms at Wild Dunes Resort. This is the place to go for relaxing, beach-oriented vacation fun, in your choice of a traditional hotel room, a house, or a villa. Bustling Mount Pleasant is only a couple minutes away, and Charleston proper not much farther.

MAP 4: 5757 Palm Blvd., 888/778-1876, www.wilddunes.com

Holiday Inn Folly Beach Oceanfront $$$

The upbeat but still cozy renovation of the Holiday Inn Folly Beach Oceanfront has locals raving. If you're going to stay on Folly Beach, this hotel—with its combination of attentive staff and great oceanfront views—is the place to be.

MAP 5: 1 Center St., 843/588-6464

★ Kiawah Island Golf Resort $$$

This beautiful island with a beautiful beach to match—about 45 minutes away from downtown Charleston—has as its main attraction the sumptuous Kiawah Island Golf Resort, a key location for PGA tournaments. But even if you don't play golf, the resort is an amazing stay. The main component is The Sanctuary, an upscale hotel featuring an opulent lobby complete with grand staircases, a large pool area overlooking the beach, tasteful Spanish Colonial-style architecture, and 255 smallish but excellently appointed guest rooms.

MAP 5: 1 Sanctuary Beach Dr., 800/654-2924, www.kiawahgolf.com

Hilton Head and the Lowcountry

For many people around the world, the Lowcountry is the first image that comes to mind when they think of the American South. For the people that live here, the Lowcountry is altogether unique. It embodies many of the region's most noteworthy qualities: an emphasis on manners, a constant look back into the past, and a slow and leisurely pace (embodied in the joking but largely accurate nickname "Slowcountry").

History hangs in the humid air where first the Spanish came to interrupt the native tribes' ancient reverie, followed by the French, and then the English. Although time, erosion, and development have erased most traces of these various occupants, you can almost hear their ghosts in the rustle of the branches in a sudden sea breeze or in the piercing call of a heron over the marsh.

Artists and arts lovers the world over are drawn here to paint, photograph, or otherwise be inspired by some of the most gorgeous wetlands in the United States, so vast that human habitation appears fleeting and intermittent. Sprawling between Beaufort and Charleston is the huge ACE (Ashepoo, Combahee, Edisto) Basin, a beautiful and important estuary and a national model for good conservation practices. In all, the defining characteristic of the Lowcountry is its liquid nature—not only literally, in the creeks and waterways that dominate every vista and the seafood cooked in all manner of ways, but figuratively too, in the slow but deep quality of life here. Once outside what passes for urban areas, you'll find yourself taking a look back through the decades to a time of roadside produce stands,

Previous: a Lowcountry road; horseback riding on Hunting Island.

Look for ★ to find
recommended sights and activities.

Highlights

★ **Henry C. Chambers Waterfront Park:** Walk the dog or while away the time on a porch swing at this clean and inviting gathering place on the serene Beaufort River (page 156).

★ **St. Helena's Episcopal Church:** To step through this Beaufort sanctuary and its walled graveyard is to walk through Lowcountry history (page 158).

★ **Penn Center:** This is not only the center of modern Gullah culture and education, it's a key site in the history of the civil rights movement as well (page 169).

★ **Hunting Island State Park:** One of the most peaceful natural getaways on the East Coast is only minutes away from the more civilized temptations of Beaufort (page 173).

★ **ACE Basin:** It can take a lifetime to learn your way around this massive, marshy estuary—or just a few hours soaking in its lush beauty (page 174).

★ **Edisto Beach State Park:** Relax at this quiet, friendly, and relatively undeveloped Sea Island, a mecca for shell collectors (page 178).

★ **Pinckney Island National Wildlife Refuge:** This well-maintained sanctuary is a major birding location and a great getaway from nearby Hilton Head (page 183).

★ **Coastal Discovery Museum at Honey Horn:** This beautifully repurposed plantation house and spacious grounds near the island's entrance are a great way to learn about Hilton Head history, both human and natural (page 183).

★ **Old Bluffton:** Gossipy and gorgeous by turns, this charming village on the May River centers on a thriving artists colony (page 200).

★ **South Carolina Artisans Center:** Visual artists and fine craftspeople from all over the state contribute work to this high-quality collective in Walterboro (page 208).

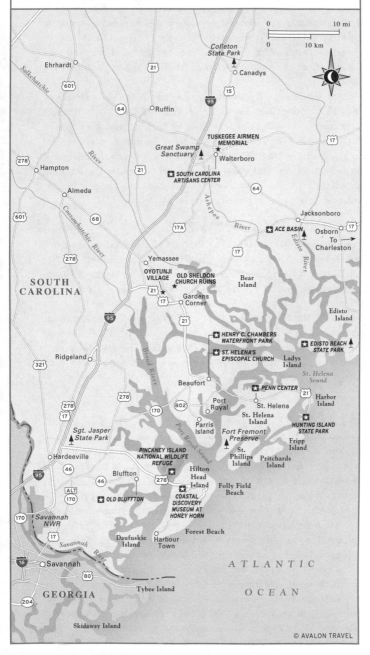

shade-tree mechanics, and men fishing and crabbing on tidal creeks—not for sport but for the family dinner. Indeed, not so very long ago, before the influx of resort development, retirement subdivisions, and tourism, much of the Lowcountry was like a flatter, more humid Appalachia—poverty-stricken and desperately underserved. While the archetypal South has been marketed in any number of ways to the rest of the world, here you get a sense that this is the real thing—timeless, endlessly alluring, but somehow very familiar.

South of Beaufort is the historically significant Port Royal area and the East Coast Marine Corps Recruit Depot of Parris Island. East of Beaufort is the center of Gullah culture, St. Helena Island, and the scenic gem of Hunting Island. Even farther south is the scenic but entirely developed golf and tennis mecca, Hilton Head Island, and Hilton Head's close neighbor but diametrical opposite in every other way, Daufuskie Island, another important Gullah center. Nestled between is the close-knit and gossipy little village of Bluffton on the gossamer May River.

PLANNING YOUR TIME

A commonsense game plan is to use centrally located Beaufort as a home base. Take at least half a day of leisure to walk all over Beaufort. Another full day should go to St. Helena's Penn Center and on to Hunting Island. If you're in the mood for a road trip, dedicate a full day to tour the surrounding area to the north and northeast, with a jaunt to the ACE Basin National Wildlife Refuge. While the New York accents fly fast and furious on Hilton Head Island, that's no reason for you to rush. Plan on at least half a day just to enjoy the fine, broad beaches alone. I recommend another half day to tour the island itself, maybe including a stop in Sea Pines for a late lunch or dinner.

Beaufort

Sandwiched halfway between the prouder, louder cities of Charleston and Savannah, Beaufort is in many ways a more authentic slice of life from the past than either of those two. Long a staple of movie crews seeking to portray some archetypal aspect of the old South (*The Prince of Tides, The Great Santini, Forrest Gump*) or just to film beautiful scenery for its own sake (*Jungle Book, Last Dance*), Beaufort—pronounced "BYOO-fert," by the way, not "BO-fort"—features many well-preserved examples of Southern architecture, most all of them in idyllic, family-friendly neighborhoods.

The pace in Beaufort is languid, slower even than the waving Spanish moss in the massive old live oak trees. The line between business and pleasure is a blurry one here. As you can tell from the signs you see on storefront doors saying things like "Back in an hour or so," time is an entirely negotiable commodity. The architecture combines the relaxed Caribbean flavor of Charleston with the Anglophilic dignity of Savannah. In fact, plenty of

Beaufort

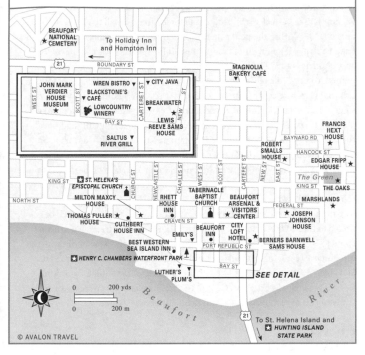

people prefer the individualistic old homes of Beaufort, seemingly tailor-made for the exact spot on which they sit, to the historic districts of either Charleston or Savannah in terms of sheer architectural delight.

While you'll run into plenty of charming and gracious locals during your time here, you might be surprised at the number of transplanted Northerners. That's due not only to the high volume of retirees who've moved to the area but the active presence of three major U.S. Navy facilities: the Marine Corps Air Station Beaufort, the Marine Corps Recruit Depot on nearby Parris Island, and the Beaufort Naval Hospital. Many is the time a former sailor or Marine has decided to put down roots in the area after being stationed here, the most famous example being author Pat Conroy's father, aka "The Great Santini."

HISTORY

This was the site of the second landing by the Spanish on the North American continent, the expedition of Captain Pedro de Salazar in 1514 (Ponce de León's more famous landing at St. Augustine was but a year earlier). A Spanish slaver made a brief stop in 1521, long enough to name the area Santa Elena. Port Royal Sound didn't get its modern name until the first serious attempt at a permanent settlement, Jean Ribault's exploration in 1562. Though ultimately disastrous, Ribault's base of Charlesfort was the first French settlement in what would become the United States.

After the French faded, Spaniards returned. But Indian forays and Francis Drake's attack on St. Augustine forced the Spanish to abandon the area in 1587. Within the next generation, British indigo planters had established a firm presence, chief among them John "Tuscarora Jack" Barnwell and Thomas Nairn. These men would go on to found the town of Beaufort, named for the Duke of Beaufort, and it was chartered in 1711 as part of the original Carolina colony. In 1776, Beaufort planter Thomas Heyward Jr. signed the Declaration of Independence. After independence, Lowcountry planters turned to cotton as the main cash crop, since England had been their prime customer for indigo. The gambit paid off, and Beaufort soon became one of the wealthiest towns in the new nation. In 1861, only seven months after secessionists fired on Fort Sumter in nearby Charleston, a Union fleet sailed into Port Royal and occupied the Lowcountry for the duration of the war.

Gradually developing their own distinct dialect and culture, much of it linked to their West African roots, isolated Lowcountry African Americans came to be known as the Gullah. Evolving from an effort by abolitionist missionaries early in the Civil War, in 1864 the Penn School was formed on St. Helena Island specifically to teach the children of the Gullah communities. Now known as the Penn Center, the facility has been a beacon for the study of this aspect of African American culture ever since.

SIGHTS

★ Henry C. Chambers Waterfront Park

A tastefully designed, well-maintained, and user-friendly mix of walkways, bandstands, and patios, **Henry C. Chambers Waterfront Park** (843/525-7054, www.cityofbeaufort.org, daily 24 hours) is a favorite gathering place for locals and visitors alike, beckoning one and all with its open green space and wonderful marsh-front views. Kids will especially enjoy the park not only because there's so much room to run around but for the charming playground at the east end near the bridge, complete with a jungle gym in the form of a Victorian home. The clean, well-appointed public restrooms are a particularly welcome feature.

John Mark Verdier House Museum

A smallish but stately Federalist building on the busiest downtown corner, the **John Mark Verdier House Museum** (801 Bay St., 843/379-6335, www.historicbeaufort.org, tours on the half hour Mon.-Sat. 10:30am-3:30pm, $5) is the only historic Beaufort home open to regular tours. Built in 1805 for the wealthy planter John Mark Verdier, its main claims to fame are acting as the Union headquarters during the long occupation of Beaufort during the Civil War and hosting Revolutionary War hero the Marquis de Lafayette, who stayed at the Verdier House on his 1825 U.S. tour.

My favorite shop in Beaufort is The Bay Street Trading Company (808 Bay St., 843/524-2000, www.baystreettrading.com, Mon.-Fri. 10am-5;30pm, Sat. 10am-5pm, Sun. noon-5pm), sometimes known simply as "The Book Shop," which has a friendly staff and the best collection of Lowcountry-themed books I've seen in one place.

Across the street, the recently renovated Old Bay Marketplace, with a facade so bright red you can't miss it, hosts a few cute shops, most notably the stylish **Lulu Burgess** (917 Bay St., 843/524-5858, Mon.-Sat. 10am-6pm, Sun. noon- 5pm), an eclectic store that brings a rich, quirky sense of humor to its otherwise tasteful assortment of gift items for the whole family.

A unique gift item, as well as something you can enjoy on your own travels, can be found at **Lowcountry Winery** (705 Bay St., 843/379-3010, Mon.-Sat. 10am-5pm). They host tastings daily in the tasting room (because of state law, they must charge a fee for the tasting, but it's only $1 pp).

Art Galleries

My favorite gallery in town is **The Gallery** (802 Bay St., 843/470-9994, www.thegallery-beaufort.com, Mon.-Sat. 11am-5pm). Deanna Bowdish brings the most cutting-edge regional contemporary artists to this large, friendly, loftlike space. A complete art experience blending the traditional with the cutting-edge is at the **I. Pinckney Simons Art Gallery** (711 Bay St., 843/379-4774, www.ipinckneysimonsgallery.com, Tues.-Fri. 11am-5pm, Sat. 11am- 3pm), which is pronounced "Simmons" despite the spelling.

Right on the water is a fun local favorite, the **Longo Gallery** (103 Charles St., 843/522-8933, Mon.-Sat. 11am-5pm). Owners Suzanne and Eric Longo provide a whimsical assortment of less traditional art than you might find in the more touristy waterfront area. Take Charles Street as it works its way toward the waterfront, and the gallery is right behind a storefront on the corner of Charles and Bay Streets.

You'll find perhaps the area's best-known gallery over the bridge on St. Helena Island. Known regionally as one of the best places to find Gullah folk art, **Red Piano Too** (870 Sea Island Pkwy., 843/838-2241, Mon.-Sat. 10am-5pm) is on the corner before you turn onto the road to the historic Penn Center. Over 150 artists from a diverse range of traditions and styles are represented in this charming little 1940 building with the red tin awning.

SPORTS AND RECREATION

Beaufort County comprises over 60 islands, so it's no surprise that nearly all recreation in the area revolves around the water, which dominates so many aspects of life in the Lowcountry. The closer to the ocean you get, the more it's a salt marsh environment. But as you explore more inland, including the sprawling ACE Basin, you'll encounter primarily blackwater.

Kayaking

The Lowcountry is tailor-made for kayaking. Most kayakers put in at the public landings in nearby **Port Royal** (1 Port Royal Landing Dr., 843/525-6664) or **Lady's Island** (73 Sea Island Pkwy., 843/522-0430), across the river from downtown Beaufort. If you don't feel comfortable with your navigation skills, it's a good idea to contact Kim and David at **Beaufort Kayak Tours** (843/525-0810, www.beaufortkayaktours.com), who rent kayaks and can guide you on a number of excellent tours of all three key areas. They charge about $40 for adults and $30 for children for a two-hour trip. A tour with Beaufort Kayak Tours is also the best (and nearly the only) way to access the historically significant ruins of the early British tabby Fort Frederick, now located on the grounds of the Beaufort Naval Hospital and inaccessible by car.

Fishing and Boating

Key marinas in the area are the **Downtown Marina** (1006 Bay St., 843/524-4422) in Beaufort, the **Lady's Island Marina** (73 Sea Island Pkwy., 843/522-0430), and the **Port Royal Landing Marina** (1 Port Royal Landing Dr., 843/525-6664). Hunting Island has a popular 1,000-foot fishing pier at the south end. A good local fishing charter service is Captain Josh Utsey's **Lowcountry Guide Service** (843/812-4919, www.beaufortscfishing.com). **Captain Ed Hardee** (843/441-6880) offers good inshore charters.

The ACE Basin is a very popular fishing, crabbing, and shrimping area. It has about two dozen public boat ramps, with colorful names like Cuckold's Creek and Steamboat Landing. There's a useful map of them all at www.acebasin.net, or look for the brown signs along the highway.

Hiking and Biking

Despite the Lowcountry's, well, lowness, biking opportunities abound. It might not get your heart rate up like a ride in the Rockies, but the area lends itself to laid-back two-wheeled enjoyment. Many local B&Bs provide bikes free for guests, and you can rent your own just across the river from Beaufort in Lady's Island at **Lowcountry Bikes** (102 Sea Island Pkwy., 843/524-9585, Mon.-Tues. and Thurs.-Fri. 10am-6pm, Wed. 10am-1pm, Sat. 10am-3pm, about $5 per hour). They can also hook you up with some good routes around the area.

ACCOMMODATIONS

Beaufort's historic district is blessed with an abundance of high-quality accommodations that blend well with their surroundings. There are plenty of budget-minded chain places, some of them acceptable, in the sprawl of Boundary Street outside of downtown, but here are some suggestions within bicycling distance of the historic district. (That's not a hypothetical, as most inns offer free bicycles to use as you please during your stay.)

The **Best Western Sea Island Inn** (1015 Bay St., 843/522-2090, www.best-western.com, $135-170) is a good value for those for whom the B&B experience is not paramount. Anchoring the southern end of the historic district in a tasteful low brick building, the Best Western offers decent service, basic amenities, and surprisingly attractive rates for the location on Beaufort's busiest street.

$150-300

Any list of upscale Beaufort lodging must highlight the **Beaufort Inn** (809 Port Republic St., 843/379-4667, www.beaufortinn.com, $152-425), consistently voted one of the best B&Bs in the nation. It's sort of a hybrid in that it comprises not only the 1897 historic central home but also a cluster of freestanding historic cottages, each with a charming little porch and rocking chairs. Within or outside the main building, each suite has a character all its own, whether it's the 1,500-square-foot Loft Apartment or one of the cozier Choice Rooms with a queen-size bed.

The 18-room, circa-1820 **Rhett House Inn** (1009 Craven St., 843/524-9030, www.rhetthouseinn.com, $175-320) is the local vacation getaway for the stars. Such arts and entertainment luminaries as Robert Redford, Julia Roberts, Ben Affleck, Barbra Streisand, Dennis Quaid, and Demi Moore have all stayed here at one time or another.

There's nothing like enjoying the view of the Beaufort River from the expansive porches of the **Cuthbert House Inn** (1203 Bay St., 843/521-1315, www.cuthberthouseinn.com, $205-250). This grand old circa-1790 Federal mansion was once the home of the wealthy Cuthbert family of rice and indigo planters. General Sherman spent a night here in 1865. Some of the king rooms have fireplaces and claw-foot tubs. Of course you get a full Southern breakfast, in addition to sunset hors d'oeuvres on the veranda.

While a stay at a B&B is the classic way to enjoy Beaufort, many travelers swear by the new **City Loft Hotel** (301 Carteret St., 843/379-5638, www.citylofthotel.com, $200). Housed in a former motel, City Loft represents a total modernist makeover, gleaming from stem to stern with chrome and various art deco touches.

FOOD

Because of Beaufort's small size and insular nature, many of its restaurants double as nightlife hot spots, with hopping bar scenes—or as hopping as it gets here, anyway—at dinner hours and beyond, often with a crowd of regulars. That said, those looking for a late-night rowdy time will be happier seeking it in the notorious party town of Charleston. Sadly, the very well-regarded restaurant within the Beaufort Inn on Port Republic Street closed for good in 2007, but there are still plenty of high-quality dining spots in town.

Lowcountry Boil or Frogmore Stew?

Near Beaufort it's called Frogmore stew after the township (now named St. Helena) just over the river. Closer to Savannah it's simply called Lowcountry boil. Supposedly the first pot of this delectable, hearty concoction was made by Richard Gay of the Gay Fish Company. As with any vernacular dish, dozens of local and family variants abound. The key ingredient that makes Lowcountry boil/Frogmore stew what it is—a well-blended mélange with a character all its own rather than just a bunch of stuff thrown together in a pot of boiling water—is some type of crab-boil seasoning. You'll find Zatarain's seasoning suggested on a lot of websites, but Old Bay is far more common in the eponymous Lowcountry where the dish originated.

In any case, here's a simple six-serving recipe to get you started. The only downside is that it's pretty much impossible to make it for just a few people. The dish is intended for large gatherings, whether a football tailgate party on a Saturday or a family afternoon after church on Sunday. Note the typical ratio of one ear of corn and 0.5 pounds each of meat and shrimp per person.

- 6 ears fresh corn on the cob, cut into 3-inch sections
- 3 pounds smoked pork sausage, cut into 3-inch sections
- 3 pounds fresh shrimp, shells on
- 5 pounds new potatoes, halved or quartered
- 6 ounces Old Bay Seasoning

Put the sausage and potato pieces, along with half of the Old Bay, in two gallons of boiling water. When the potatoes are about halfway done, about 15 minutes in, add the corn and boil for about half that time, seven minutes. Add the shrimp and boil for another three minutes, until they just turn pink. Do not overcook the shrimp. Take the pot off the heat and drain; serve immediately. If you cook the shrimp just right, the oil from the sausage will cause those shells to slip right off.

This is but one of dozens of recipes. Some cooks add some lemon juice and beer in the water as it's coming to a boil; others add onion, garlic, or green peppers.

Breakfast and Brunch

One of the best breakfasts I've had anywhere was a humble two-egg plate for five bucks at Beaufort's most popular morning hangout, **Blackstone's Café** (205 Scott St., 843/524-4330, Mon.-Sat. 7:30am-2:30pm, Sun. 7:30am-2pm, under $10), complete with tasty hash browns, a comparative rarity in this part of the country, where grits rule as the breakfast starch of choice.

Burgers and Sandwiches

Another lunch favorite is **Magnolia Bakery Café** (703 Congress St., 843/524-1961, Mon.-Sat. 9am-5pm, under $10). Lump crab cakes are a specialty item, but you can't go wrong with any of the lunch sandwiches. Vegetarian diners are particularly well taken care of with a large selection of black-bean burger plates. As the name indicates, the range of desserts here is tantalizing, with the added bonus of a serious espresso bar.

It's a 20-minute drive out of downtown, but **Maggie's Pub** (17 Market

St., 843/379-1719, www.maggiespub.net, Tues.-Sat. 5-9pm, $12)—within a small shopping center in the new residential development of Habersham—is not only a happening neighborhood tavern, it also has the best grass-fed burgers in town and some excellent fish-and-chips. While a very friendly place, be aware it's a heavily local crowd. Get here by taking Boundary Street/Highway 21 west out of downtown, a left onto Parris Island Gateway/Highway 280, a right on Broad River Boulevard, and then a right on Joe Frazier Road. Veer onto Cherokee Farms Road and then left into the Habersham Marketplace area.

Coffee, Tea, and Sweets

The closest thing to a hipster coffeehouse in Beaufort is **City Java and News** (301 Carteret St., 843/379-5282, Mon.-Sat. 6am-6:30pm, Sun. 7am-6:30pm), a sunny and well-kept little modernist space next to the similarly modernist City Loft Hotel. Their espresso is big-city quality, their periodicals are timely, and their pastries and sandwiches are good for tiding you over when you need some quick energy for more walking around town.

New Southern

The stylishly appointed **Wren Bistro, Bar and Market** (210 Carteret St., 843/524-9463, www.wrenbistroandbar.com, Mon.-Sat. 11am-11pm, $15-25) is known for any of its chicken dishes. While the food is great, the interior is particularly well done, simultaneously warm and classy. As seems to be typical of Beaufort, the lunches are as good as the dinners, and the bar scene is quite active.

Seafood

The hottest dinner table in town is at the **Saltus River Grill** (802 Bay St., 843/379-3474, Sun.-Thurs. 5pm-9pm, Fri.-Sat. 5pm-10pm, $10-39), famous throughout the state for its raw bar menu. Other specialties include she-crab bisque, lump crab cakes, and the ubiquitous shrimp and grits. The Saltus River Grill is more upscale in feel and in price than most Lowcountry places, with a very see-and-be-seen attitude and a hopping bar. Reservations are recommended.

The short and focused menu at **Plum's** (904½ Bay St., 843/525-1946, lunch daily 11am-4pm, dinner daily 5pm-10pm, $15-25) keys in on entrées highlighting local ingredients, such as the shrimp penne *al'amatriciana* and fresh black mussel pasta. Because of the outstanding microbrew selection, Plum's is a big nightlife hangout as well; be aware that after 10pm, when food service ends but the bar remains open until 2am, it's no longer smoke-free.

An up-and-comer downtown is **Breakwater Restaurant & Bar** (203 Carteret St., 843/379-0052, www.breakwatersc.com, dinner Thurs.-Sat. 6-9:30pm, bar until 2am, $10-20). The concise menu makes up in good taste what it lacks in comprehensiveness, with an emphasis on seafood, of course.

Steaks

Luther's Rare & Well Done (910 Bay St., 843/521-1888, daily 10am-midnight, from $8) on the waterfront is the kind of meat-lover's place where even the French onion soup has a morsel of rib eye in it. While the patented succulent rubbed steaks are a no-brainer here, the handcrafted specialty pizzas are also quite popular. Housed in a historic pharmacy building, Luther's is also a great place for late eats after many other places in this quiet town have rolled up the sidewalk. A limited menu of appetizers and bar food to nosh on at the inviting and popular bar is available after 10pm.

Tapas

Right around the corner from Breakwater is **Emily's** (906 Port Republic St., 843/522-1866, www.emilysrestaurantandtapasbar.com, dinner Mon.-Sat. 4pm-10pm, bar until 2am, $10-20), a very popular fine-dining spot that specializes in a more traditional brand of rich, tasty tapas and is known for its active bar scene.

INFORMATION AND SERVICES

The **Beaufort Visitors Information Center** (713 Craven St., 843/986-5400, www.beaufortsc.org, daily 9am-5:30pm), the headquarters of the Beaufort Chamber of Commerce and Convention and Visitors Bureau, has relocated from its old Carteret Street location and can now be found within the Beaufort Arsenal, once home to the now-closed Beaufort Museum.

GETTING THERE AND AROUND

While the Marines can fly their F-18s directly into Beaufort Naval Air Station, you won't have that luxury. The closest major airport to Beaufort is the **Savannah/Hilton Head International Airport** (SAV, 400 Airways Ave., 912/964-0514, www.savannahairport.com) off I-95 outside Savannah. From there it's about an hour to Beaufort. If you're not going into Savannah for any reason, the easiest route to the Beaufort area from the airport is to take I-95's exit 8, and from there take U.S. 278 east to Highway 170.

Alternately, you could fly into **Charleston International Airport** (CHS, 5500 International Blvd., 843/767-1100, www.chs-airport.com), but because that facility is on the far north side of Charleston, it will take a bit longer (about an hour and 20 minutes) to get to Beaufort. From the Charleston Airport the best route south to Beaufort is U.S. 17 south, exiting onto U.S. 21 at Gardens Corner and then into Beaufort.

If you're coming into the region by car, I-95 will be your likely primary route, with your main point of entry being exit 8 off I-95 connecting to U.S. 278 east to Highway 170. Beaufort is a little over an hour from Charleston.

Don't be discouraged by the big-box sprawl that assaults you on the approaches to Beaufort on Boundary Street, lined with the usual discount megastores, fast-food outlets, and budget motels. After you make the big 90-degree bend where Boundary turns into Carteret Street—known locally as the "Bellamy Curve"—it's like entering a whole new world of slow-paced,

Spanish moss-lined avenues, friendly people, gentle breezes, and inviting storefronts.

While you can make your way to downtown by taking Carteret Street all the way to Bay Street—don't continue over the big bridge unless you want to go straight to Lady's Island and St. Helena Island—I suggest availing yourself of one of the "Downtown Access" signs before you get that far. Because Carteret Street is the only way to that bridge, it can get backed up at rush hour. By taking a quick right and then a left all the way to Bay Street, you can come into town from the other, quieter end, with your first glimpse of downtown proper being its timelessly beguiling views of the Beaufort River.

Unlike Charleston or Savannah, any visitor in reasonably good shape can walk the entire length and breadth of Beaufort's 300-acre downtown with little trouble. In fact, that's by far the best way to experience it.

There's no public transportation to speak of in Beaufort, but that's okay—the historic section is quite small and can be traversed in an afternoon. A favorite mode of transport is by bicycle, often complimentary to bed-and-breakfast guests. You can also rent one at **Lowcountry Bikes** (102 Sea Island Pkwy., 843/524-9585, Mon.-Tues. and Thurs.-Fri. 10am-6pm, Wed. 10am-1pm, Sat. 10am-3pm, about $5 per hour) in Lady's Island just over the bridge.

Outside Beaufort

The areas outside tourist-traveled Beaufort can take you even further back into sepia-toned Americana, into a time of sharecropper homesteads, sturdy oyster gatherers, and an altogether variable and subjective sense of time.

About 15 minutes east of Beaufort is the center of Gullah culture, St. Helena Island, and the scenic gem of Hunting Island. Just a few minutes south of Beaufort is the East Coast Marine Corps Recruit Depot of Parris Island. About 10 minutes away is the little community of Port Royal.

SIGHTS
★ Penn Center

By going across the Richard V. Woods Memorial Bridge over the Beaufort River on the Sea Island Parkway (which turns into U.S. 21), you'll pass through Lady's Island and reach St. Helena Island. Known to old-timers as Frogmore, the area took back its old Spanish-derived place name in the 1980s. Today St. Helena Island is most famous for the **Penn Center** (16 Dr. Martin Luther King Jr. Dr., 843/838-2474, www.penncenter.com, Mon.-Sat. 11am-4pm, $4 adults, $2 seniors and children), the spiritual home of Gullah culture and history. When you visit here among the live oaks and humble but well-preserved buildings, you'll instantly see why Martin Luther King Jr. chose this as one of his major retreat and planning sites during the civil rights era. The dream began as early as 1862, when a group of abolitionist Quakers from Philadelphia came during the Union occupation with the goal of teaching recently freed slave children. They were soon joined by African American educator Charlotte Forten. After Reconstruction, the Penn School continued its mission by offering teaching as well as agricultural and industrial trade curricula. In the late 1960s, the Southern Christian Leadership Conference used the school as a retreat and planning site, with both the Peace Corps and the Conscientious Objector Programs training here. The Penn Center continues to serve an important civil rights role by providing legal counsel to African American homeowners in St. Helena. Because clear title is difficult to acquire in the area due to the fact that so much of the land has stayed in the families of former slaves, developers are constantly making shady offers so that ancestral land can be opened up to upscale development.

The 50-acre campus is part of the Penn School Historic District, a National Historic Landmark comprising 19 buildings, most of key historical significance. The Retreat House was intended for Dr. King to continue his strategy meetings, but he was assassinated before being able to stay there. The museum and bookshop are housed in the Cope Building, now called the York W. Bailey Museum, situated right along MLK Jr. Drive.

To get to the Penn Center from Beaufort (about 10 miles), proceed over the bridge until you get to St. Helena Island. Take a right onto MLK Jr. Drive when you see the Red Piano Too Art Gallery. The Penn Center is a few hundred yards down on your right. If you drive past the Penn Center and continue a few hundred yards down MLK Jr. Drive, look for the ancient tabby ruins on the left side of the road. This is the **Chapel of Ease,** the remnant of a 1740 church destroyed by forest fire in the late 1800s.

Fort Fremont Preserve

Military historians and sightseers of a particularly adventurous type will want to drive several miles past the Penn Center on St. Helena Island to visit **Fort Fremont Preserve** (Lands End Rd., www.fortfremont.org, daily 9am-dusk, free). Two artillery batteries remain of this Spanish-American War-era coastal defense fort (an adjacent private residence is actually the old army hospital). The big guns are long gone, but the concrete emplacements—along with many very dark tunnels and small rooms—are still here. Bring a flashlight and be warned that there are no facilities of any kind, including lights and guardrails.

Old Sheldon Church Ruins

About 20 minutes north of Beaufort are the poignantly desolate ruins of the once-magnificent **Old Sheldon Church** (Old Sheldon Church Rd., off U.S. 17 just past Gardens Corner, daily dawn-dusk, free). One of the first Greek Revival structures in the United States, the house of worship held its first service in 1757. The sanctuary was first burned by the British in 1779. After being rebuilt in 1826, the sanctuary survived until General Sherman's arrival in 1865, whereupon Union troops razed it once more.

The Lost Art of Tabby

Tabby is the unique construction technique combining oyster shells, lime, water, and sand found along the South Carolina and Georgia coast.

It did not originate with Native Americans. The confusion is due to the fact that the native population left behind many middens, or trash heaps, of oyster shells. While these middens indeed provided the bulk of the shells for tabby buildings to come, Native Americans had little else to do with it.

Although the Spanish were responsible for the first use of tabby in the Americas, almost all remaining tabby in the area dates from later English settlement. The British first fell in love with tabby after the siege of Spanish-held St. Augustine, Florida, and quickly began building with it in their colonies to the north.

Scholars are divided as to whether tabby was invented by West Africans or its use spread to Africa from Spain and Portugal, coming to the United States through the knowledge of imported slaves. The origin of the word itself is also unclear, as similar words exist in Spanish, Portuguese, Gullah, and Arabic to describe various types of wall.

The primary technique was to burn alternating layers of oyster shells and logs in a deep hole in the ground, creating lime. The lime was then mixed with oyster shells, sand, and freshwater and poured into wooden molds, or "forms," to dry and then be used as building blocks, like large bricks. Tabby walls were usually plastered with stucco. Tabby is remarkably strong and resilient, able to survive hurricanes. It also stays cool in the summer and is insect-resistant.

Following are some great examples of true tabby you can see today on the South Carolina and Georgia coasts, from north to south:

- **Dorchester State Historic Site** in Summerville, north of Charleston, contains a well-preserved tabby fort.

- Several younger tabby buildings still exist in downtown Beaufort: the **Barnwell-Gough House** (705 Washington St.); the Thomas Fuller House, or **"Tabby Manse"** (1211 Bay St.); and the **Saltus House** (800 block of Bay St.), perhaps the tallest surviving tabby structure.

- The **Chapel of Ease** on St. Helena Island dates from the 1740s. If someone tells you Sherman burned it down, don't believe it; the culprit was a forest fire.

- The **Stoney-Baynard Ruins** in Sea Pines Plantation on Hilton Head are all that's left of the home of the old Braddock's Point Plantation. Foundations of a slave quarters are nearby.

- **Wormsloe Plantation** across the Georgia state line near Savannah has the remains of Noble Jones's fortification on the Skidaway Narrows.

- **St. Cyprian's Episcopal Church** in Darien, Georgia, is one of the largest tabby structures still in use.

- **Fort Frederica** on St. Simons Island, Georgia, has not only the remains of a tabby fort but many foundations of tabby houses in the surrounding settlement.

- The remarkably intact walls of the **Horton-DuBignon House** on Jekyll Island, Georgia, date from 1738, and the house was occupied into the 1850s.

Nothing remains now but these towering walls and columns, made of red brick instead of the tabby often seen in similar ruins on the coast. It's now owned by the nearby St. Helena's Episcopal Church in Beaufort, which holds outdoor services here the second Sunday after Easter.

Oyotunji Village

Continuing north of the Sheldon Church a short way, the more adventurous can find a quirky Lowcountry attraction, **Oyotunji Village** (56 Bryant Ln., 843/846-8900, www.oyotunji.org, daily 11am-dusk, $10). Built in 1970 by self-proclaimed "King" Ofuntola Oseijeman Adelabu Adefunmi I, a former used car dealer with an interesting past, Oyotunji claims to be North America's only authentic African village, and also claims to be a separate kingdom and not a part of the United States—though I'm sure the State Department begs to differ. Take U.S. 17 north out of Beaufort; about 25 minutes later Oyotunji Village will be on your right.

Port Royal

This sleepy hamlet between Beaufort and Parris Island touts itself as a leader in "small-town New Urbanism," with an emphasis on livability, retro-themed shopping areas, and relaxing walking trails. However, **Port Royal** is still pretty sleepy—but not without very real charms, not the least of which is the fact that everything is within easy walking distance of everything else. The highlight of the year is the annual Softshell Crab Festival, held each April to mark the short-lived harvesting season for that favorite crustacean.

While much of the tiny historic district has a scrubbed, tidy feel, the main historic structure is the charming little **Union Church** (11th St., 843/524-4333, Mon.-Fri. 10am-4pm, donation), one of the oldest buildings in town, with guided docent tours.

Don't miss the boardwalk and observation tower at **The Sands** municipal beach and boat ramp. The 50-foot-tall structure provides a commanding view of Battery Creek. To get to The Sands, head east onto 7th Street off the main drag of Parris Avenue. Seventh Street turns into Sands Beach Road for a brief stretch and then merges with 6th Street, taking you directly to The Sands.

Another environmentally oriented point of pride is the **Lowcountry Estuarium** (1402 Paris Ave., 843/524-6600, www.lowcountryestuarium. org, Wed.-Sat. 10am-5pm, feedings 11:30am and 3pm, $5 adults, $3 children). The point of the facility is to give visitors hands-on opportunities to learn more about the flora and fauna of the various ecosystems of the Lowcountry, such as salt marshes, beaches, and estuaries.

If you get hungry in Port Royal, try the waterfront seafood haven **11th Street Dockside** (1699 11th St., 843/524-7433, daily 4:30-10pm, $17-27). The Dockside Dinner is a great sampler plate with lobster tail, scallops, crab legs, and shrimp. The views of the waterfront and the adjoining shrimp-boat docks are relaxing and beautiful.

To get to Port Royal, take Ribault (REE-bo) Road south out of Beaufort, then a left onto Parris Avenue, which takes you directly into downtown Port Royal for a total drive of about 10 minutes.

Parris Island

Though more commonly known as the home of the legendary **Marine Corps Recruit Depot Parris Island** (283 Blvd. de France, 843/228-3650, www.mcrdpi.usmc.mil, free), the island is also of historic significance as the site of some of the earliest European presence in the New World. Today it's where all female U.S. Marine recruits and all male recruits east of the Mississippi River go through the grueling 13-week boot camp. Almost every Friday during the year marks the graduation of a company of newly minted Marines. That's why you might notice an influx of visitors to the area each Thursday, aka "Family Day," with the requisite amount of celebration on Fridays after that morning's ceremony.

Unlike many military facilities in the post-9/11 era, Parris Island still hosts plenty of visitors. Just check in with the sentry at the gate and show your valid driver's license, registration, and proof of insurance. Rental car drivers must show a copy of the rental agreement. On your way to the depot proper, there are a couple of beautiful picnic areas. Once inside, stop first at the **Douglas Visitor Center** (Bldg. 283, Blvd. de France, 843/228-3650, Mon. 7:30am-noon, Tues.-Wed. 7:30am-4:30pm, Thurs. 6:30am-7pm, Fri. 7:30am-3pm), a great place to find maps and information. As you go by the big parade ground, or "deck," be sure to check out the beautiful sculpture re-creating the famous photo of Marines raising the flag on Iwo Jima. A short ways ahead is the **Parris Island Museum** (Bldg. 111, 111 Panama St., 843/228-2951, www.parrisislandmuseum.com, daily 10am-4:30pm, free).

The Spanish built Santa Elena directly on top of the original French settlement, Charlesfort. They then built two other settlements, San Felipe and San Marcos. The Santa Elena-Charlesfort site, now on the circa-1950s depot golf course, is a National Historic Landmark. Many artifacts are viewable at the nearby **clubhouse-interpretive center** (daily 7am-5pm, free). You can take a self-guided tour; to get to the site from the museum, continue on Panama Street and take a right on Cuba Street. Follow the signs to the golf course and continue through the main parking lot of the course.

To make the 15-minute drive to Parris Island from Beaufort, take Ribault Road south, which turns into U.S. 21. Continue through and out of Port Royal and follow the signs for the Parris Island Gateway.

★ Hunting Island State Park

Rumored to be a hideaway for Blackbeard himself, the aptly named Hunting Island was indeed for many years a notable hunting preserve, and its abundance of wildlife remains to this day. The island is one of the East Coast's best birding spots and also hosts dolphins, loggerheads, alligators, and deer. Thanks to preservation efforts by President Franklin Roosevelt and the Civilian Conservation Corps, however, the island is no longer for hunting but for sheer enjoyment. And enjoy it people do, to the tune of one million visitors per year. A true family-friendly outdoor adventure spot, **Hunting Island State Park** (2555 Sea Island Pkwy., 866/345-7275, www.huntingisland.com, winter daily 6am-6pm, during daylight saving time daily 6am-9pm, $5 adults, $3 children) has something for everyone—kids, parents, and newlyweds. Yet it still retains a certain sense of lush wildness—so much so that it doubled as Vietnam in the movie *Forrest Gump*.

At the north end past the campground is the island's main landmark, the historic **Hunting Island Light,** which dates from 1875. Although the lighthouse ceased operations in 1933, a rotating light—not strong enough to serve as an actual navigational aid—is turned on at night. While the 167-step trek to the top (donation $2 pp) is strenuous, the view is stunning. At the south end of the island is a marsh walk, nature trail, and a fishing pier complete with a cute little nature center. Hunting Island's three miles of beautiful beaches also serve as a major center of loggerhead turtle nesting and hatching, a process that begins around June as the mothers lay their eggs and culminates in late summer and early fall, when the hatchlings make their daring dash to the sea. At all phases the turtles are strictly protected, and while there are organized events to witness the hatching of the eggs, it is strictly forbidden to touch or otherwise disturb the turtles or their nests. Contact the park ranger for more detailed information. The tropical-looking inlet running through the park is a great place to kayak or canoe.

Getting to Hunting Island couldn't be easier—just take the Sea Island Parkway (U.S. 21 East) about 20 minutes beyond Beaufort and you'll run right into it.

★ ACE Basin

Occupying pretty much the entire area between Beaufort and Charleston, the **ACE Basin**—the acronym signifies its role as the collective estuary of the Ashepoo, Combahee, and Edisto Rivers—is one of the most enriching natural experiences the country has to offer. The ACE Basin's three core rivers, the Edisto being the largest, are the framework for a matrix of waterways crisscrossing its approximately 350,000 acres of salt marsh. It's the intimate relationship with the tides that makes the area so enjoyable, and also what attracted so many plantations throughout its history (canals and dikes from the old paddy fields are still visible throughout). Other uses have included growing tobacco and corn, and lumbering. While the ACE Basin can in no way be called "pristine," it's a testament to the power of nature that after 6,000 years of human presence and often intense cultivation, the basin manages to retain much of its untamed feel. The ACE Basin is so big that it is actually divided into several parts for management purposes under the umbrella of the ACE Basin Project (www.acebasin.net), a task force begun in 1988 by the state of South Carolina, the U.S. Fish and Wildlife Service, and various private firms and conservation groups. The project is now considered a model for responsible watershed preservation techniques in a time of often rampant coastal development. A host of species,

Clockwise from top left: Sheldon Ruins; Penn Center; the Grove Plantation House in the ACE Basin.

both common and endangered, thrive in the area, including wood storks, alligators, sturgeon, loggerheads, teals, and bald eagles.

About 12,000 acres of the ACE Basin Project comprise the **Ernest F. Hollings ACE Basin National Wildlife Refuge** (8675 Willtown Rd., 843/889-3084, www.fws.gov/acebasin, grounds year-round daily dawn-dusk, office Mon.-Fri. 7:30am-4pm, free), run by the U.S. Fish and Wildlife Service. The historic 1828 **Grove Plantation House** is in this portion of the basin and houses the refuge's headquarters. Sometimes featured on local tours of homes, it's one of only three antebellum homes left in the ACE Basin. Surrounded by lush, ancient oak trees, it's really a sight in and of itself.

This section of the refuge, the **Edisto Unit,** is about an hour's drive from Beaufort. It is almost entirely composed of paddies from the area's role as a rice plantation before the Civil War. To get to the Edisto Unit of the Hollings ACE Basin National Wildlife Refuge, take U.S. 17 to Highway 174 (going all the way down this route takes you to Edisto Island) and turn right onto Willtown Road. The unpaved entrance road is about two miles ahead on the left. There are restrooms and a few picnic tables.

You can also visit the two parts of the **Combahee Unit** of the refuge, which offers a similar scene of trails among impounded wetlands along the Combahee River, with parking; it's farther west near Yemassee. The Combahee Unit is about 30 minutes from Beaufort. Get here by taking a left off U.S. 17 onto Highway 33. The larger portion of the Combahee Unit is soon after the turnoff, and the smaller, more northerly portion is about five miles up the road.

About 135,000 acres of the entire ACE Basin falls under the protection of the South Carolina Department of Natural Resources (DNR) as part of the **National Estuarine Research Reserve System** (www.nerrs.noaa.gov/acebasin). The DNR also runs two Wildlife Management Areas (WMAs), **Donnelly WMA** (843/844-8957, www.dnr.sc.gov, year-round Mon.-Sat. 8am-5pm) and **Bear Island WMA** (843/844-8957, www.dnr.sc.gov, Feb. 1-Oct. 14 Mon.-Sat. dawn-dusk), both of which provide rich opportunities for birding and wildlife observation.

Recreation

Kayaking

You can put in at the ramp at the **Lady's Island Marina** (73 Sea Island Pkwy., 843/522-0430) just across the bridge from Beaufort. **Hunting Island State Park** (2555 Sea Island Pkwy., 866/345-7275, www.huntingisland.com, winter daily 6am-6pm, during daylight saving time daily 6am-9pm, $5 adults, $3 children) has a wonderful inlet that is very popular with kayakers.

A good service for rentals and knowledgeable guided tours of the ACE Basin is **Outpost Moe's** (843/844-2514, www.geocities.ws/outpostmoe), where the basic 2.5-hour tour costs $40 pp, and an all-day extravaganza through the basin is $80. Moe's provides lunch for most of its tours. Another premier local outfitter for ACE Basin tours is **Carolina Heritage Outfitters** (U.S. 15 in Canadys, 843/563-5051, www.canoesc.com), which focuses on the Edisto River trail. In addition to guided tours ($30) and rentals, you can camp overnight in their cute tree houses ($125) along the kayak routes. They load you up with your gear and drive you 22 miles upriver; then you paddle downriver to the tree house for the evening. The next day, you paddle yourself the rest of the way downriver back to home base.

To have a drier experience of the ACE Basin from the deck of a larger vessel, try **ACE Basin Tours** (1 Coosaw River Dr., Beaufort, 843/521-3099, www.acebasintours.com, Mar.-Nov. Wed. and Sat. 10am, $35 adults, $15 children), which will take you on a three-hour tour in the 40-passenger *Dixie Lady*. To get to their dock from Beaufort, take Carteret Street over the bridge to St. Helena Island, and then take a left on Highway 802 east (Sam's Point Rd.). Continue until you cross Lucy Point Creek; the ACE Basin Tours marina is on your immediate left after you cross the bridge.

The state of South Carolina has conveniently gathered some of the best self-guided kayak trips at www.acebasin.net/canoe.

Golf

Golf is much bigger in Hilton Head than in the Beaufort area, but there are some local highlights. The best-regarded public course in the area, and indeed one of the best military courses in the world, is **Legends at Parris Island** (Bldg. 299, Parris Island, 843/228-2240, www.mccssc.com, $30). Call in advance for a tee time.

Another popular public course is **South Carolina National Golf Club** (8 Waveland Ave., Cat Island, 843/524-0300, www.scnational.com, $70). Get to secluded Cat Island by taking the Sea Island Parkway onto Lady's Island and continuing south as it turns into Lady's Island Drive. Turn onto Island Causeway and continue for about three miles.

Camping

Hunting Island State Park (2555 Sea Island Pkwy., 866/345-7275, www. huntingisland.com, winter daily 6am-6pm, during daylight saving time daily 6am-9pm, $5 adults, $3 children, $25 RV sites, $19 tent sites, $87-172 cabin) has 200 campsites on the north end of the island, with individual water and electric hookups. There used to be plenty of cabins for rent, but beach erosion has sadly made the ones near the water uninhabitable. One cabin near the lighthouse is still available for rent, and it is in such high demand that the park encourages you to camp instead.

Another neat place to camp is **Tuck in the Wood** (22 Tuc In De Wood Ln., St. Helena, 843/838-2267, $25), a very well-maintained 74-site private campground just past the Penn Center on St. Helena Island.

Edisto Island

One of the last truly unspoiled places in the Lowcountry, Edisto Island has been highly regarded as a getaway spot since the Edisto people first started coming here for shellfish. In fact, locals here swear that the island was settled by English-speaking colonists even before Charleston was settled in 1670.

Now this barrier island, for the moment unthreatened by the encroachment of planned communities and private resorts so endemic to the Carolina coast, is a nice getaway for area residents in addition to being a great—if a little isolated—place to live for its 800 or so full-time residents, who operate on "Edisto Time," with a *mañana* philosophy (i.e., it'll get done when it gets done) that results in a mellow pace of life out in these parts.

★ EDISTO BEACH STATE PARK

Edisto Beach State Park (8377 State Cabin Rd., 843/869-2156, www.south-carolinaparks.com, Nov.-mid-Mar. daily 8am-6pm, mid-Mar.-Oct. daily 6am-10pm, $5 adults, $3 children, free under age 6) is one of the world's foremost destinations for shell collectors. Largely because of fresh loads of silt from the adjacent ACE Basin, there are always new specimens, many of them fossils, washing ashore. The park stretches almost three miles and features the state's longest system of fully accessible hiking and biking trails, including one leading to the 4,000-year-old shell midden, now much eroded from past millennia. The new and particularly well-done **interpretive center** (Tues.-Sat. 9am-4pm) has plenty of interesting exhibits about the nature and history of the park as well as the surrounding ACE Basin.

OTHER SIGHTS

The **Edisto Museum** (8123 Chisolm Plantation Rd., 843/869-1954, www.edistomuseum.org, Tues.-Sat. noon-5pm, $4 adults, $2 children, free under age 10), a project of the Edisto Island Historic Preservation Society, has recently expanded and incorporated a nearby slave cabin. Its well-done exhibits of local lore and history are complemented by a gift shop. The Edisto Museum is before you get to the main part of the island, off Highway 174.

Opened in 1999 by local snake-hunters the Clamp brothers, the **Edisto Island Serpentarium** (1374 Hwy. 174, 843/869-1171, www.edistoserpentarium.com, hours vary, $14.95 adults, $10.95 ages 4-12, free under age 3) is educational and fun, taking you up close and personal with a variety of reptilian creatures native to the area. They usually close Labor Day-April 30.

The **Botany Bay Wildlife Management Area** (www.preserveedisto.org, Wed.-Mon. dawn-dusk, free) is a great way to enjoy the unspoiled nature of Edisto Island. On the grounds of two former rice and indigo plantations comprising 4,000 acres, Botany Bay features several historic remains of the old plantations and a small, wonderful beach. There are no facilities to speak of, so pack and plan accordingly. Botany Bay is closed on hunt days, which vary depending on the hunting season but are fairly rare.

TOURS

Edisto has many beautiful plantation homes, relics of the island's longtime role as host to cotton plantations. While all are in private hands and therefore off limits to the public, an exception is offered through **Edisto Island Tours & T'ings** (843/869-9092, $20 adults, $10 under age 13). You'll take a van tour around Edisto's beautiful churches and old plantations.

SPORTS AND RECREATION

As the largest river of the ACE (Ashepoo, Combahee, Edisto) Basin complex, the Edisto River figures large in the lifestyle of residents and visitors. A good public landing is at Steamboat Creek off Highway 174 on the way down to the island. Take Steamboat Landing Road (Hwy. 968) from Highway 174 near the James Edwards School. Live Oak Landing is farther up Big Bay Creek near the Interpretive Center at the state park. The **Edisto Marina** (3702 Docksite Rd., 843/869-3504) is on the far west side of the island.

Captain Ron Elliott of **Edisto Island Tours** (843/869-1937) offers various ecotours and fishing trips as well as canoe and kayak rentals for about $25 per day. A typical kayak tour runs about $35 pp for a 1.5- to 2-hour trip, and he offers a "beachcombing" trip for $15 pp. **Ugly Ducklin'** (843/869-1580) offers creek and inshore fishing charters. You can get gear as well as reserve boat and kayak tours of the entire area, including into the ACE Basin, at **Edisto Watersports & Tackle** (3731 Docksite Rd., 843/869-0663, www.edistowatersports.com). Their guided tours run about $30 pp, with a two-hour rental running about $20.

Riding a bike on Edisto Beach and all around the island is a great and relaxing way to get some exercise and enjoy its scenic, laid-back beauty. The best place to rent a bike—or a kayak or canoe, for that matter—is **Island Bikes and Outfitters** (140 Jungle Rd., 843/869-4444, Mon.-Sat. 9am-4pm). Bike rentals run about $16 per day; single kayaks are about $60 per day.

SHOPPING

Not only a convenient place to pick up odds and ends, the **Edistonian Gift Shop & Gallery** (406 Hwy. 174, 843/869-4466, daily 9am-7pm) is also an important landmark, as the primary supply point before you get into the main part of town. Think of a really nice convenience store with an attached gift shop and you'll get the picture.

For various ocean gear, try the **Edisto Surf Shop** (145 Jungle Rd., 843/869-9283, daily 9am-5pm). You can find whimsical Lowcountry-themed art for enjoyment or purchase at **Fish or Cut Bait Gallery** (142 Jungle Rd., 843/869-2511, www.fishorcutbaitgallery.com, Tues.-Sat. 10am-5pm).

For fresh seafood, try **Flowers Seafood Company** (1914 Hwy. 174, 843/869-0033, Mon.-Sat. 9am-7pm, Sun. 9am-5pm).

ACCOMMODATIONS AND FOOD

A great thing about Edisto Island is the total absence of ugly chain lodging or beachfront condo development. My recommended option is staying at **Edisto Beach State Park** (843/869-2156, www.southcarolinaparks.com, $25 tent sites, $75-100 cabins) itself, either at a campsite on the Atlantic side or in a marsh-front cabin on the northern edge. During high season (Apr.-Nov.), there's a minimum weeklong stay in the cabins; during the off-season, the minimum stay is two days. You can book cabins up to 11 months in advance.

If you want something a little more plush, there are rental homes galore on Edisto Island. Because of the aforementioned lack of hotels, this is the most popular option for most vacationers here—indeed, it's just about the only option. Contact **Edisto Sales and Rentals Realty** (1405 Palmetto Blvd., 800/868-5398, www.edistorealty.com).

One of the all-time great barbecue places in South Carolina is on Edisto: **Po Pigs Bo-B-Q** (2410 Hwy. 174, 843/869-9003, Wed.-Sat. 11:30am-9pm, $4-10), on the way into town. This is the real thing, the full pig cooked in all its many ways: white meat, dark meat, cracklin's, and hash, served in the local style of "all you care to eat." Unlike many barbecue spots, they do serve beer and wine.

Another popular joint on the island is **Whaley's** (2801 Myrtle St., 843/869-2161, Tues.-Sat. 11:30am-2pm and 5-9pm, bar daily 5pm-2am, $5-15), a down-home place in an old gas station a few blocks off the beach. This is a good place for casual seafood like boiled shrimp, washed down with a lot of beer. The bar is open seven days a week.

The legendary **Old Post Office** (1442 Hwy. 174, 843/869-2339, www.the-oldpostofficerestaurant.com, Tues.-Sun. 5:30pm-10pm, $20), a Lowcountry-style fine-dining spot, served a devoted clientele for 20 years. It recently reopened with a bang and thankfully kept its old-school mystique intact. Specialties include fine crab cakes drizzled with mousseline sauce, the pecan-encrusted Veal Edistonian, and a Carolina rib eye topped with a pimiento cheese sauce.

GETTING THERE AND AROUND

Edisto Island is basically halfway between Beaufort and Charleston. There's one main land route here, south on Highway 174 off U.S. 17. It's a long way down from U.S. 17 to Edisto, but the 20- to 30-minute drive is scenic and enjoyable. Most activity on the island centers on the township of Edisto Beach, which voted to align itself with Colleton County for its lower taxes (the rest of Edisto Island is part of Charleston County).

Once in town, there are two main routes to keep in mind. Palmetto Boulevard runs parallel to the beach and is noteworthy for the lack of high-rise development so common in other beach areas of South Carolina. Jungle Road runs parallel to Palmetto Boulevard several blocks inland and contains the tiny business district.

Literally the prototype of the modern planned resort community, Hilton Head Island is also a case study in how a landscape can change when money is introduced. From Reconstruction until the post-World War II era, the island consisted almost entirely of African Americans with deep roots in the area. In the mid-1950s Hilton Head began its transformation into an almost all-Caucasian, upscale golf, tennis, and shopping mecca populated largely by Northern transplants and retirees. As you can imagine, the flavor here is now quite different from surrounding areas of the Lowcountry, to say the least, with an emphasis on material excellence, top prices, get-it-done-yesterday punctuality, and the attendant aggressive traffic.

One of the unsung positive aspects of modern Hilton Head is its dedication to sustainable living. With the support of voters, the town routinely buys large tracts of land to preserve as open space. Hilton Head was the first municipality in the country to mandate the burying of all power lines and one of the first to regularly use covenants and deed restrictions. All new development must conform to rigid guidelines on setbacks and tree canopy. It has one of the most comprehensive signage ordinances in the country as well, which means no garish commercial displays will disrupt your views of the night sky. If those are "elite" values, then certainly we might do well in making them more mainstream.

HISTORY

The second-largest barrier island on the East Coast was named in 1663 by adventurer Sir William Hilton, who thoughtfully named the island—with its notable headland or "Head"—after himself. Later it gained fame as the first growing location of the legendary "Sea Island cotton," a long-grain variety that, following its introduction in 1790 by William Elliott II of the Myrtle Bank Plantation, would soon be the dominant version of the cash crop.

Nearby Bluffton was settled by planters from Hilton Head Island and the surrounding area in the early 1800s as a summer retreat. Though Charleston likes to claim the label today, Bluffton was actually the genuine "cradle of secession." Indeed, locals still joke that the town motto is "Divided We Stand."

Though it seems unlikely given the island's modern demographics, Hilton Head was almost entirely African American through much of the 20th century. When Union troops occupied the island at the outbreak of the Civil War, freed and escaped slaves flocked there, and most of the dwindling number of African Americans on the island today are descendants of this original Gullah population.

In the 1950s the Fraser family bought 19,000 of the island's 25,000 acres with the intent to continue forestry on them. But in 1956—not at all coincidentally the same year the first bridge to the island was built—Charles Fraser convinced his father to sell him the southern tip. Fraser's brainchild and decades-long labor of love—some said his obsession—Sea Pines

Hilton Head Island

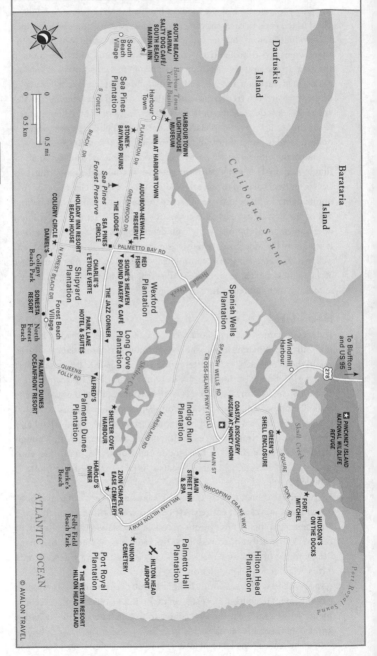

© AVALON TRAVEL

Plantation became the prototype for the golf-oriented resort communities so common today on both U.S. coasts. Fraser himself was killed in a boating accident in 2002 and is buried under the famous Liberty Oak in Harbour Town.

SIGHTS

Contrary to what many think, there are things to do on Hilton Head that don't involve swinging a club at a little white ball or shopping for designer labels, but instead celebrate the area's history and natural setting. The following are some of those attractions, arranged in geographical order from where you first access the island.

★ Pinckney Island National Wildlife Refuge

Actually consisting of many islands and hammocks, **Pinckney Island National Wildlife Refuge** (912/652-4415, daily dawn-dusk, free) is the only part of this small but very well-managed 4,000-acre refuge that's open to the public. Almost 70 percent of the former rice plantation is salt marsh and tidal creeks, making it a perfect microcosm for the Lowcountry as a whole, as well as a great place to kayak or canoe. Native Americans liked the area as well, with a 10,000-year presence and over 100 archaeological sites being identified to date. Like many coastal refuges, it was a private game preserve for much of the 20th century. Some of the state's richest birding opportunities abound here, with observers able to spot gorgeous white ibis and rare wood storks, along with herons, egrets, eagles, and ospreys, with little trouble from the refuge's miles of trails. Getting here is easy: On U.S. 278 east to Hilton Head, the refuge entrance is right between the two bridges onto the island.

Green's Shell Enclosure

Less known than the larger Native American shell ring farther south at Sea Pines, **Green's Shell Enclosure** (803/734-3886, daily dawn-dusk) is certainly easier to find, and you don't have to pay $5 to enter the area, as with Sea Pines. This three-acre heritage preserve dates back to at least the 1300s. The heart of the site comprises a low embankment, part of the original fortified village. To get here, take a left at the intersection of U.S. 278 and Squire Pope Road. Turn left into Green's Park, pass the office on the left, and park. The entrance to the shell enclosure is on the left behind a fence. You'll see a small community cemetery that has nothing to do with the shell ring; veer to your right to get to the short trail entrance.

★ Coastal Discovery Museum at Honey Horn

With the acquisition of Honey Horn's 70-acre spread of historic plantation land, Hilton Head finally has a full-fledged museum worthy of the name, and the magnificent **Coastal Discovery Museum** (70 Honey Horn Dr., 843/689-6767, www.coastaldiscovery.org, Mon.-Sat. 9am-4:30pm, Sun. 11am-3pm, free) is a must-see, even for those who came to the island mostly to golf and soak up sun.

The facility centers on the expertly restored Discovery House, the only antebellum house still existing on Hilton Head, with exhibits and displays devoted to the history of the island. The museum is also a great one-stop place to sign up for a variety of specialty on-site and off-site guided tours, such as birding and Gullah history tours. The cost for most on-site tours is a reasonable $10 adults and $5 children.

But the real draw is the 0.5-mile trail through the Honey Horn grounds, including several boardwalk viewpoints over the marsh, a neat little butterfly habitat, a few gardens, and a stable and pasture that host Honey Horn May and Tadpole, the museum's two Marsh Tackies—short, tough little ponies descended from Spanish horses and used to great effect by Francis "Swamp Fox" Marion and his freedom fighters in the American Revolution. The trail even features a replica of an ancient Native American shell ring of oyster shells, but do be aware that it is not a genuine shell ring (you can find the real thing at Green's Shell Enclosure a bit farther west on Highway 278 and in Sea Pines at the south end of the island).

While a glance at a map and area signage might convince you that you must pay the $1.25 toll on the Cross Island Parkway to get to Honey Horn, that isn't so. The exit to Honey Horn on the parkway is actually before you get to the toll plaza, therefore access is free.

Union Cemetery

A modest but key aspect of African American history on Hilton Head is at **Union Cemetery** (Union Cemetery Rd.), a small burial ground featuring several graves of African American Union Army troops (you can tell by the designation "USCI" on the tombstone, for "United States Colored Infantry"). Also of interest are the charming, hand-carved cement tombstones of nonveterans. To get here, turn north off of William Hilton Parkway onto Union Cemetery Road. The cemetery is a short way ahead on the left. There is no signage or site interpretation.

Zion Chapel of Ease Cemetery

More like one of the gloriously desolate scenes common to the rest of the Lowcountry, this little cemetery in full view of the William Hilton Parkway at Folly Field Road is all that remains of one of the "Chapels of Ease," a string of chapels set up in the 1700s. The **Zion Chapel of Ease Cemetery** (daily dawn-dusk, free) is said to be haunted by the ghost of William Baynard, whose final resting place is in a mausoleum on the site (the remains of his ancestral home are farther south at Sea Pines Plantation).

Audubon-Newhall Preserve

Plant lovers shouldn't miss this small but very well-maintained 50-acre wooded tract in the south-central part of the island on Palmetto Bay Road between the Cross Island Parkway and the Sea Pines Circle. Almost all plantlife, even that in the water, is helpfully marked and identified. The **Audubon-Newhall Preserve** (year-round dawn-dusk, free) is open to the

Clockwise from top left: the Coastal Discovery Museum; the Audubon-Newhall Preserve; biking on the beach at Hilton Head.

public, but you can't camp here. For more information, call the **Hilton Head Audubon Society** (843/842-9246).

Sea Pines Plantation

This private residential resort development at the extreme west end of the island—the first on Hilton Head and the prototype for every other such development in the country—hosts several attractions that collectively are well worth the $5 per vehicle "road use" fee, which you pay at the main entrance gate.

Harbour Town

It's not particularly historic and not all that natural, but **Harbour Town** is still pretty cool. The dominant element is the squat, colorful **Harbour Town Lighthouse Museum** (149 Lighthouse Rd., 843/671-2810, www.harbourtownlighthouse.com, daily 10am-dusk, $3), which has never really helped a ship navigate its way near the island. The 90-foot structure was built in 1970 purely to give visitors a little atmosphere, and that it does, as kids especially love climbing the stairs to the top ($2 pp) and looking out over the island's expanse.

Stoney-Baynard Ruins

The **Stoney-Baynard Ruins** (Plantation Dr., dawn-dusk, free), tabby ruins in a residential neighborhood, are what remains of the circa-1790 central building of the old Braddock's Point Plantation, first owned by patriot and raconteur Captain "Saucy Jack" Stoney and later by the Baynard family. Active during the island's heyday as a cotton center, the plantation was destroyed after the Civil War. Two other foundations are nearby, one for slave quarters and one whose use is still unknown.

Sea Pines Forest Preserve

The **Sea Pines Forest Preserve** (175 Greenwood Dr., 843/363-4530, free) is set amid the Sea Pines Plantation golf resort development, but you don't need a bag of clubs to enjoy this 600-acre preserve, which is built on the site of an old rice plantation (dikes and logging trails are still visible). Here you can ride a horse, fish, or just take a walk on the eight miles of trails (dawn-dusk) and enjoy the natural beauty around you. No bike riding is allowed on the trails, however.

In addition to the Native American shell ring farther north off Squire Pope Road, the Sea Pines Forest Preserve also boasts a shell ring set within a canopy of tall pines. Scientists date the ring itself to about 1450 BC, although human habitation on the island goes as far back as 8000 BC.

Tours and Cruises

Most guided tours on Hilton Head focus on the water. **Harbour Town Cruises** (843/363-9023, www.vagabondcruise.com, $30-60) offers several sightseeing tours as well as excursions to Daufuskie and Savannah. They also offer a tour on a former America's Cup racing yacht.

"Dolphin tours" are extremely popular on Hilton Head, and there is no shortage of operators. **Dolphin Watch Nature Cruises** (843/785-4558, $25 adults, $10 children) departs from Shelter Cove, as does **Lowcountry Nature Tours** (843/683-0187, www.lowcountrynaturetours.com, $40 adults, $35 children, free under age 3). The *Gypsy* (843/363-2900, www.bitemybait.com, $15 adults, $7 children) sails out of South Beach Marina, taking you all around peaceful Calibogue Sound. Two dolphin tours are based on Broad Creek, the large body of water that almost bisects the island through the middle. "Captain Jim" runs **Island Explorer Tours** (843/785-2100, www.dolphintourshiltonhead.com, two-hour tour $45 pp) from a dock behind the old Oyster Factory on Marshland Road. Not to be outdone, "Captain Dave" leads tours at **Dolphin Discoveries** (843/681-1911, two-hour tour $40 adults, $30 under age 13), leaving out of Simmons Landing next to the Broad Creek Marina on Marshland Road. **Outside Hilton Head** (843/686-6996, www.outsidehiltonhead.com) runs a variety of water eco-tours and dolphin tours as well as a guided day-trip excursion to Daufuskie, complete with golf cart rental.

There is a notable land-based tour by **Gullah Heritage Trail Tours** (leaves from Coastal Discovery Museum at Honey Horn, 843/681-7066, www.gullahheritage.com, $32 adults, $15 children) delving into the island's rich, if poorly preserved, African American history, from slavery through the time of the freedmen.

ENTERTAINMENT AND EVENTS
Nightlife
The most high-quality live entertainment on the island is at **The Jazz Corner** (1000 William Hilton Pkwy., 843/842-8620, www.thejazzcorner.com, dinner daily 6pm-9pm, late-night menu after 9pm, dinner $15-20, cover varies), which brings in the best names in the country—and outstanding regulars like Bob Masteller and Howard Paul—to perform in this space in the unlikely setting of a boutique mall, the Village at Wexford. The dinners are actually quite good, but the attraction is definitely the music. Reservations are recommended. Live music starts around 7pm.

For years islanders have jokingly referred to the "Barmuda Triangle," an area named for the preponderance of bars within walking distance of Sea Pines Circle. While some of the names have changed over the years, the longtime anchor of the Barmuda Triangle is the **Tiki Hut** (1 S. Forest Beach Dr., 843/785-5126, Sun.-Thurs. 11am-8pm, Fri.-Sat. 11am-10pm, bar until 2am), actually part of the Holiday Inn Oceanfront Hotel at the entrance to Sea Pines. This popular watering hole is the only beachfront bar on the island, which technically makes it the only place you can legally drink alcohol on a Hilton Head beach. Another Barmuda Triangle staple is **Hilton Head Brewing Company** (7 Greenwood Dr., 843/785-3900, daily 11am-2am), the only brewpub on the island and indeed South Carolina's first microbrewery since Prohibition. They offer a wide range of handcrafted brews, from a Blueberry Wheat to a Mocha Porter. Another longtime Triangle fave is **The Lodge** (7 Greenwood

Dr., 843/842-8966, www.hiltonheadlodge.com, daily 11:30am-midnight). After the martini and cigar craze waned, this popular spot successfully remade itself into a beer-centric place with 36 rotating taps. They still mix a mean martini, though. Also nearby is **Murphy's Irish Pub** (81 Pope Ave., 843/842-3448, Mon. 5pm-10pm, Tues.-Thurs. 3pm-midnight, Fri.-Sat. noon-4am, Sun. 11am-10pm), where the name pretty much says it all (unlike most pubs with made-up Irish names, this one's actually run by a guy named Murphy). There is great bangers and mash in this frequent rugby players' hangout.

Despite its location in the upscale strip mall of the Village at Wexford, the **British Open Pub** (1000 William Hilton Pkwy./Hwy. 278, 843/686-6736, daily 11am-10pm) offers a fairly convincing English vibe with, as the name suggests, a heavy golf theme. The fish-and-chips and shepherd's pie are both magnificent.

Inside Sea Pines is the **Quarterdeck Lounge and Patio** (843/842-1999, www.seapines.com, Sun.-Thurs. 5:30pm-10pm, Fri.-Sat. 5:30pm-midnight) at the base of the Harbour Town Lighthouse. This is where the party's at after a long day on the fairways during the Heritage golf tournament. Within Sea Pines at the South Beach Marina is also where you'll find **The Salty Dog Cafe** (232 S. Sea Pines Dr., 843/671-2233, www.saltydog.com, lunch daily 11am-3pm, dinner daily 5pm-10pm, bar daily until 2am), one of the area's most popular institutions (some might even call it a tourist trap) and something akin to an island empire, with popular T-shirts, a gift shop, books, and an ice cream shop, all overlooking the marina. My suggestion, however, is to make the short walk to the affiliated **Wreck of the Salty Dog** (843/671-7327, daily until 2am) where the marsh views are better and the atmosphere not quite so tacky.

There's only one bona fide gay club on Hilton Head, **Vibe** (32 Palmetto Bay Rd., 843/341-6933, Mon.-Fri. 8pm-3am, Sat. 8pm-2am). Wednesday is karaoke night, and Thursdays bring an amateur drag revue.

Performing Arts

Because so many residents migrated here from art-savvy metropolitan areas in the Northeast, Hilton Head maintains a very high standard of top-quality entertainment. Much of the activity centers on the multimillion-dollar **Arts Center of Coastal Carolina** (14 Shelter Cove Ln., 843/842-2787, www.artshhi.com), which hosts touring shows, resident companies, musical concerts, dance performances, and visual arts exhibits.

Now over a quarter-century old and under the direction of maestro John Morris Russell, the **Hilton Head Symphony Orchestra** (843/842-2055, www.hhso.org) performs a year-round season of masterworks and pops programs at various venues, primarily the First Presbyterian Church (540 William Hilton Pkwy./Hwy. 278). They also take their show on the road with several concerts in Bluffton and even perform several "Symphony Under the Stars" programs at Shelter Cove. **Chamber Music Hilton Head** (www.cmhh.org) performs throughout the year with selections ranging from Brahms to Smetana at All Saints Episcopal Church (3001 Meeting St.).

There's an art house on Hilton Head, the charming **Coligny Theatre** (843/686-3500, www.colignytheatre.com) in the Coligny Plaza shopping center before you get to Sea Pines. For years this was the only movie theater for miles around, but it has reincarnated as a primarily indie film venue. Look for the entertaining murals by local artist Ralph Sutton. Showtimes are Monday 11:30am and 4pm, Tuesday and Friday 11:30am, 4pm, and 7pm, Wednesday-Thursday and Saturday-Sunday 4pm and 7pm.

Festivals and Events

Late February-early March brings the **Hilton Head Wine and Food Festival** (www.hiltonheadhospitality.org), culminating in what they call "The East Coast's Largest Outdoor Public Tasting and Auction," which is generally held at the Coastal Discovery Museum at Honey Horn. Some events charge admission.

Hilton Head's premier event is the **RBC Heritage Classic Golf Tournament** (843/671-2248, http://theheritagegolfsc.com), held each April (usually the week after the Masters) at the Harbour Town Golf Links on Sea Pines Plantation. Formerly known as the Verizon Heritage Classic, the event is South Carolina's only PGA Tour event and brings thousands of visitors to town.

A fun and fondly anticipated yearly event is the **Kiwanis Club Chili Cookoff** (www.hiltonheadkiwanis.org), held each October at Honey Horn on the south end. A low admission price gets you all the chili you can eat plus free antacids. All funds go to charity, and all excess chili goes to a local food bank.

Every November brings Hilton Head's second-largest event, the **Hilton Head Concours d'Elegance & Motoring Festival** (www.hhiconcours. com), a multiday event bringing together vintage car clubs from throughout the nation and culminating in a prestigious "Best of Show" competition. It started as a fund-raiser for the Hilton Head Symphony, but now people come from all over the country to see these fine vintage cars in a beautiful setting.

SHOPPING

As you'd expect, Hilton Head is a shopper's delight, with an emphasis on upscale stores and prices to match. Keep in mind that hours may be shortened in the off-season (Nov.-Mar.). Here's a rundown of the main island shopping areas in the order you'll encounter them as you enter the island.

Shelter Cove

As of this writing, the **Mall at Shelter Cove** is being completely repurposed, with plans for boutique retail centered around a Belk anchor store. The other two shopping entities at this shopping area on Broad Creek right off the William Hilton Parkway are the **Plaza at Shelter Cove** and the dockside **Shelter Cove Harbour.** The most interesting store at the Plaza is the flagship location of **Outside Hilton Head** (843/686-6996, www.out-sidehiltonhead.com, Mon.-Sat. 10am-5:30pm, Sun. 11am-5:30pm), a complete outdoor outfitter with a thoroughly knowledgeable staff. Whatever outdoor gear you need and whatever tour you want to take, they can most likely hook you up. Shelter Cove Harbour hosts a few cute shops hewing to its overall nautical-vacation theme, such as the clothing stores **Camp Hilton Head** (843/842-3666, Mon.-Sat. 10am-9pm, Sun. noon-5pm) and the marine supplier **Ship's Store** (843/842-7001, Mon.-Sat. 7:30am-5pm, Sun. 7:30am-4pm).

Village at Wexford

Easily my favorite place to shop on Hilton Head, this well-shaded shopping center on William Hilton Parkway (Hwy. 278) hosts plenty of well-tended shops, including the foodie equipment store **Le Cookery** (843/785-7171, Mon.-Sat. 10am-6pm), the Lily Pulitzer signature women's store **S. M. Bradford Co.** (843/686-6161, Mon.-Sat. 10am-6pm) and the aromatic **Scents of Hilton Head** (843/842-7866, Mon.-Fri. 10am-6pm, Sat. 10am-5pm).

My favorite shop on all Hilton Head is at Wexford, **The Oilerie** (843/681-2722, www.oilerie.com, Mon.-Sat. 10am-7pm, Sun. noon-5pm). This franchise provides free samples of all its high-quality Italian olive oils and vinegars. After you taste around awhile, you pick what you want and the friendly staff bottles it for you in souvenir-quality glassware. They also have a selection of spices, soaps, and other goodies.

Coligny Circle

This is the closest Hilton Head comes to funkier beach towns like Folly Beach, although it doesn't really come that close. You'll find dozens of delightful and somewhat quirky stores here, many keeping long hours in the summer, like the self-explanatory **Coligny Kite & Flag Co.** (843/785-5483, Mon.-Sat. 10am-9pm, Sun. 11am-6pm), the hippie-fashion **Loose Lucy's** (843/785-8093, Mon.-Sat. 10am-6pm, Sun. 11am-5pm), and the Caribbean-flavored **Jamaican Me Crazy** (843/785-9006, daily 10am-10pm). Kids will love both **The Shell Shop** (843/785-4900, Mon.-Sat. 10am-9pm, Sun. noon-9pm) and **Black Market Minerals** (843/785-7090, Mon.-Sat. 10am-10pm, Sun. 11am-8pm).

Harbour Town

The **Shoppes at Harbour Town** (www.seapines.com) are a collection of about 20 mostly boutique stores along Lighthouse Road in Sea Pines Plantation. At **Planet Hilton Head** (843/363-5177, www.planethiltonhead.com, daily 10am-9pm) you'll find some cute, eclectic gifts and home goods. Other clothing highlights include **Knickers Men's Store** (843/671-2291, daily 10am-9pm) and **Radiance** (843/363-5176, Mon.-Tues. 10am-5pm, Wed.-Sat. 10am.-9pm, Sun. 11am-9pm), a very cute and fashion-forward women's store.

The **Top of the Lighthouse Shoppe** (843/671-2810, www.harbourtown-lighthouse.com, daily 10am-9pm) is where many a climbing visitor has been coaxed to part with some of disposable income. And, of course, as you'd expect being near the legendary Harbour Town links, there's the **Harbour Town Pro Shop** (843/671-4485), routinely voted one of the best pro shops in the nation.

South Beach Marina

On South Sea Pines Drive at the marina you'll find several worthwhile shops, including a good ship's store and all-around grocery dealer **South Beach General Store** (843/671-6784, daily 8am-10pm). I like to stop in **Blue Water Bait and Tackle** (843/671-3060, daily 7am-8pm) and check out the cool nautical stuff. They can also hook you up with a variety of kayak trips and fishing charters. And, of course, right on the water there's the ever-popular **Salty Dog Cafe** (843/671-2233, www.saltydog.com, lunch daily 11am-3pm, dinner daily 5pm-10pm), whose ubiquitous T-shirts seem to adorn every other person on the island.

Art Galleries

Despite the abundant wealth apparent in some quarters here, there's no freestanding art museum in the area, that role being filled by independent galleries. A good representative example is **Morris & Whiteside Galleries** (220 Cordillo Pkwy., 843/842-4433, www.morris-whiteside.com, Mon.-Fri. 9am-5pm, Sat. 10am-4pm), in the historic Red Piano Art Gallery building, which features a variety of paintings and sculpture, heavy on landscapes but also showing some fine figurative work. The nonprofit **Art League of Hilton Head** (14 Shelter Cove Ln., 843/681-5060, Mon.-Sat. 10am-6pm) is housed in the Walter Greer Art Gallery within the Arts Center of Coastal Carolina and displays work by member artists in all media. The **Nash Gallery** (13 Harboursise Ln., 843/785-6424, Mon.-Fri. 10am-9pm, Sat. 10am-8pm, Sun. 11am-5pm) in Shelter Cove Harbour deals more in North American craft styles. Hilton Head art isn't exactly known for its avant-garde nature, but you can find some whimsical stuff at **Picture This** (78D Arrow Rd., 843/842-5299, Mon.-Fri. 9:30am-5:30pm, Sat. 9:30am-12:30pm), including a selection of Gullah craft items. A wide range of regional painters, sculptors, and glass artists is featured at **Endangered Arts** (841 William Hilton Pkwy., 843/785-5075, www.endangeredarts.com).

SPORTS AND RECREATION
Beaches

First, the good news: Hilton Head Island has 12 miles of some of the most beautiful, safe beaches you'll find anywhere. The bad news is that there are only a few ways to gain access, generally at locations referred to as "beach parks." Don't just drive into a residential neighborhood and think you'll be able to park and find your way to the beach; for better or worse, Hilton Head is not set up for that kind of casual access.

Driessen Beach Park has 207 long-term parking spaces, costing $0.25 for 30 minutes. There's free parking but fewer spaces at the Coligny Beach Park entrance and at Fish Haul Creek Park. Also, there are 22 metered spaces at Alder Lane Beach Access, 51 at Folly Field Beach Park, and 13 at Burkes Beach Road. Most other beach parks have permit parking only. Clean, well-maintained public restrooms are available at all the beach parks. You can find beach information at 843/342-4580 and www.hiltonheadislandsc. gov. Beach park hours vary: Coligny Beach Park is open daily 24 hours; all other beach parks are open March-September daily 6am-8pm and October-February daily 6am-5pm.

Alcohol is strictly prohibited on Hilton Head's beaches. There are lifeguards on all the beaches during the summer, but be aware that the worst undertow is on the northern stretches. Also remember to leave the sand dollars where they are; their population is dwindling due to souvenir hunting.

Kayaking

Kayakers will enjoy Hilton Head Island, which offers several gorgeous routes, including Calibogue Sound to the south and west and Port Royal Sound to the north. For particularly good views of life on the salt marsh, try Broad Creek, which nearly bisects Hilton Head Island, and Skull Creek, which separates Hilton Head from the natural beauty of Pinckney Island. Broad Creek Marina is a good place to put in. There are also two public landings, Haigh Landing and Buckingham Landing, on Mackay Creek at the entrance to the island, one on either side of the bridge.

If you want a guided tour, there are plenty of great kayak tour outfits to choose from in the area. Chief among them is **Outside Hilton Head** (32 Shelter Cove Ln., 800/686-6996, www.outsidehiltonhead.com). They offer a wide range of guided trips, including "The Outback," in which you're first boated to a private island and then taken on a tour of tidal creeks, and five- or seven-hour "Ultimate Lowcountry Day" trips to Daufuskie, Bluffton, or Bull Creek. Other good places to book a tour or just rent a kayak are **Water-Dog Outfitters** (Broad Creek Marina, 843/686-3554) and **Kayak Hilton Head** (Broad Creek Marina, 843/684-1910). Leaving out of the Harbour Town Yacht Basin is **H2O Sports** (843/671-4386, www.h2o-sportsonline.com), which offers 90-minute guided kayak tours ($30) and rents kayaks for about $20 per hour. Within **Palmetto Dunes Oceanfront Resort** (4 Queens Folly Rd., 800/827-3006, www.palmettodunes.com) is **Palmetto Dunes Outfitters** (843/785-2449, www.pdoutfitters.com, daily 9am-5pm), which rents kayaks and canoes and offers lessons on the resort's 11-mile-long lagoon.

Fishing and Boating

As you'd expect, anglers and boaters love the Hilton Head-Bluffton area, which offers all kinds of saltwater, freshwater, and fly-fishing opportunities. Captain Brian Vaughn runs **Off the Hook Charters** (68 Helmsman Way, 843/298-4376, www.offthehookcharters.com), which offers fully licensed half-day trips ($400). **Miss Carolina Sportfishing** (168 Palmetto Bay Rd., 843/298-2628, www.misscarolinafishing.com) offers deep-sea action at a little over $100 per hour. Captain Dave Fleming of **Mighty Mako Sport Fishing Charters** (164 Palmetto Bay Rd., 843/785-6028, www.mightymako.com) can take you saltwater fishing, both backwater and near-shore, on the 25-foot *Mighty Mako* for about $400 for a half-day. If you're at the South Beach Marina area of Sea Pines Plantation, head into **Blue Water Bait and Tackle** (843/671-3060, daily 7am-8pm) and see if they can hook you up with a trip.

Public landings in the Hilton Head area include the Marshland Road Boat Landing and the Broad Creek Boat Ramp under the Charles Fraser Bridge, and the Haigh Landing on Mackay Creek.

Hiking and Biking

Although the very flat terrain is not challenging, Hilton Head provides some scenic and relaxing cycling opportunities. Thanks to wise planning and foresight, the island has an extensive and award-winning 50-mile network of biking trails that does a great job of keeping cyclists out of traffic. A big plus is the long bike path paralleling the William Hilton Parkway, enabling cyclists to use that key artery without braving its traffic. There is even an underground bike path beneath the parkway to facilitate crossing that busy road. In addition, there are also routes along Pope Avenue as well as North and South Forest Beach Drive. Go to www.hiltonheadisland.org/biking to download a map of the island's entire bike path network.

Palmetto Dunes Oceanfront Resort (4 Queens Folly Rd., 800/827-3006, www.palmettodunes.com) has a particularly nice 25-mile network of bike paths that all link up to the island's larger framework. Within the resort is **Palmetto Dunes Outfitters** (843/785-2449, www.pdoutfitters.com, daily 9am-5pm), which will rent you any type of bike you might need. Sea Pines Plantation also has an extensive 17-mile network of bike trails; you can pick up a map at most information kiosks within the plantation.

But the best bike path on Hilton Head is the simplest of all, and where no one will ask you where you're staying that night: the beach. For a few hours before and after low tide, the beach effectively becomes a 12-mile bike path around most of the island, and a pleasant morning or afternoon ride may well prove to be the highlight of your trip.

There's a plethora of bike rental facilities on Hilton Head with competitive rates. Be sure to ask if they offer free pickup and delivery. Try **Hilton Head Bicycle Company** (112 Arrow Rd., 843/686-6888, daily 9am-5pm, $16/day).

Hikers will particularly enjoy **Pinckney Island National Wildlife Refuge** (U.S. 278 east, just before Hilton Head, 912/652-4415, www.fws.gov, free), which takes you through several key Lowcountry ecosystems, from maritime forest to salt marsh. Other peaceful, if nonchallenging, trails are at the **Audubon-Newhall Preserve** (Palmetto Bay Road between the

Cross Island Parkway and the Sea Pines Circle, 843/842-9246, year-round dawn-dusk, free).

Horseback Riding

Within the Sea Pines Forest Preserve is **Lawton Stables** (190 Greenwood Dr., 843/671-2586, www.lawtonstableshhi.com), which features pony rides, a small-animal farm, and guided horseback rides through the preserve. You don't need any riding experience, but you do need reservations.

Bird-Watching

The premier birding locale in the area is the **Pinckney Island National Wildlife Refuge** (U.S. 278 east, just before Hilton Head, 912/652-4415, www.fws.gov, free). You can see bald eagles, ibis, wood storks, painted buntings, and many more species. Birding is best in spring and fall. The refuge has several freshwater ponds that serve as wading bird rookeries. During migration season, so many beautiful birds make such a ruckus that you'll think you've wandered onto an Animal Planet shoot.

Golf

Hilton Head is one of the world's great golf centers, with no less than 23 courses, and one could easily write a book about nothing but that. This, however, is not that book. Perhaps contrary to what you might expect, most courses on the island are public, and some are downright affordable. All courses are 18 holes unless otherwise described; greens fees are averages and vary with season and tee time.

The best-regarded course, with prices to match, is **Harbour Town Golf Links** (Sea Pines Plantation, 843/363-4485, www.seapines.com, $239). It's on the island's south end at Sea Pines and is the home of the annual RBC Heritage Classic, far and away the island's number-one tourist draw.

There are two Arthur Hills-designed courses on the island, **Arthur Hills at Palmetto Dunes Resort** (843/785-1140, www.palmettodunes.com, $125) and **Arthur Hills at Palmetto Hall** (Palmetto Hall Plantation, 843/689-4100, www.palmettohallgolf.com, $130), both of which now offer the use of Segway vehicles on the fairways. The reasonably priced **Barony Course** at Port Royal Plantation (843/686-8801, www.portroyalgolfclub.com, $98) also boasts some of the toughest greens on the island. Another challenging and affordable course is the **George Fazio** at Palmetto Dunes Resort (843/785-1130, www.palmettodunes.com, $105).

Hilton Head National Golf Club (60 Hilton Head National Dr., 843/842-5900, www.golfhiltonheadnational.com), which is actually on the mainland just before you cross the bridge to Hilton Head, is still highly rated for both condition and service, despite recently losing nine holes to a road widening project. *Golf Week* has named it one of the country's best golf courses. The 18-hole course is public and greens fees are below $100.

It's a good idea to book tee times through the **Golf Island Call Center**

Tennis

One of the top tennis destinations in the country, Hilton Head has over 20 tennis clubs, some of which offer court time to the public (walk-on rates vary; call for information). They are: **Palmetto Dunes Tennis Center** (Palmetto Dunes Resort, 843/785-1152, www.palmettodunes.com, $30 per hour), **Port Royal Racquet Club** (Port Royal Plantation, 843/686-8803, www.portroyalgolfclub.com, $25 per hour), **Sea Pines Racquet Club** (Sea Pines Plantation, 843/363-4495, www.seapines.com, $25 per hour), **South Beach Racquet Club** (Sea Pines Plantation, 843/671-2215, www.seapines.com, $25 per hour), and **Shipyard Racquet Club** (Shipyard Plantation, 843/686-8804, $25 per hour).

Free, first-come, first-served play is available at the following public courts, maintained by the Island Recreation Association (www.islandrec-center.org): **Chaplin Community Park** (Singleton Beach Rd., four courts, lighted), **Cordillo Courts** (Cordillo Pkwy., four courts, lighted), **Fairfield Square** (Adrianna Ln., two courts), **Hilton Head High School** (School Rd., six courts), and **Hilton Head Middle School** (Wilborn Rd., four courts).

Zip Line

Billing itself as the only zip line experience within 250 miles, the new **Zip Line Hilton Head** (33 Broad Creek Marina Way, 843/682-6000, www.ziplinehiltonhead.com) offers an extensive canopy tour making great use of the area's natural scenery and features. You generally "fly" in groups of about eight. Reservations strongly encouraged. The newest offering is "Aerial Adventure," a challenging two-hour trip ($50) with about 50 obstacles.

ACCOMMODATIONS

Generally speaking, accommodations on Hilton Head are often surprisingly affordable given their overall high quality and the breadth of their amenities.

Under $150

You can't beat the price at **Park Lane Hotel and Suites** (12 Park Ln., 843/686-5700, www.hiltonheadparklanehotel.com, $130). This is your basic suite-type hotel (formerly a Residence Inn) with kitchens, laundry, a pool, and a tennis court. The allure here is the price, hard to find anywhere these days at a resort location. For a nonrefundable fee, you can bring your pet. The one drawback is that the beach is a good distance away. The hotel does offer a free shuttle, however, so it would be wise to take advantage of that and avoid the usual beach-parking hassles. As you'd expect given the price, rooms here tend to go quickly; reserve early.

By Hilton Head standards, the **Main Street Inn & Spa** (2200 Main St., 800/471-3001, www.mainstreetinn.com, $160-210) can be considered a bargain stay, and with high quality to boot. With the old-world touches, sumptuous appointments, charming atmosphere, and attentive service, this 33-room inn and attached spa on the grounds of Hilton Head Plantation seem like they would be more at home in Charleston than Hilton Head. The inn serves a great full breakfast—not continental—daily 7:30am-10:30am.

Another good place for the price is the **South Beach Marina Inn** (232 S. Sea Pines Dr., 843/671-6498, www.sbinn.com, $186) in Sea Pines. Near the famous Salty Dog Cafe and outfitted in a similar nautical theme, the inn not only has some pretty large guest rooms for the price, it offers a great view of the marina and has a very friendly feel. As with all Sea Pines accommodations, staying on the plantation means you don't have to wait in line with other visitors to pay the $5-per-day "road fee." Sea Pines also offers a free trolley to get around the plantation.

One of Hilton Head's favorite hotels for beach lovers is the **Holiday Inn Oceanfront** (1 S. Forest Beach Dr., 843/785-5126, www.hihiltonhead. com, $200), home of the famed Tiki Hut bar on the beach. Staff turnover is less frequent here than at other local accommodations, and while it's no Ritz-Carlton and occasionally shows signs of wear, it's a good value in a bustling area of the island.

One of the better resort-type places for those who prefer the putter and the racquet to the Frisbee and the surfboard is the **Inn at Harbour Town** (7 Lighthouse Ln., 843/363-8100, www.seapines.com, $199) in Sea Pines. The big draw here is the impeccable service, delivered by a staff of "butlers" in kilts, mostly Europeans who take the venerable trade quite seriously. While it's not on the beach, you can take advantage of the free Sea Pines Trolley every 20 minutes.

Recently rated the number-one family resort in the United States by *Travel + Leisure,* the well-run **Palmetto Dunes Oceanfront Resort** (4 Queens Folly Rd., 800/827-3006, www.palmettodunes.com, $150-300) offers something for everybody in terms of lodging. There are small, cozy condos by the beach or larger villas overlooking the golf course and pretty much everything in between. The prices are perhaps disarmingly affordable considering the relative luxury and copious recreational amenities, which include 25 miles of very well-done bike trails, 11 miles of kayak and canoe trails, and, of course, three signature links. As with most developments of this type on Hilton Head, most of the condos are privately owned, and therefore each has its own particular set of guidelines and cleaning schedules.

A little farther down the island you'll find the **Sonesta Resort** (130 Shipyard Dr., 843/842-2400, www.sonesta.com/hiltonheadisland, $160-200), which styles itself as Hilton Head's only green-certified accommodations. The guest rooms are indeed state-of-the-art, and the expansive, shaded grounds near the beach are great for relaxation. No on-site golf here, but immediately adjacent is a well-regarded tennis facility with 20 courts.

Another good resort-style experience heavy on the golf is on the grounds of the Port Royal Plantation on the island's north side, **The Westin Resort Hilton Head Island** (2 Grasslawn Ave., 843/681-4000, www.westin.com/hiltonhead, from $200), which hosts three PGA-caliber links. The beach is also but a short walk away. This AAA four diamond-winning Westin offers a mix of suites and larger villas.

Vacation Rentals

Many visitors to Hilton Head choose to rent a home or villa for an extended stay, and there is no scarcity of availability. Try **Resort Rentals of Hilton Head** (www.hhivacations.com) or **Destination Vacation** (www.destinationvacationhhi.com).

FOOD

Because of the cosmopolitan nature of the population, with so many transplants from the northeastern United States and Europe, there is uniformly high quality in Hilton Head restaurants. And because of another demographic quirk of the area, its large percentage of senior citizens, you can also find some great deals by looking for some of the common "early bird" dinner specials, usually starting around 5pm.

Breakfast and Brunch

There are a couple of great diner-style places on the island. Though known more for its hamburgers and Philly cheesesteaks, **Harold's Diner** (641 William Hilton Pkwy., 843/842-9292, Mon.-Sat. 7am-3pm, $4-6) has great pancakes as well as its trademark brand of sarcastic service. Unpretentious and authentic in a place where those two adjectives are rarely used, it has been said of Harold's that "the lack of atmosphere *is* the atmosphere." The place is small, popular, and does not take reservations.

If you need a bite in the Coligny Plaza area, go to **Skillets** (1 N. Forest Beach Dr., 843/785-3131, www.skilletscafe.com, breakfast daily 7am-5pm, dinner daily 5pm-9pm, $5-23) in Coligny Plaza. Their eponymous stock-in-trade is a layered breakfast dish of sautéed ingredients served in a porcelain skillet, like the "Kitchen Sink" (pancakes ringed with potatoes, sausage, and bacon, topped with two poached eggs).

A great all-day breakfast place with a twist is **Signe's Heaven Bound Bakery & Café** (93 Arrow Rd., 843/785-9118, www.signesbakery.com, Mon.-Fri. 8am-4pm, Sat. 9am-2pm, $5-10). Breakfast is tasty dishes like frittatas and breakfast polenta, while the twist is the extensive artisanal bakery, with delicious specialties like the signature key lime pound cake. You'll be surprised at the quality of the food for the low prices. Expect a wait during peak periods.

A fairly well-kept local secret is the **French Bakery and Courtyard Cafe** (430 William Hilton Pkwy./U.S. 278, 843/342-5420, www.frenchbakeryhiltonhead.com, Mon.-Sat. 8:30am-4pm, $5). Set inside the Pineland Station shopping center and with nice open-air seating, French Bakery offers a full range of fresh-baked goods like quiches, croissants, paninis, artisanal breads, cakes, and gourmet pastries.

German

I'm pretty sure you didn't come all the way to South Carolina to eat traditional German food, but while you're here...check out **Alfred's** (807 William Hilton Pkwy./Hwy. 278, 843/341-3117, wwww.alfredsofhiltonhead.com, $20-30), one of the more unique spots on Hilton Head and a big favorite with the locals. Expect a wait. Bratwurst, veal cordon bleu, and of course Wiener schnitzel are all standouts. I recommend the German Mix Platter ($25), which features a brat, some sauerbraten, and a schnitzel.

Mediterranean

For upscale Italian, try **Bistro Mezzaluna** (55 New Orleans Rd., 843/842-5011, daily 5-9:30pm, $18-25). Known far and wide for its osso buco as well as its impeccable service, there's also a great little bar for cocktails before or after dinner.

Mexican

There are a couple of excellent and authentic Mexican restaurants on the island. Just off the William Hilton Parkway near the island's entrance is **Mi Tierra** (160 Fairfield Square, 843/342-3409, lunch daily 11am-4pm, dinner Mon.-Fri. 4pm-9pm, Sat.-Sun. 4pm-10pm, $3-15). You'll find lots of traditional seafood dishes, like ceviche, octopus, shrimp, and oysters. On Mondays there is often a real mariachi band.

Middle Eastern

Hard to describe but well worth the visit, **Daniel's Restaurant and Lounge** (2 N. Forest Beach Dr., 843/341-9379, http://danielshhi.com, daily 4pm-2am, tapas $10-12) combines elements of a traditional Middle Eastern eatery, an upscale tapas place, a beach spot, and a swank bar scene to create one of the more memorable food-and-beverage experiences on the island. Add in the fact that the prices are actually quite accessible and you've got a must-visit. Their "big small plates," meaning larger-portion tapas, run about $10-12 per plate. While they market their Middle Eastern flavor with plates like the cinnamon lamb kebab, their tapas have a cosmopolitan feel; they range from a Caribbean salmon steak to chicken pesto sliders.

Seafood

Not to be confused with Charley's Crab House next door to Hudson's, seafood lovers will enjoy the experience down near Sea Pines at **Charlie's L'Etoile Verte** (8 New Orleans Rd., 843/785-9277, http://charliesgreenstar.com, lunch Tues.-Sat. 11:30am-2pm, dinner Mon.-Sat. 5:30pm-10pm, $25-40), which is considered by many connoisseurs to be Hilton Head's single best restaurant. The emphasis here is on "French country kitchen" cuisine—think Provence, not Paris. In keeping with that theme, each day's menu is concocted from scratch and handwritten. Listen to these recent entrées and feel your mouth water: flounder sauté meunière, grilled wild coho salmon with basil pesto, and breast of duck in a raspberry demi-glace. Get the picture? Of course, you'll want to start with the escargot and leeks vol-au-vent, the house pâté, or even some pan-roasted Bluffton oysters. Reservations are essential.

A longtime Hilton Head favorite is **Red Fish** (8 Archer Rd., 843/686-3388, www.redfishofhiltonhead.com, lunch Mon.-Sat. 11:30am-2pm, dinner daily beginning with early-bird specials at 5pm, $20-37). Strongly Caribbean in decor as well as menu, with romanticism and panache to match, this is a great place for couples. The creative but accessible menu by executive chef Sean Walsh incorporates unique spices, fruits, and vegetables for a fresh, zesty palette. Reservations are essential.

Fresh seafood lovers will enjoy one of Hilton Head's staples, the huge **Hudson's on the Docks** (1 Hudson Rd., 843/681-2772, www.hudsonson-thedocks.com, lunch daily 11am-4pm, dinner daily from 5pm, $14-23) on Skull Creek just off Squire Pope Road on the less-developed north side. Much of the catch—though not all of it, by any means—comes directly off the boats you'll see dockside. Try the stuffed shrimp filled with crabmeat. Leave room for one of the homemade desserts crafted by Ms. Bessie, a 30-year veteran employee of Hudson's.

INFORMATION AND SERVICES

The best place to get information on Hilton Head, book a room, or secure a tee time is just as you come onto the island at the **Hilton Head Island Chamber of Commerce Welcome Center** (100 William Hilton Pkwy., 843/785-3673, www.hiltonheadisland.org, daily 9am-6pm).

GETTING THERE AND AROUND

A few years back, the **Savannah/Hilton Head International Airport** (SAV, 400 Airways Ave., Savannah, 912/964-0514, www.savannahairport.com) added Hilton Head to its name specifically to identify itself with that lucrative market. The move has been a success, and this facility remains the closest large airport to Hilton Head Island and Bluffton. However, it's not actually *that* close: Keep in mind that when your plane touches down in Savannah, you're still about a 45-minute drive to Hilton Head proper. From the airport, go north on I-95 into South Carolina, and take exit 8 onto U.S. 278 east.

There is a local regional airport as well, the **Hilton Head Island Airport** (HXD, 120 Beach City Rd., 843/689-5400, www.bcgov.net). While attractive and convenient, keep in mind that it only hosts propeller-driven commuter planes because of the runway length and concerns about noise.

Hilton Head is about 30 minutes from I-95. If you're entering the area by car, the best route is exit 8 off I-95 onto U.S. 278, which takes you by Bluffton and right into Hilton Head. Near Bluffton, U.S. 278 is called

Fording Island Road, and on Hilton Head proper it becomes the William Hilton Parkway business route.

Hilton Head Islanders have long referred to their island as the "shoe" and speak of driving to the toe or going to the heel. If you take a look at a map, you'll see why: Hilton Head bears an uncanny resemblance to a running shoe pointed toward the southwest, with the aptly named Broad Creek forming a near facsimile of the Nike "swoosh" symbol.

Running the length and circumference of the shoe is the main drag, U.S. 278 Business (William Hilton Pkwy.), which crosses onto Hilton Head right at the "tongue" of the shoe, a relatively undeveloped area. The Cross Island Parkway toll route (U.S. 278), beginning up toward the ankle as you first get on the island, is a quicker route straight to the toe near Sea Pines.

While it is technically the business spur, when locals say "278" they're talking about the William Hilton Parkway. It takes you along the entire sole of the shoe, including the beaches, and on down to the toe, where you'll find a confusing, crazy British-style roundabout called Sea Pines Circle. It's also the site of the Harbour Town Marina and the island's oldest planned development, Sea Pines Plantation.

While making your way around the island, always keep in mind that the bulk of it consists of private developments, and local law enforcement frowns on people who aimlessly wander among the condos and villas.

Other than taxi services, there is no public transportation to speak of on Hilton Head, unless you want to count the free shuttle around Sea Pines Plantation. Taxi services include **Yellow Cab** (843/686-6666), **Island Taxi** (843/683-6363), and **Ferguson Transportation** (843/842-8088).

Bluffton and Daufuskie Island

Just outside Hilton Head are two of the Lowcountry's true gems, Bluffton and Daufuskie Island. While Bluffton's outskirts have been taken over by the same gated community and upscale strip-mall sprawl spreading throughout the coast, at its core is a delightfully charming little community on the quiet May River, now called Old Bluffton, where you'd swear you just entered a time warp.

Daufuskie Island still maintains much of its age-old isolated, timeless personality, and the island—even today accessible only by boat—remains one of the spiritual centers of the Gullah culture and lifestyle.

★ OLD BLUFFTON

Similar to Beaufort, but even quieter and smaller, historic Bluffton is an idyllic village on the banks of the serene and well-preserved May River. Bluffton was the original hotbed of secession, with Charleston diarist Mary Chesnut famously referring to the town as "the center spot of the fire eaters." While its outskirts (so-called "Greater Bluffton") are now a haven for planned communities hoping to mimic some aspect of Bluffton's historic patina, the town center itself remains an authentic look at old South Carolina. Retro cuts both ways, however, and Bluffton has been a notorious speed trap for generations. Always obey the speed limit. During their Civil War occupation, Union troops repaid the favor of those original Bluffton secessionists, which is why only nine homes in Bluffton are of antebellum vintage; the rest were torched in a search for Confederate guerrillas.

The center of tourist activity focuses on the **Old Bluffton Historic District,** several blocks of 1800s-vintage buildings clustered between the parallel Boundary and Calhoun Streets (old-timers sometimes call this "the original square mile"). Many of the buildings are private residences, but most have been converted into art studios and antiques stores.

Heyward House Historic Center

The **Heyward House Historic Center** (70 Boundary St., 843/757-6293, www.heywardhouse.org, Mon.-Fri. 10am-5pm, Sat. 10am-4pm, tours $5 adults, $2 students) is not only open to tours but also serves as Bluffton's visitors center. Built in 1840 as a summer home for the owner of Moreland Plantation, John Cole, the house was later owned by George Cuthbert Heyward, grandson of Declaration of Independence signer Thomas Heyward Jr. (Remarkably, it stayed in the family until the 1990s.) Of note are the intact slave quarters on the grounds.

The Heyward House also sponsors walking tours of the historic district (by appointment only, $15). Download your own walking tour map at www.heywardhouse.org.

Church of the Cross

Don't fail to go all the way to the end of Calhoun Street, as it dead-ends on a high bluff on the May River at the Bluffton Public Dock. Overlooking this peaceful marsh-front vista is the photogenic **Church of the Cross** (110 Calhoun St., 843/757-2661, www.thechurchofthecross.net, tours Mon.-Sat. 10am-2pm, free). The current sanctuary was built in 1854 and is one of only two local churches not burned in the Civil War. The parish itself began in 1767, with the first services on this spot held in the late 1830s. While the church looks as if it were made of cypress, it's actually constructed of heart pine.

Bluffton Oyster Company

You might want to get a gander at the state's last remaining working oyster house, the **Bluffton Oyster Company** (63 Wharf St., 843/757-4010, www.blufftonoyster.com, Mon.-Sat. 9am-5:30pm), and possibly purchase some of their maritime bounty. Larry and Tina Toomer continue to oversee the oyster harvesting-and-shucking family enterprise, which has roots going back to the early 1900s.

SHOPPING

Bluffton's eccentric little art studios, most clustered in a two-block stretch on Calhoun Street, are by far its main shopping draw. Named for the Lowcountry phenomenon you find in the marsh at low tide among the fiddler crabs, Bluffton's **Pluff Mudd Art** (27 Calhoun St., 843/757-5551, Mon.-Sat. 10am-5:30pm) is a cooperative of 16 great young painters and photographers from throughout the area. The **Guild of Bluffton Artists** (20 Calhoun St., 843/757-5590, Mon.-Sat. 10am-4:30pm) features works from many local artists, as does the outstanding **Society of Bluffton Artists** (48 Boundary St., 843/757-6586, Mon.-Sat. 10am-5pm, Sun. 11:30am-3pm). For cool, custom handcrafted pottery, try **Preston Pottery and Gallery** (10 Church St., 843/757-3084, Tues.-Sat. 10am-5pm). Another great Bluffton place is the hard-to-define **Eggs'n'tricities** (71 Calhoun St., 843/757-3446, Mon.-Sat. 10am-5pm). The name pretty much says it all for this fun and eclectic vintage, junk, jewelry, and folk art store.

If you want to score some fresh local seafood for your own culinary adventure, the no-brainer choice is the **Bluffton Oyster Company** (63 Wharf St., 843/757-4010, www.blufftonoyster.com, Mon.-Sat. 9am-5:30pm), the state's only active oyster facility. They also have shrimp, crab, clams, and fish, nearly all of it from the nearly pristine May River on whose banks the facility sits.

For a much more commercially intense experience, head just outside of town on U.S. 278 on the way to Hilton Head to find the dual **Tanger Outlet Centers** (1414 Fording Island Rd., 843/837-4339, Mon.-Sat. 10am-9pm, Sun. 11am-6pm), an outlet-shopper's paradise with virtually every major brand represented.

SPORTS AND RECREATION

A key kayaking outfitter in Bluffton is **Native Guide Kayak Tours** (8 2nd St., 843/757-5411, www.nativeguidetours.com), which features tours of the May and New Rivers led by native Ben Turner. Another good outfit is **Swamp Girls Kayak Tours** (843/784-2249, www.swampgirls.com), the labor of love of Sue Chapman and Linda Etchells.

To put in your own kayak or canoe on the scenic, well-preserved May River, go to the **Alljoy Landing** at the eastern terminus of Alljoy Road along the river. Or try the dock at the end of Calhoun Street near the Church of the Cross. There's also a rough put-in area at the Bluffton Oyster Company (63 Wharf St.), which has a public park adjacent to it. For fishing, public landings include the dock on Calhoun Street, Alljoy Landing, and Bluffton Oyster Company.

The closest public golf courses to Bluffton are the Arnold Palmer-designed **Crescent Pointe Golf Club** (1 Crescent Pointe Dr., 888/292-7778, www.crescentpointegolf.com, $90) and the nine-hole **Old Carolina Golf Club** (89 Old Carolina Rd., 888/785-7274, www.oldcarolinagolf.com, $26), certainly one of the best golf deals in the region.

Under $150

A quality bargain stay right between Bluffton and Hilton Head is the **Holiday Inn Express Bluffton** (35 Bluffton Rd., 843/757-2002, www.ichotelsgroup.com, $120), on U.S. 278 as you make the run onto Hilton Head proper. It's not close to the beach or to Old Town Bluffton, so you'll definitely be using your car, but its central location will appeal to those who want to keep their options open.

Over $300

For an ultra-upscale spa and golf resort environment near Bluffton, the clear pick is the **Inn at Palmetto Bluff** (476 Mt. Pelia Rd., 843/706-6500, www.palmettobluffresort.com, $650-900) just across the May River. This Auberge property was picked recently as the number-two U.S. resort by *Condé Nast Traveler* magazine. Lodging is dispersed among a series of cottages and "village home" rentals. There are three top-flight dining options on the grounds: the fine-dining **River House Restaurant** (843/706-6542, breakfast daily 7am-11am, lunch or "porch" menu daily 11am-10pm, dinner daily 6pm-10pm, $30-40); the **May River Grill** (Tues.-Sat. 11am-4pm, $9-13) at the golf clubhouse; and the casual **Buffalo's** (843/706-6630, Sun.-Tues. 11:30am-5pm, Wed.-Sat. 11:30am-9pm, $10-15).

FOOD

Breakfast and Brunch

No discussion of Bluffton cuisine is complete without the famous **Squat 'n' Gobble** (1231 May River Rd., 843/757-4242, daily 24 hours), a local phenomenon not to be confused with a similarly named chain of eateries in California. Long a site of gossiping and politicking as well as, um, squatting and gobbling, this humble diner on May River Road is an indelible part of the local consciousness. They specialize in the usual "American" menu of eggs, bacon, hamburgers, hot dogs, and fries.

French

Most dining in Bluffton is pretty casual, but you'll get the white tablecloth treatment at **Claude & Uli's Signature Bistro** (1533 Fording Island Rd., 843/837-3336, lunch Mon.-Fri. 11:30am-2:30pm, dinner Mon.-Sat. from 5pm, $18-25) just outside of town in Moss Village. Chef Claude does a great veal cordon bleu as well as a number of fine seafood entrées, such as an almond-crusted tilapia and an excellent seafood pasta. Don't miss their specialty soufflé for dessert; order it with dinner, as it takes almost half an hour to bake.

Mexican

My favorite restaurant in Bluffton by far is a near-copy of an equally fine Mexican restaurant in Hilton Head, **Mi Tierra** (101 Mellichamp Center, 843/757-7200, lunch daily 11am-4pm, dinner Mon.-Fri. 4pm-9pm, Sat.-Sun.

Clockwise from top left: Church of the Cross; the Squat 'n' Gobble restaurant; Bluffton Oyster Company.

4pm-10pm, $3-15). They have very high-quality Tex-Mex-style food in a fun atmosphere at great prices. Another highly regarded Mexican place in Bluffton is **Amigo's Café Y Cantina** (133 Towne Dr., 843/815-8226, Mon.-Sat. 11am-9pm, $8).

GETTING THERE AND AROUND

To make the 40-minute drive to Bluffton from Beaufort, take Highway 170 south to U.S. 278 east. Bluffton is a short 15 minutes away from Hilton Head, taking U.S. 278 west.

DAUFUSKIE ISLAND

Sitting between Hilton Head Island and Savannah and accessible only by water, Daufuskie (da-FUSK-ee) Island has about 500 full-time residents, most of whom ride around on golf carts or bikes (there's only one paved road, Haig Point Road, and cars are a rare sight), and all of whom are very laid-back. Once the home of rice and indigo plantations and rich oyster beds—the latter destroyed by pollution and overharvesting—the two up-scale residential resort communities on the island, begun in the 1980s, give a clue as to where the future might lie, although the recent global economic downturn, perhaps thankfully, slowed development to a standstill.

The area of prime interest to visitors is the unincorporated western portion, or **Historic District,** the old stomping grounds of Pat Conroy during his stint as a teacher of resident African American children. His old one-room schoolhouse of *The Water is Wide* fame, the **Mary Field School,** is still here, as is the adjacent 140-year-old **Union Baptist Church,** but Daufuskie students now have a surprisingly modern new facility (middle school students are still ferried to mainland schools every day). Farther north on Haig Point Road is the new **Billie Burn Museum,** housed in the old Mt. Carmel Church and named after the island's resident historian. On the southern end you'll find the **Bloody Point Lighthouse,** named for the vicious battle fought nearby during the Yamasee War of 1815 (the light was actually moved inland in the early 1900s). Other areas of interest throughout the island include Native American sites, tabby ruins, the old Baptist Church, and a couple cemeteries.

Download a very well-done, free self-guided tour of Daufuskie's historic sites at www.hiltonheadisland.org; look for the "Robert Kennedy Historic Trail Guide" (not a nod to the former attorney general and U.S. senator, but a longtime island resident and historian).

The **Melrose Beach Golf Club** (55 Avenue of the Oaks, 888/851-4971, www.melroseonthebeach.com) is back in operation, an iteration of the long-troubled Melrose golf resort that recently went through an extended bankruptcy. While not everything is back up and running, you can play golf on the Jack Nicklaus-designed course; to schedule a tee time call the club. Lodging is not available at Melrose as of this writing.

For overnight stays, you can rent a humble but cozy cabin at **Freeport**

Marina (843/785-8242, $100-150, golf cart $60 extra per day), near the ferry dock and overlooking the water. There are vacation rental options island-wide as well; go to www.daufuskieislandrentals.com for info on a wide variety of offerings. Sorry, no camping available!

There are no grocery stores as commonly understood on Daufuskie, only

Who Are the Gullah?

A language, a culture, and a people with a shared history, Gullah is more than that—it's also a state of mind. The Gullah are African Americans of the Sea Islands of South Carolina and Georgia. (In Georgia, the term *Geechee,* from the Ogeechee River, is more or less interchangeable.) Protected from outside influence by the isolation of this coastal region after the Civil War, Gullah culture is the closest living cousin to the West African traditions of those brought to this country as slaves.

While you might hear that *Gullah* is a corruption of "Angola," some linguists think it simply means "people" in a West African language. In any case, the Gullah speak what is known as a creole language, meaning one derived from several sources. Gullah combines elements of Elizabethan English, Jamaican patois, and several West African dialects; for example "goober" (peanut) comes from the Congo *n'guba.* Another creole element is a word with multiple uses; for example, Gullah's *shum* could mean "see them," "see him," "see her," or "see it" in either past or present tense, depending on context. Lorenzo Dow Turner's groundbreaking *Africanisms in the Gullah Dialect,* published in 1949, traced elements of the language to Sierra Leone in West Africa and more than 300 Gullah words directly to Africa.

Gullah is typically spoken very rapidly, which only adds to its impenetrability to the outsider. Gullah also relies on colorful turns of phrase. *"E tru mout"* ("He true mouth") means the speaker is referring to someone who doesn't lie. *"Ie een crack muh teet"* ("I

didn't even crack my teeth") means "I kept quiet." A forgetful person might say, *"Mah head leab me"* ("My head left me").

Gullah music, as practiced by the world-famous Hallelujah Singers of St. Helena Island, also uses many distinctly African techniques, such as call-and-response (the folk hymn "Michael Row the Boat Ashore" is a good example). The most famous Americans with Gullah roots are boxer Joe Frazier (Beaufort), hip-hop star Jazzy Jay (Beaufort), NFL great Jim Brown (St. Simons Island, Georgia), and Supreme Court Justice Clarence Thomas (Pin Point, Georgia, near Savannah).

Upscale development continues to claim more and more traditional Gullah areas, generally by pricing the Gullah out through rapidly increasing property values. Today, the major pockets of living Gullah culture in South Carolina are in Beaufort, St. Helena Island, Daufuskie Island, Edisto Island, and a northern section of Hilton Head Island.

Several key institutions are keeping alive the spirit of Gullah: the **Penn Center** (16 Dr. Martin Luther King Jr. Dr., St. Helena, 843/838-2474, www.penncenter.com, Mon.-Sat. 11am-4pm, $4 adults, $2 seniors and children) on St. Helena Island near Beaufort; the **Avery Research Center** (66 George St., Charleston, 843/953-7609, www.cofc.edu/avery, Mon.-Fri. 10am-5pm, Sat. noon-5pm) at the College of Charleston; and **Geechee Kunda** (622 Ways Temple Rd., Riceboro, Georgia, 912/884-4440, www.geecheekunda.com) near Midway off U.S. 17.

a couple of "general store" type places. So if you've booked a vacation rental, most grocery items will need to be brought in with you.

For the freshest island seafood, check out the **Old Daufuskie Crab Company** (Freeport Marina, 843/785-6652, daily 11:30am-9pm, $8-22). The deviled crab is the house specialty, The other place to dine out on the island is **Marshside Mama's** (15 Haig Pt. Rd., 843/785-4755, www.marshsidemamas.com, hours change frequently, $10-15), a laid-back spot to enjoy grouper, gumbo, and Lowcountry boil. Reservations strongly encouraged.

For handcrafted island art, go to **Iron Fish Gallery** (168 Benjies Point Rd., 843/842-9448, call ahead for hours), featuring the work of Chase Allen. His "coastal sculptures" include fanciful depictions of fish, stingrays, and even mermaids.

Getting There and Around

The main public ferry between Daufuskie and Hilton Head is **Calibogue Cruises** (18 Simmons Rd., 843/342-8687, www.daufuskiefreeport.com). Taking off from Broad Creek Marina on Hilton Head, the pleasant, short ride—a half hour each way—brings you in on the landward side of the island. Cost is $33 per person round-trip, or $64 per person round-trip including a meal at the Old Daufuskie Crab Company and a golf cart rental. Ferries run three times a day Mondays, Wednesdays, and Fridays, and twice a day Tuesdays, Thursdays, Saturdays, and Sundays. Ferry reservations are essential!

While the ferry trip and many vacation rentals include the rental of a golf cart, for *a la carte* service—get it?—rent one near Freeport Marina by calling 843/342-8687 (rates vary but hover around $30 per person per day). As the amount of golf carts is limited, I strongly recommend reserving yours in advance. All standard rules of the road apply, including needing a valid driver's license.

Points Inland

It's likely that at some point you'll find yourself traveling inland from Beaufort, given that area's proximity to I-95. While this area is generally more known for offering interstate drivers a bite to eat and a place to rest their heads, there are several spots worth checking out in their own right, especially Walterboro and the Savannah National Wildlife Refuge.

WALTERBORO

The very picture of the slow, moss-drenched Lowcountry town—indeed, the municipal logo is the silhouette of a live oak tree—Walterboro is a delightful, artsy oasis. Right off I-95, Walterboro serves as a gateway of sorts to the Lowcountry, and the cheap commercial sprawl on the interstate shows it. But don't be put off by this ugliness—once you get into town it's as charming as they come, with roots dating back to 1783.

Walterboro is chiefly known to the world at large for being one of the best antiquing locales on the East Coast. Indeed, many of the high-dollar antiques shops on Charleston's King Street actually do their picking right here in the local stores, selling their finds at a significant markup in Charleston! (Another advantage Walterboro antiques shopping has over Charleston: plenty of free parking.)

Convenient and walkable, the two-block **Arts and Antiques District** on Washington Street centers on more than a dozen antiques and collectible stores, interspersed with a few gift shops and eateries. The best shop, though by no means the only one you should check out, is **Bachelor Hill Antiques** (255 E. Washington St., 843/549-1300, Mon.-Sat. 9am-6pm, Sun. 9am-4pm), which has several rooms packed with interesting and unique items, from collectibles to furniture to most everything in between.

Walterboro is about a 45-minute drive from Beaufort. Take U.S. 21 north to I-95, then take exit 53 or 57. Walterboro is about an hour's drive from Charleston.

Sights

★ South Carolina Artisans Center

If you're in town, don't miss the **South Carolina Artisans Center** (334 Wichman St., 843/549-0011, www.scartisanscenter.com, Mon.-Sat. 9am-5pm, Sun. 1pm-5pm, free), an expansive and vibrant collection of the best work of local and regional painters, sculptors, jewelers, and other craftspeople, for sale and for enjoyment. Imagine a big-city folk art gallery, except without the pretension, and you get the idea. You can find most any genre represented here, including jewelry, watercolors, shawls, photography, and sweetgrass baskets. The Artisans Center hosts numerous receptions, and every third Saturday of the month they hold live artist demonstrations 11am-3pm.

Museums

Walterboro boasts three small museums. The newly relocated and upgraded **Colleton Museum** (506 E. Washington St., 843/549-2303, www.cm-fm.org, Tues. noon-6pm, Wed.-Fri. 10am-5pm, Sat. 10am-2pm, free) is one of the best examples of a small-town museum you're likely to find anywhere. It has a lot of surprisingly well-curated exhibits about local history, from Native American days through the colonial and Civil War periods through the present day. Adjacent is the Farmers Market, open from May until the end of October on Tuesdays 2pm-6pm and on Saturdays 10am-2pm.

The **Bedon-Lucas House Museum** (205 Church St., 843/549-9633, Thurs.-Sat. 1pm-4pm, $3 adults, free under age 8) was built by a local planter in 1820. An example of the local style of "high house," built off the ground to escape mosquitoes and catch the breeze, the house today is a nice mix of period furnishings and unadorned simplicity.

The **Slave Relic Museum** (208 Carn St., 843/549-9130, www.slaverelics.

houses the Center for Research and Preservation of the African American Culture. It features artifacts, photos, and documents detailing the Atlantic passage, slave life, and the Underground Railroad.

Tuskegee Airmen Memorial

Yes, the Tuskegee Airmen of World War II fame were from Alabama, not South Carolina. But a contingent trained in Walterboro, at the site of the present-day **Lowcountry Regional Airport** (537 Aviation Way, 843/549-2549) a short ways south of downtown on U.S. 17. Today, on a publicly accessible, low-security area of the airport stands the **Tuskegee Airmen Memorial,** an outdoor monument to these brave flyers. There's a bronze statue and several interpretive exhibits.

Great Swamp Sanctuary

A short ways out of town in the other direction is the **Great Swamp Sanctuary** (www.thegreatswamp.org, daily dawn-dusk, free), a still-developing ecotourism project focusing on the Lowcountry environment. Located in one of the few braided-creek habitats accessible to the public, the 842-acre sanctuary has three miles of walking and biking trails, some along the path of the old Charleston-Savannah stagecoach route. Kayakers and canoeists can paddle more than two miles of winding creeks. There are three entry points to the Great Swamp Sanctuary, all off Jefferies Boulevard. In west-to-east order from I-95: north onto Beach Road, north onto Detreville Street (this is considered the main entrance), and west onto Washington Street.

Festivals and Events

In keeping with South Carolina's tradition of towns hosting annual events to celebrate signature crops and products, Walterboro's **Colleton County Rice Festival** (http://thericefestival.org, free) happens every April. There's a parade, live music, a 5K run, and the crowning of the year's "Rice Queen," and you just might find yourself learning something about the unique coastal lifestyle built around this ultimate cash crop of the early South.

Accommodations and Food

If you're looking for big-box lodging, the section of Walterboro close to I-95 is chockablock with it. The quality is surprisingly good, perhaps because they tend to cater to Northerners on their way to and from Florida. A good choice is **Holiday Inn Express & Suites** (1834 Sniders Hwy., 843/538-2700, www.hiexpress.com, $85), or try the **Comfort Inn & Suites** (97 Downs Ln., 843/538-5911, www.choicehotels.com, $95).

If you'd like something with a bit more character, there are two B&Bs on Hampton Street downtown. **Old Academy Bed & Breakfast** (904 Hampton St., 843/549-3232, www.oldacademybandb.com, $80-115) has four guest rooms housed in Walterboro's first school building. They offer a

Tuskegee Airmen in Walterboro

In a state where all too often African American history is studied in the context of slavery, a refreshing change is the tale of the Tuskegee Airmen, one of the most lauded American military units of World War II. Though named for their origins at Alabama's Tuskegee Institute, the pilots of the famed 332nd Fighter Group actually completed their final training in South Carolina at Walterboro Army Airfield, where the regional airport now sits.

The U.S. military was segregated during World War II, with African Americans mostly relegated to support roles. An interesting exception was the case of the 332nd, formed in 1941 as the 99th Pursuit Squadron by an act of Congress and the only all-African American flying unit in the U.S. military at the time. For the most part flying P-47 Thunderbolts and P-51 Mustangs, the pilots of the 332nd had one of the toughest missions of the war: escorting bombers over the skies of Germany and protecting them from Luftwaffe fighters. Though initially viewed with skepticism, the Tuskegee Airmen wasted no time in proving their mettle.

In fact, it wasn't long before U.S. bomber crews—who were, needless to say, not African American—specifically requested that they be escorted by the airmen, who were given the nickname "Red-tail Angels" because of the distinctive markings of their aircraft. While legend has it that the 332nd never lost a bomber, this claim has been debunked. But as Tuskegee Airman Bill Holloman said, "The Tuskegee story is about pilots who rose above adversity and discrimination and opened a door once closed to black America, not about whether their record is perfect." The 332nd's reputation for aggressiveness in air combat was so widely known that the Germans also had a nickname for them—*Schwartze Vogelmenschen*, or "Black Birdmen."

Today Walterboro honors the airmen with a monument on the grounds of the Lowcountry Regional Airport, on U.S. 17 just northeast of town. In an easily accessible part of the airport grounds, the monument features a bronze statue and several interpretive exhibits. Another place to catch up on Tuskegee Airmen history is at the **Colleton Museum** (506 E. Washington St., 843/549-2303, www. cm-fm.org, Tues. noon-6pm, Wed.-Fri. 10am-5pm, Sat. 10am-2pm, free), which has a permanent exhibit on the pilots and their history in the Walterboro area.

Walterboro Army Airfield's contribution to the war effort was not limited to the Tuskegee Airmen. Seven of the famed Doolittle Raiders were trained here, there was a compound for holding German prisoners of war, and it was also the site of the U.S. military's largest camouflage school.

full continental breakfast. Note that credit cards are not accepted. Although built recently (by local standards), the 1912 **Hampton House Bed and Breakfast** (500 Hampton St., 843/542-9498, www.hamptonhousebandb. com, $125-145) has three well-appointed guest rooms and offers a full country breakfast. By appointment only, you can see the Forde Doll and Dollhouse Collection, with over 50 dollhouses and oodles of antique dolls.

The story of food in Walterboro revolves around **Duke's Barbecue** (949 Robertson Blvd., 843/549-1446, $7), one of the best-regarded barbecue spots in the Lowcountry and one of the top two joints named "Duke's" in the state (the other, by common consensus, is in Orangeburg). The pulled pork is delectable, cooked with the indigenous South Carolina mustard-based sauce. Unlike most area barbecue restaurants, some attention is devoted to the veggies, such as collard greens, green beans, and black-eyed peas with rice.

HARDEEVILLE

For most travelers, Hardeeville is known for its plethora of low-budget lodging and garish fireworks stores at the intersection of I-95 and U.S. 17. Truth be told, that's about all that's here. However, train buffs will enjoy getting a gander at the rare and excellently restored **Narrow Gauge Locomotive** near the intersection of U.S. 17 and Highway 46. Donated by the Argent Lumber Company in 1960, Engine No. 7 memorializes the role of the timber industry in the area.

If you're hungry in Hardeeville, go straight to **Mi Tierrita** (U.S. 17 and I-95, 843/784-5011, $5), an excellent, authentic Mexican restaurant near the confluence of I-95 and U.S. 17. It's pretty beat-up on the inside, but the food is delicious and many steps above the typical watered-down Tex-Mex you find in the Southeast.

If barbecue is your thing, go on Highway 170A on the "backside" of Hardeeville in the hamlet of Levy to **The Pink Pig** (3508 S. Okatie Hwy., 843/784-3635, www.the-pink-pig.com, Tues.-Wed. and Sat. 11am-3pm, Thurs.-Fri. 11am-3pm and 5-7pm, $5-15). They offer three sauces: honey mustard, spicy, and "Gullah." The place is surprisingly hip, with good music piped in and a suitably cutesy, kid-friendly decor with plenty of the eponymous rosy porcine figures.

Hardeeville is about a half-hour drive from Beaufort, at the intersection of I-95 and U.S. 17.

SAVANNAH NATIONAL WILDLIFE REFUGE

Roughly equally divided between Georgia and South Carolina, the sprawling, 30,000-acre **Savannah National Wildlife Refuge** (912/652-4415, www.fws.gov/savannah, daily dawn-dusk, free) is one of the premier bird-watching and nature-observing locales in the Southeast. The system of dikes and paddy fields once used to grow rice now helps make this an attractive stopover for migrating birds. Bird-watching is best October-April. While you can kayak on your own on miles of creeks, you can also call **Swamp Girls Kayak Tours** (843/784-2249, www.swampgirls.com), who work out of nearby Hardeeville, for a guided tour. The wildlife refuge is about two hours from Charleston and an hour from Beaufort. To get here, take exit 5 off I-95 onto U.S. 17. Go south to U.S. 170 and look for Laurel Hill Wildlife Drive. Be sure to stop by the brand-new visitors center (off U.S. 170 at Laurel Hill Wildlife Drive, Mon.-Sat. 9am-4:30pm).

Background

The Landscape

GEOGRAPHY

The area covered by this guide falls within the **Coastal Plain** region of the southeastern United States, which contains some of the most unique ecosystems in North America. It's a place where water is never far away and features large in the daily lives, economy, and folkways of the region's people.

Although it's hundreds of miles away, the Appalachian mountain chain has a major influence on the southeastern coast. It's in Appalachia where so much of the coast's freshwater—in the form of rain—comes together and flows southeast—in the form of rivers—to the Atlantic Ocean. Moving east, the next level down from the Appalachians is the hilly **Piedmont** region, the eroded remains of an ancient mountain chain.

At the Piedmont's eastern edge is the **fall line,** so named because it's where rivers make a drop toward the sea, generally becoming navigable. Around the fall line zone in the **Upper Coastal Plain** you can sometimes spot **sand hills,** usually only a few feet in elevation, generally thought to be the vestigial remains of primordial sand dunes and offshore sandbars. Well beyond the fall line and the sometimes nearly invisible sand hills lies the **Lower Coastal Plain,** gradually built up over a 150-million-year span by sedimentary runoff from the Appalachian Mountains, which at that time were as high or even higher than the modern-day Himalayas.

The Coastal Plain was sea bottom for much of the earth's history, and in some eroded areas you can see dramatic proof of this in the form of prehistoric shells, shark's teeth, and fossilized whale bones and oyster beds, often many miles inland. Sea level has fluctuated wildly with climate and geological changes through the eons. At various times over the last 50 million years, the Coastal Plain has submerged, surfaced, and submerged again. At the height of the last major ice age, when global sea levels were very low, the east coast of North America extended out nearly 100 miles farther than the present shoreline. (We now call this former coastal region the **continental shelf.**) The Coastal Plain has been roughly in its current form for about the last 15,000 years.

Rivers

Visitors from drier climates are sometimes shocked to see how huge the rivers can get in coastal South Carolina. Wide and voluminous as they saunter to the sea, their seemingly slow speed belies the massive power they contain. South Carolina's big **alluvial,** or sediment-bearing, rivers originate in the region of the Appalachian mountain chain.

The headwaters of the Savannah River, for example, are near Tallulah

---

Gorge in extreme north Georgia. Some rivers form out of the confluence of smaller rivers, such as Georgia's mighty Altamaha River, actually the child of the Ocmulgee and Oconee Rivers in the middle of the state. Others, like the Ashley and Cooper Rivers in South Carolina, originate much closer to the coast in the Piedmont.

The **blackwater river** is a particularly interesting Southern phenomenon, duplicated only in South America and in one example each in New York and Michigan. While alluvial rivers generally originate in highlands and carry with them a large amount of sediment, blackwater rivers originate in low-lying areas and move slowly toward the sea, carrying with them very little sediment. Rather, their dark tea color comes from the tannic acid of decaying vegetation all along their banks, washed out by the slow, inexorable movement of the river toward the sea. A blackwater course featured prominently in this guide is the Edisto River, the longest blackwater river in the world.

The Intracoastal Waterway

You'll often see its acronym, ICW, on signs—and sadly you'll probably hear the locals mispronounce it "intercoastal"—but the casual visitor might actually find the Intracoastal Waterway difficult to spot. Relying on a natural network of interconnected estuaries and channels, combined with artificial **cuts,** the ICW often blends in rather subtly with the region's already extensive network of creeks and rivers.

Mandated by Congress in 1919 and maintained by the U.S. Army Corps of Engineers, the Atlantic portion of the ICW runs from Key West, Florida, to Boston and carries recreational and barge traffic away from the perils of offshore currents and weather. Even if they don't use it specifically, kayakers and boaters often find themselves on it at some point during their nautical adventures.

Estuaries

Most biologists will tell you that the Coastal Plain is where things get interesting. The place where a river interfaces with the ocean is called an estuary, and it's perhaps the most interesting place of all. Estuaries are heavily tidal in nature (indeed, the word derives from *aestus,* Latin for "tide"), and feature brackish water and heavy silt content. This portion of the U.S. coast typically has about a 6- to 8-foot tidal range, and the coastal ecosystem depends on this steady ebb and flow for life. At high tide, shellfish open and feed. At low tide, they literally clam up, keeping saltwater inside their shells until the next tide comes. Waterbirds and small mammals feed on shellfish and other animals at low tide, when their prey is exposed. High tide brings an influx of fish and nutrients from the sea, in turn drawing predators like dolphins, who often come into tidal creeks to feed. In the region covered by this guide, key estuaries from north to south are: Cape Romain, Charleston Harbor, the ACE (Ashepoo, Combahee, Edisto) Basin, Beaufort River, May River, Calibogue Sound, and the Savannah River.

All this water action in both directions—freshwater coming from inland, saltwater encroaching from the Atlantic—results in the phenomenon of the salt marsh, the single most recognizable and iconic geographic feature of the South Carolina coast, also known simply as "wetlands." (Freshwater marshes are rarer, Florida's Everglades being perhaps the premier example.) Far more than just a transitional zone between land and water, marsh is also nature's nursery. Plant and animal life in marshes tends not only to be diverse but encompasses multitudes.

You may not see its denizens easily, but on close inspection you'll find the marsh absolutely teeming with creatures. Visually, the main identifying feature of a salt marsh is its distinctive, reedlike marsh grasses, adapted to survive in brackish water. Like estuaries, marshes and all life in them are heavily influenced by the tides, which bring in nutrients.

The marsh has also played a key role in human history as well, for it was here that the massive rice and indigo plantations grew their signature crops, aided by the natural ebb and flow of the tides. While most marsh you see will look quite undisturbed, very little of it could be called pristine. In the heyday of the rice plantations, much of the coastal salt marsh was criss-crossed by the canal-and-dike system of the paddy fields.

You can still see evidence almost everywhere in this area if you look hard enough (the best time to look is right after takeoff or before land-ing in an airplane, since many approaches to regional airports take you over wetlands). Anytime you see a low, straight ridge running through a marsh, that's likely the eroded, overgrown remnant of an old paddy field dike. Kayakers occasionally find old wooden sluice gates on their paddles.

In the Lowcountry, you'll often hear the term **pluff mud.** This refers to the area's distinctive variety of soft, dark mud in the salt marsh, which often has an equally distinctive odor that locals love but some visitors have a hard time getting used to. Extraordinarily rich in nutrients, pluff mud helped make rice such a successful crop in the marshes of the Lowcountry.

In addition to their vital role as wildlife incubators and sanctuaries, wet-lands are also one of the most important natural protectors of the health of the coastal region. They serve as natural filters, cleansing runoff from the land of toxins and pollutants before it hits the ocean. They also help humans by serving as natural hurricane barriers, their porous nature help-ing to ease the brunt of the damaging storm surge.

Beaches and Barrier Islands

The beautiful, broad beaches of South Carolina are almost all situated on barrier islands, long islands parallel to the shoreline and separated from the mainland by a sheltered body of water. Because they're formed from the de-posit of sediment by offshore currents, they change shape over the years, with the general pattern of deposit going from north to south (meaning the north-ern end will begin eroding first). Most of the barrier islands are geologically quite young, only having formed within the last 25,000 years or so. Natural erosion by currents and by storms, combined with the accelerating effects of dredging for local port activity, has quickened the decline of many barrier islands. Many beaches in the area are subject to a mitigation of erosion called **beach renourishment,** which generally involves redistributing dredged material closely offshore so that it will wash up on and around the beach.

As the name indicates, barrier islands are another of nature's safeguards against hurricane damage. Historically, the barrier islands have borne the vast bulk of the damage done by hurricanes in the region. Sullivan's Island near Charleston was submerged by 1989's Hurricane Hugo. Like the marshes, barrier islands also help protect the mainland by absorbing the brunt of the storm's wind and surging water.

CLIMATE

One word comes to mind when one thinks about the Southern climate: *hot.* That's the first word that occurs to Southerners as well, but virtually every survey of why residents are attracted to the area puts the climate at the top of the list. Go figure. How hot is hot? The average high for July, the region's hottest month is about 89°F. While that's nothing compared to Tucson or Death Valley, when coupled with the region's notoriously high **humidity** it can have an altogether miserable effect.

Heat aside, there's no doubt that one of the most difficult things for an outsider to adjust to in the South is the humidity. The average annual humidity in Charleston is about 55 percent in the afternoons and a whopping 85 percent in the mornings. The most humid months are August and September. There is no real antidote to humidity—other than air-conditioning, that is—although many film crews and other outside workers swear by the use of Sea Breeze astringent. If you and your traveling companions can deal with the strong minty odor, dampen a hand towel with the astringent, drape it across the back of your neck, and go about your business.

Don't assume that because it's humid you shouldn't drink fluids. Just as in any hot climate, you should drink lots of water if you're going to be out in the Southern heat.

August and September are by far the wettest months in terms of rainfall, with averages well over six inches for each of those months. July is also quite wet, coming in at over five inches on average.

Winters here are pretty mild but can seem much colder than they actually are because of the dampness in the air. The coldest month is January, with a high of about 58°F for the month and 42°F the average low. You're highly unlikely to encounter snow in the area, and if you do, it will likely be only skimpy flurries that a resident of the Great Lakes region wouldn't even notice as snow. But don't let this lull you into a false sense of security.

If such a tiny flurry were to hit, be aware that most people down here have no clue how to drive in rough weather and will not be prepared for even such a small amount of snowfall. Visitors from snow country are often surprised, sometimes bordering on shock, by how completely a Southern city will shut down when that once-in-a-decade few tenths of an inch of snow finally hits.

The major weather phenomenon of concern for residents and visitors alike is the mighty hurricane. These massive storms, with counterclockwise-rotating bands of clouds and winds that can push 200 mph, are an ever-present danger to the southeast coast June-November each year.

In any case, as most everyone is aware of now from the horrific, well-documented damage from such killer storms as Hugo, Andrew, and Katrina, hurricanes are not to be trifled with. Old-fashioned drunken "hurricane parties" are a thing of the past for the most part, the images of cataclysmic destruction everyone has seen on TV having long since eliminated any lingering romanticism about riding out the storm.

Tornadoes—especially those that come in the "back door" through the Gulf of Mexico and overland to the Carolina coast—are a very present danger with hurricanes. As hurricanes die out over land, they can spawn dozens of tornadoes, which in many cases prove more destructive than the hurricanes that produced them.

Local TV, websites, and print media can be counted on to give more than ample warning in the event a hurricane is approaching the area during your visit. Whatever you do, do not discount the warnings; it's not worth it. If the locals are preparing to leave, you should too. Typically when a storm is likely to hit the area, there will first be a suggested evacuation. But if authorities determine there's an overwhelming likelihood of imminent hurricane damage, they will issue a **mandatory evacuation order.** What this means in practice is that if you do choose to stay behind, you cannot count on any type of emergency services or help whatsoever.

Generally speaking, the most lethal element of a hurricane is not the wind but the **storm surge,** the wall of ocean water that the winds drive before them onto the coast. During 1989's Hurricane Hugo, Charleston's Battery was inundated with a storm surge of over 12 feet, with an amazing 20 feet reported farther north at Cape Romain.

In the wake of such devastation, local governments have dramatically improved their once tepid disaster-response plans.

ENVIRONMENTAL ISSUES

The coast of South Carolina is currently experiencing a double whammy, environmentally speaking: Not only are its distinctive wetlands extraordinarily sensitive to human interference, this is one of the most rapidly developing parts of the country. New and often poorly planned subdivisions and resort communities are popping up all over the place. Vastly increased port activity is also taking a devastating toll on the salt marsh and surrounding barrier islands. Combine all that with the South's often skeptical attitude toward environmental activism and you have a recipe for potential ecological disaster.

Thankfully, there are some bright spots. More and more communities are seeing the value of responsible planning and not green-lighting every new development sight unseen. Land trusts and other conservation organizations are growing in size, number, funding, and influence. The large number of marine biologists in these areas at various research and educational institutions means there's a wealth of education and talent available to advise local governments and citizens on how best to conserve the area's natural beauty.

Here's a closer look at some of the most urgent environmental issues facing the region today:

Marsh Dieback

The dominant species of marsh grass, *Spartina alterniflora* and *Juncus roemerianus,* thrive in the typically brackish water of the coastal marsh estuaries, their structural presence helping to stem erosion of banks and dunes. While drought and blight have taken their toll on the grass, increased coastal development and continued channel deepening have also led to a steady creep of ocean saltwater farther and farther into remaining marsh stands.

The Paper Industry

Early in the 20th century, the Southeast's abundance of cheap undeveloped land and plentiful free water led to the establishment of massive pine tree farms to feed coastal pulp and paper mills. Chances are, if you used a paper grocery bag recently, it was made in a paper mill in the South.

But in addition to making a whole lot of paper bags and providing lots of employment for residents through the decades, the paper industry also gave the area lots of air and water pollution, stressed local rivers (it takes a lot of freshwater to make paper from trees), and took away natural species diversity from the area by devoting so much acreage to a single crop, pine trees.

When driving near rivers in this region, anytime you see a large industrial facility on the riverside it's probably a paper mill. The rotten egg smell that comes next is from the sulfurous discharge from its smokestacks.

Aquifers

Unlike parts of the western United States, where individuals can enforce private property rights to water, the South has generally held that the region's water is a publicly held resource. The upside of this is that everybody has equal claim to drinking water without regard to status or income or how long they've lived here. The downside is that industry also has the same free claim to the water that citizens do—and they use a heck of a lot more of it.

Currently most of the South Carolina coast gets their water from aquifers, which are basically huge underground caverns made of limestone. Receiving **groundwater** drip by drip, century after century, from rainfall farther inland, the aquifers essentially act as massive sterile warehouses for freshwater, accessible through wells.

The aquifers have human benefit only if their water remains fresh. Once saltwater from the ocean begins intruding into an aquifer, it doesn't take

But nearly a century ago, paper mills began pumping millions and millions of gallons of water out of coastal aquifers. Combined with the dramatic rise in coastal residential development and a continuing push to deepen existing shipping channels, the natural water pressure of the aquifers has decreased, leading to measurable saltwater intrusion at several points under the coast.

Currently, local and state governments are increasing their reliance on **surface water** (treated water from rivers and creeks) to relieve the strain on the underground aquifer system. But it's too soon to tell if that has contained the threat from saltwater intrusion.

Air Pollution

Despite growing awareness of the issue, air pollution is still a big problem in the coastal region. Paper mills still operate, putting out their distinctive rotten egg odor, and auto emissions standards are notoriously lax in South Carolina. The biggest culprits, though, are coal-powered electric plants, which are the norm throughout the region and which continue to pour large amounts of toxins into the atmosphere.

Plants and Animals

PLANTS

Probably the most iconic plantlife of the coastal region is the **Southern live oak** (*Quercus virginiana*). Named because of its evergreen nature, a live oak is technically any of a number of evergreens in the *Quercus* genus, many of which reside on the South Carolina coast, but in local practice almost always refers to the Southern live oak.

Capable of living over 1,000 years and possessing wood of legendary resilience, the Southern live oak is one of nature's most magnificent creations. The timber value of live oaks has been well known since the earliest days of the North American shipbuilding industry—when the oak dominated the entire coast inland of the marsh—but their value as a canopy tree has finally been widely recognized by local and state governments.

Fittingly, the other iconic plantlife of the coastal region grows on the branches of the live oak. Contrary to popular opinion, **Spanish moss** (*Tillandsia usneoides*) is neither Spanish nor moss. It's an air plant, a wholly indigenous cousin to the pineapple. Also contrary to folklore, Spanish moss is not a parasite nor does it harbor parasites while living on an oak tree— although it can after it has already fallen to the ground.

Also growing on the bark of a live oak, especially right after a rain shower, is the **resurrection fern** (*Polypodium polypodioides*), which can stay dormant for amazingly long periods of time, only to spring back to

Top: colorful blooming azaleas. **Bottom:** live oak tree.

recognizable by the little balls of sediment at the entrances (the cra[b] out the balls after sifting through the sand for food).

One charming beach inhabitant, the **sand dollar** (*Mellita quinquies forata*), has seen its numbers decline drastically due to being entirely t[oo] charming for its own good. Beachcombers are now asked to enjoy thes[e] flat little cousins to the sea urchin in their natural habitat and to refrain from taking them home. Besides, they start to smell bad when they dry out.

The **sea nettle** (*Chrysaora quinquecirrha*), a less-than-charming beach inhabitant, is a jellyfish that stings thousands of people on the coast each year (although only for those with severe allergies are the stings potentially life-threatening). Stinging their prey before transporting it into their waiting mouths, the jellyfish also sting when disturbed or frightened. Most often, people are stung by stepping on the bodies of jellyfish washed up on the sand. If you're stung by a jellyfish, don't panic. You'll probably experience a stinging rash for about half an hour. Locals say applying a little baking soda or vinegar helps cut the sting. (Some also swear fresh urine will do the trick, and I pass that tip along to you purely in the interest of thoroughness.)

In the Air

When enjoying the marshlands of the coast, consider yourself fortunate to see a **wood stork** (*Mycteria americana*), very recently taken off the endangered species list. The only storks to breed in North America, these graceful long-lived birds (routinely living over 10 years) are usually seen on a low flight path across the marsh, although at some birding spots beginning in late summer you can find them at a **roost,** sometimes numbering over 100 birds. Resting at high tide, they fan out over the marsh to feed at low tide on foot. Old-timers sometimes call them "Spanish buzzards" or simply "the preacher."

Often confused with the wood stork is the gorgeous **white ibis** (*Eudocimus albus*), distinguishable by its orange bill and black wingtips. Like the wood stork, the ibis is a communal bird that roosts in colonies.

Other similar-looking coastal denizens are the white-feathered **great egret** (*Ardea alba*) and **snowy egret** (*Egretta thula*), the former distinguishable by its yellow bill and the latter by its black bill and the tuft of plumes on the back of its head. Egrets are in the same family as herons.

The most magnificent in that family is the **great blue heron** (*Ardea herodias*). Despite their imposing height—up to four feet tall—these waders are shy. Often you hear them rather than see them, a loud shriek of alarm that echoes over the marsh.

So how to tell the difference between all these wading birds at a glance? It's actually easiest when they're in flight. Egrets and herons fly with their necks tucked in, while storks and ibis fly with their necks extended.

Dozens of species of shorebirds comb the beaches, including **sandpipers, plovers,** and the wonderful and rare **American oystercatcher** (*Haematopus palliatus*), instantly recognizable for its prancing walk,

Top: horse on the grounds of Hilton Head's Coastal Discovery Museum. Bottom: waterfowl along the coast.

dark-brown back, stark white underside, and long bright-orange bill. **Gulls** and **terns** also hang out wherever there's water. They can frequently be seen swarming around incoming shrimp boats, attracted by the catch of little crustaceans.

The chief raptor of the salt marsh is the fish-eating **osprey** (*Pandion haliaetus*). These large grayish birds of prey are similar to eagles but adapted to a maritime environment, with a reversible outer toe on each talon (the better for catching wriggly fish) and closable nostrils so they can dive into the water after prey. Very common all along the coast, they like to build big nests on top of buoys and channel markers in addition to trees.

The **bald eagle** (*Haliaeetus leucocephalus*) is making a comeback in the area thanks to increased federal regulation and better education of trigger-happy locals. Apparently not as all-American as their bumper stickers might sometimes indicate, local farmers would often regard the national symbol as more of a nuisance and fire away anytime they saw one. Of course, as we all should have learned in school, the bald eagle is not actually bald but has a head adorned with white feathers. Like the osprey, bald eagles prefer fish, but unlike the osprey will settle for rodents and rabbits.

Inland among the pines you'll find the most common area woodpecker, the huge **pileated woodpecker** (*Dryocopus pileatus*) with its large crest. Less common is the smaller, more subtly marked **red-cockaded woodpecker** (*Picoides borealis*). Once common in the vast primordial pine forests of the Southeast, the species is now endangered, its last real refuge being the big tracts of relatively undisturbed land on military bases.

Insects

Down here they say that God invented bugs to keep the Yankees from completely taking over the South. And insects are probably the most unpleasant fact of life in the southeastern coastal region. The list of annoying indigenous insects must begin with the infamous **sand gnat** (*Culicoides furens*). This tiny and persistent nuisance, a member of the midge family, lacks the precision of the mosquito with its long proboscis. No, the sand gnat is more torture master than surgeon, brutally gouging and digging away its victim's skin until it hits a source of blood. Most prevalent in the spring and fall, the sand gnat is drawn to its prey by the carbon dioxide trail of its breath. While long sleeves and long pants are one way to keep gnats at bay, the only real antidote to the sand gnat's assault—other than never breathing—is the Avon skin-care product Skin So Soft, which has taken on a new and wholly unplanned life as the South's favorite anti-gnat lotion. In calmer moments, grow to appreciate the great contribution sand gnats make to the salt marsh ecosystem—as food for birds and bats.

Running a close second to the sand gnat are the over three dozen species of highly aggressive **mosquito,** which breeds anywhere a few drops of water lie stagnant. Not surprisingly, massive populations blossom in the rainiest months, in late spring and late summer, feeding in the morning and late afternoon. Like the gnat, the mosquito—the biters are always female—homes in on its victim by trailing the plume of carbon dioxide exhaled in the breath. More than just a biting nuisance, mosquitoes are now carrying West Nile disease to the Lowcountry, signaling a possibly dire threat to public health. Alas, Skin So Soft has little effect on the mosquito. Try over-the-counter sprays, anything smelling of citronella, and wearing long sleeves and long pants when weather permits.

But undoubtedly the most viscerally loathed of all pests on the Lowcountry coast is the so-called "palmetto bug," or **American cockroach** (*Periplaneta americana*). These black, shiny, and sometimes grotesquely massive insects—up to two inches long—are living fossils, virtually unchanged over hundreds of millions of years. And perfectly adapted as they are to life in and among wet, decaying vegetation, they're unlikely to change a bit in 100 million more years. While they spend most of their time crawling around, usually under rotting leaves and tree bark, American cockroaches can indeed fly—sort of. There are few more hilarious sights than a room full of people frantically trying to dodge a palmetto bug that has just clumsily launched itself off a high point on the wall. Because the cockroach doesn't know any better than you do where it's going, it can be a particularly bracing event—though the insect does not bite and poses few real health hazards.

Popular regional use of the term *palmetto bug* undoubtedly has its roots in a desire for polite Southern society to avoid using the ugly word *roach* and its connotations of filth and unclean environments. But the colloquialism actually has a basis in reality. Contrary to what anyone tells you, the natural habitat of the American cockroach—unlike its kitchen-dwelling, much-smaller cousin the German cockroach—is outdoors, often up in trees. They only come inside human dwellings when it's especially hot, especially cold, or especially dry outside. Like you, the palmetto bug is easily driven indoors by extreme temperatures and by thirst.

Other than visiting the Southeast during the winter, when the roaches go dormant, there's no convenient antidote for their presence. The best way to keep them out of your life is to stay away from decaying vegetation and keep doors and windows closed on especially hot nights.

History

BEFORE THE EUROPEANS

Based on artifacts found throughout the state, anthropologists know the first humans arrived on the coast of South Carolina at least 13,000 years ago, at the tail end of the last ice age. During this **Paleo-Indian Period,** sea levels were over 200 feet lower than present levels, and large mammals such as woolly mammoths, horses, and camels were hunted for food and skins. However, rapidly increasing temperatures, rising sea levels, and efficient hunting techniques combined to quickly kill off these large mammals,

relics of the Pleistocene Era, ushering in the **Archaic Period.** Still hunter-
gatherers, Archaic Period Indians began turning to small game such as
deer, bears, and turkeys, supplemented with fruit and nuts. The latter part
of the Archaic era saw more habitation on the coasts, with an increasing
reliance on fish and shellfish. It's to this time that the great **shell middens**
of the South Carolina coast trace their origins. Basically serving as trash
heaps for discarded oyster shells, as the middens grew in size they also took
on a ceremonial status, often being used as sites for important rituals and
meetings. Such sites are often called **shell rings,** and the largest yet found
was over nine feet high and 300 feet in diameter.

The introduction of agriculture and improved pottery techniques about
3,000 years ago led to the **Woodland Period** of Native American settlement. Extended clan groups were much less migratory, establishing year-
round communities of up to 50 people, who began the practice of clearing
land to grow crops. The ancient shell middens of their ancestors were not
abandoned, however, and were continually added onto. Native Americans
had been cremating or burying their dead for years, a practice that eventually gave rise to the construction of the first **mounds** during the Woodland
Period. Essentially built-up earthworks sometimes marked with spiritual
symbols, often in the form of animal shapes, mounds not only contained
the remains of the deceased but items like pottery to accompany the deceased into the afterlife.

Increased agriculture led to increased population, and with that population growth came competition over resources and a more formal notion
of warfare. This period, about AD 800-1600, is termed the **Mississippian
Period.** It was the Mississippians who would be the first Native Americans
in what's now the continental United States to encounter European explorers and settlers after Columbus. The Native Americans who would later be
called **Creek Indians** were the direct descendants of the Mississippians in
lineage, language, and lifestyle. Native American social structure north of
Mexico reached its apex with the Mississippians, who were not only prodigious mound builders but constructed elaborate wooden villages and
evolved a top-down class system. The defensive palisades surrounding
some of the villages attest to the increasingly martial nature of the groups
and their chieftains, or *micos.*

Described by later European accounts as a tall, proud people, the
Mississippians often wore elaborate body art and, like the indigenous
inhabitants of Central and South America, used the practice of **head
shaping,** whereby an infant's skull was deliberately deformed into an elon-
gated shape by tying the baby's head to a board for about a year.

THE SPANISH ARRIVE

The first known contact by Europeans on the southeastern coast came
in 1521, roughly concurrent with Cortés's conquest of Mexico. A party
of Spanish slavers ventured into what's now Port Royal Sound, South
Carolina, from Santo Domingo in the Caribbean. Naming the area Santa

Elena, they kidnapped a few Indian slaves and left, ranging as far north as the Cape Fear River in present-day North Carolina.

The first serious exploration of the coast came in 1526, when Lucas Vázquez de Ayllón and about 600 colonists made landfall at Winyah Bay in South Carolina, near present-day Georgetown. They didn't stay long, however, immediately moving down the coast and trying to set down roots in the St. Catherine's Sound area of modern-day Liberty County, Georgia.

That colony—called San Miguel de Gualdape—was the first European settlement in North America since the Vikings (the continent's oldest continuously occupied settlement, St. Augustine, Florida, wasn't founded until 1565). The colony also brought with it the seed of a future nation's dissolution: slaves from Africa. While San Miguel lasted only six weeks due to political tension and a slave uprising, artifacts from its brief life have been discovered in the area.

Hernando de Soto's ill-fated trek of 1539-1543 from Florida through Georgia to Alabama (where De Soto died of a fever) did not find the gold he anticipated, nor did it enter the coastal region covered in this guide. But De Soto's legacy was indeed soon felt there and throughout the Southeast in the form of various diseases for which the Mississippian people had no immunity whatsoever: smallpox, typhus, influenza, measles, yellow fever, whooping cough, diphtheria, tuberculosis, and bubonic plague.

While the cruelties of the Spanish certainly took their toll, these deadly diseases were far more damaging to a population totally unprepared for them. Within a few years, the Mississippian people—already in a state of internal decline—were losing huge percentages of their population to disease, echoing what had already happened on a massive scale to the indigenous people of the Caribbean after Christopher Columbus's expeditions. As the viruses they introduced ran rampant, the Europeans themselves stayed away for a couple of decades after the ignominious end of De Soto's fruitless quest.

During that quarter-century, the once-proud Mississippian culture continued to disintegrate, dwindling into a shadow of its former greatness. In all, disease would claim the lives of at least 80 percent of all indigenous inhabitants of the Western Hemisphere.

THE FRENCH MISADVENTURE

The next European presence on the South Carolina coast was another ill-fated attempt, the establishment of Charlesfort in 1562 by French Huguenots under Jean Ribault on present-day Parris Island, South Carolina. Part of a covert effort by the Protestant French admiral Gaspard II de Coligny to send Huguenot colonists around the globe, Ribault's crew of 150 first explored the mouth of the St. Johns River near present-day Jacksonville, Florida, before heading north.

After establishing Charlesfort, Ribault returned to France for supplies. In his absence, religious war had broken out in his home country. Ribault sought sanctuary in England but was clapped in irons anyway. Meanwhile, most of Charlesfort's colonists grew so demoralized they joined another French expedition led by René Laudonnière at Fort Caroline on the St. Johns River. The remaining 27 built a ship to sail from Charlesfort back to France; 20 of them survived the journey, which was cut short in the English Channel when they had to be rescued.

Ribault himself was dispatched to reinforce Fort Caroline, but was headed off by a contingent from the new Spanish settlement at St. Augustine. The fate of the French presence on the southeast coast was sealed when not only did the Spanish take Fort Caroline but a storm destroyed Ribault's reinforcing fleet; Ribault and all survivors were killed as soon as they came ashore. To keep the French away for good and cement Spain's hold on this northernmost part of their province of La Florida, the Spanish built the fort of Santa Elena directly on top of Charlesfort. Both layers are currently being excavated and studied.

THE MISSION ERA

With Spanish dominance of the region ensured for the near future, the lengthy mission era began. It's rarely mentioned as a key part of U.S. history, but the Spanish missionary presence on the Georgia coast was longer and more comprehensive than its much more widely known counterpart in California. St. Augustine's governor Pedro Menéndez de Avilés—sharing "biscuits with honey" on the beach at St. Catherine's Island with a local *mico*—negotiated for the right to establish a system of Jesuit missions in two coastal chiefdoms: the Mocama on and around Cumberland Island, and the Guale (WALL-ie) to the north. Those early missions, the first north of Mexico, were largely unsuccessful. But a renewed, organized effort by the Franciscan Order came to fruition during the 1580s. Starting with Santa Catalina de Guale on St. Catherine's Island, missions were established all along the Georgia coast.

The looming invasion threat to St. Augustine from English adventurer and privateer Sir Francis Drake was a harbinger of trouble to come, as was a Guale uprising in 1597. The Spanish consolidated their positions near St. Augustine, and Santa Elena was abandoned. As Spanish power waned, in 1629 Charles I of England laid formal claim to what is now the Carolinas, Georgia, and much of Florida, but made no effort to colonize the area. Largely left to their own devices and facing an indigenous population dying from disease, the missions in the Georgia interior nonetheless carried on. A devastating Indian raid in 1661 on a mission at the mouth of the Altamaha River, possibly aided by the English, persuaded the Spanish to pull the mission effort to the barrier islands. But even as late as 1667, right before the founding of Charles Towne far to the north, there were 70 missions still extant in the old Guale kingdom.

Pirate raids and slave uprisings finished off the Georgia missions for good by 1684. By 1706 the Spanish mission effort in the Southeast had fully retreated to St. Augustine. In an interesting postscript, 89 Native Americans—the only surviving descendants of Spain's Georgia missions—evacuated to Cuba with the final Spanish exodus from Florida in 1763.

ER THE ENGLISH

With the native populations in steep decline due to disease and a wholesale retrenchment by European powers, a sort of vacuum came to the southeastern coast. Into the vacuum came the first English-speaking settlers of South Carolina. The first attempt was an expedition by a Barbadian colonist, William Hilton, in 1663. While he didn't establish a new colony, he did leave his name on the most notable geographic feature he saw—Hilton Head Island.

In 1665 King Charles II gave a charter to eight **Lords Proprietors** to establish a colony, generously to be named Carolina after the monarch himself. (One of the Proprietors, Lord Ashley Cooper, would see not one but both rivers in the Charleston area named after him.) Remarkably, none of the Proprietors ever set foot in the colony they established for their own profit. Before their colony was even set up, the Proprietors themselves set the stage for the vast human disaster that would eventually befall it. They encouraged slavery by promising that each colonist would receive 20 acres of land for every male African slave and 10 acres for every female African slave brought to the colony within the first year.

In 1666 explorer Robert Sandford officially claimed Carolina for the king. The Proprietors then sent out a fleet of three ships from England, only one of which, the *Carolina,* would make it the whole way. After stops in the thriving English colonies of Barbados and Bermuda, the ship landed in Port Royal. The settlers were greeted without violence, but the fact that the local indigenous people spoke Spanish led the colonists to conclude that perhaps the site was too close for comfort to Spain's sphere of influence.

A Kiawah chief, eager for allies against the fierce, slave-trading Westo people, invited the colonists north to settle instead. So the colonists—148 of them, including three African slaves—moved 80 miles up the coast and in 1670 pitched camp on the Ashley River at a place they dubbed Albemarle Point after one of their lost ships. Living within the palisades of the camp—you can visit it today at the Charles Towne Landing State Historic Site just outside Charleston—the colonists farmed 10-acre plots outside the walls.

A few years later some colonists from Barbados, which was beginning to suffer the effects of overpopulation, joined the Carolinians. The Barbadian influence, with an emphasis on large-scale slave labor and a caste system, would have an indelible imprint on the colony. Indeed, within a generation a majority of settlers in the new colony would be African slaves.

By 1680, however, Albemarle Point was feeling growing pains as well, and the Proprietors ordered the site moved to Oyster Point at the confluence of the Ashley and Cooper Rivers (the present-day Battery). Within a year Albemarle Point was abandoned, and the walls of Charles Towne were built a few hundred yards up from Oyster Point on the banks of the Cooper River.

The original Anglican settlers were quickly joined by various **Dissenters,** among them French Huguenots, Quakers, Congregationalists, and Jews. A group of Scottish Presbyterians established the short-lived Stuart Town near Port Royal in 1684. Recognizing this diversity, the colony in 1697 granted religious liberty to all "except Papists," meaning Catholics. The Anglicans attempted a crackdown on Dissenters in 1704, but two years later Queen Anne stepped in and ensured religious freedom for all Carolinians (again

Henry Woodward, Colonial Indiana Jones

He's virtually unsung in the history books, and there are no movies made about him, but Dr. Henry Woodward, the first English settler in South Carolina, lived a life that is the stuff of novels and screenplays. Educated in medicine in London, Woodward first tried his hand in the colony of Barbados. Still in his teens, Woodward left Barbados in Captain Robert Sandford's 1664 expedition to Carolina. In 1666, in what is perhaps the New World's first "cultural exchange program," Woodward volunteered to stay behind while the rest of the expedition returned to England.

Woodward learned the local language and established relations with Native Americans, actions for which the Lords Proprietors granted him temporary "formall possession of the whole Country to hold as Ténnant att Will." The Spanish kidnapped the young Englishman, taking him to the Spanish stronghold of St. Augustine in Florida. Woodward was popular and treated well. During that time, he studied Spanish government, commerce, and culture, with the same diligence with which he had studied the Indians a year earlier. In 1668, Woodward was "rescued" by English pirates under the command of Robert Searle. Woodward's sojourn with the pirates would last two years, during which he was kept on board as ship's surgeon.

In 1670 Woodward was rescued when the pirates shipwrecked on the Caribbean island of Nevis. His rescuers were none other than settlers on their way to found Charles Towne. Woodward used his previous experience to direct the colonists to an area of less Spanish influence. That same year he began a series of expeditions to contact Native Americans in the Carolina interior—the first non-Spanish European to set foot in the area. Using information gained from the Spanish, Woodward's goal was to jump-start the trade in deerskins that would be the bulwark of the Charles Towne colony. Woodward's 1674 alliance with the aggressive Westo people was instrumental in this burgeoning trade. As if all this weren't enough, in 1680 Woodward, now with property of his own on Johns Island, would introduce local farmers to a certain crop recently imported from Madagascar: rice.

Woodward made enemies of settlers who were envious of his growing affluence and suspicious of his friendship with the Westo. His outspoken disgust with the spread of Indian slavery brought a charge against him of undermining the interests of the crown. But Woodward, by now a celebrity of sorts, returned to England to plead his case directly to the Lords Proprietors. They not only pardoned him but made him their official Indian agent—with a 20 percent share of the profits.

Woodward returned to the American colonies to trek inland, making alliances with groups of Creek Indians in Spanish-held territory. Hounded by Spanish troops, Woodward fell ill of a fever somewhere in the Savannah River valley. He made it to Charleston and safety but never fully recovered and died around 1690.

with the exception of Catholics, who wouldn't be a factor in the colony until after the American Revolution).

THE YAMASEE WAR

Within 20 years the English presence had expanded throughout the Lowcountry to include Port Royal and Beaufort. Charles Towne became a thriving commercial center, dealing in deerskins with traders in the interior and with foreign concerns from England to South America. Its success was not without a backlash, as the local Yamasee people became increasingly disgruntled at the settlers' growing monopolies on deerskin and the trade in Native American slaves.

As rumors of war spread, on Good Friday, 1715, a delegation of six Carolinians went to the Yamasee village of Pocataligo to address some of the Native Americans' grievances in the hopes of forestalling violence. Their effort was in vain, however, as warriors murdered four of them in their sleep, the remaining two escaping to sound the alarm.

The treacherous attack signaled the beginning of the two-year Yamasee War, which would claim the lives of nearly 10 percent of the colony's population and an unknown number of Native Americans—making it one of the bloodiest conflicts fought on American soil.

Energized and ready for war, the Yamasee attacked Charles Towne itself and killed almost all the European traders in the interior, effectively ending commerce in the area. As Charles Towne began to swell with refugees from the hinterland, water and supplies ran low, and the colony's very existence was in peril.

After an initially poor performance by the Carolina militia, a professional army—including armed African slaves—was raised. Well trained and well led, the new army more than held its own despite being outnumbered. A key alliance with local Cherokees was all the advantage the colonists needed to turn the tide. While the Cherokee never received the overt military backing from the settlers that they sought, they did garner enough supplies and influence to convince their Creek rivals, the Yamasee, to begin the peace process. The war-weary settlers, eager to get back to life and to business, were glad to negotiate with them, offering goods as a sign of their earnest intent. By 1717 the Yamasee threat had subsided, and trade in the region began flourishing anew.

No sooner had the Yamasee War ended, however, than a new threat emerged: the dreaded pirate Edward Teach, aka Blackbeard. Entering Charleston Harbor in May 1718 with his flagship *Queen Anne's Revenge* and three other vessels, he promptly plundered five ships and began a full-scale blockade of the entire settlement. He took a number of prominent citizens hostage before finally departing northward.

SLAVERY

For the colonists, the Blackbeard episode was the final straw. Already disgusted by the lack of support from the Lords Proprietors during the

Yamasee War, the humiliation of the pirate blockade was too much to ta▪
To almost universal agreement in the colony, the settlers threw off the ru▪
of the Proprietors and lobbied in 1719 to become a crown colony, an effort
that came to final fruition in 1729.

While this outward-looking and energetic Charleston was originally
built on the backs of merchants, with the introduction of the rice and indigo crops in the early 1700s it would increasingly be built on the backs of
slaves. For all the wealth gained through the planting of rice and cotton
seeds, another seed was sown by the Lowcountry plantation culture. The
area's total dependence on slave labor would ultimately lead to a disastrous
war, a conflict signaled for decades to those smart enough to read the signs.

By the early 18th century Charleston and Savannah were firmly established as the key American ports for the importation of African slaves, with
about 40 percent of the trade centered in Charleston alone. As a result, the
African population of the coast outnumbered the European population
by more than three to one, and much more than that in some areas. The
fear of violent slave uprisings had a great influence over not only politics
but day-to-day affairs.

These fears were eventually realized in the **Stono Rebellion** on
September 9, 1739. Twenty African American slaves led by an Angolan
known only as Jemmy met near the Stono River near Charleston. Marching
with a banner that read "Liberty," they seized guns with the plan of marching all the way to Spanish Florida and finding sanctuary in the wilderness.
On the way they burned seven plantations and killed 20 more settlers. A militia eventually caught up with them, killing 44 escaped slaves while losing
20 of their own. The prisoners were decapitated and had their heads spiked
on every milepost between the spot of that final battle and Charleston.
Inspired by the rebellion, at least two other uprisings would take place over
the next two years in South Carolina and Georgia.

OGLETHORPE'S VISION

In 1729, Carolina was divided into north and south. In 1731, a colony to
be known as Georgia, after the new English king, was carved out of the
southern part of the Carolina land grant. A young general, aristocrat, and
humanitarian named James Edward Oglethorpe gathered together a group
of Trustees—similar to Carolina's Lords Proprietors—to take advantage.

While Oglethorpe would go on to found Georgia, his wasn't the first
English presence in the area. A garrison built Fort King George in modern-
day Darien, Georgia, in 1721, which you can visit today. A cypress block-
house surrounded by palisaded earthworks, the fort defended the southern
reaches of England's claim for seven years before being abandoned in 1728.

On February 12, 1733, after stops in Beaufort and Charleston, the ship
Anne with its 114 passengers made its way to the highest bluff on the
Savannah River. The area was controlled by the peaceful Yamacraw people,
who had been encouraged by the powers-that-be in Charleston to settle on
this vacant land 12 miles up the Savannah River to serve as a buffer for the

Pirates of the Atlantic

Pirates were among the earliest explorers of the Atlantic seaboard of North America and, other than Native American chiefs, were the only real authority in the area for decades. The creeks and barrier islands of the southeastern coast provided important, hard-to-find sanctuaries away from the regular pirate circuit in the booty-laden Spanish Caribbean.

A real-life pirate story from the earliest days of the Charleston seems almost too unbelievable. The encounter was at the hands of the infamous Edward Teach, aka Blackbeard. A tall, terrifying bully, the legendary pirate also had a flair for the dramatic. Given to twisting flaming wads of cloth when he attacked, Blackbeard was also quite eccentric. In May 1718, Blackbeard, driven north from his usual hunting grounds in the Bahamas by a concerted effort of the British Navy, approached Charleston Harbor in his flagship *Queen Anne's Revenge,* accompanied by three smaller vessels. He seized several ships and kidnapped several leading citizens, including Councilman Samuel Wragg and his four-year-old son. He sent one captive ashore with the message that unless his demand was met, the heads of Wragg and son would soon be delivered to the colonial governor's doorstep. Blackbeard's demand? A chest of medicine. For what purpose is still unknown. The medicines were delivered in short order, and Blackbeard released his hostages and sailed north to Ocracoke Island, North Carolina, to enjoy a royal pardon he'd just received.

One of the pirates serving under Blackbeard during the Charleston escapade was Stede Bonnet, a contrasting figure in his debonair nature and posh finery. When Charleston's Colonel William Rhett got wind that Bonnet and crew were still a-pirating off Cape Fear, North Carolina, he set out to bring him to justice. And that he did, bringing pirate and crew back to Charleston for a trial that almost didn't happen after Bonnet escaped from custody dressed as a woman. The dashing Bonnet garnered quite a bit of public sympathy—especially when he begged not to be hanged—but it wasn't enough to forestall the grim fate of the pirate and his crew: public execution at White Point, the bodies left as a warning to other buccaneers. Another coastal menace, Richard Worley, was also hanged in Charleston.

Though Savannah is home to the famous Pirate's House restaurant and got a shout-out in Robert Louis Stevenson's *Treasure Island,* actual pirate history here is hard to nail down. There seems little doubt that a host of ne'er-do-wells made their way onto the rowdy Savannah waterfront, but the port's location nearly 20 miles upriver would have made it less-than-ideal territory for a true buccaneer, who always needed a fast getaway handy.

As for Blackbeard, his retirement plans were interrupted by a contingent of Virginians who tracked him down and killed him near Ocracoke. However, his legend lives to this day on Blackbeard Island, Georgia, a gorgeous, undeveloped barrier island that has changed little since the days when Teach himself allegedly stopped over between pirate raids. The legends even say he left some treasure there, but don't try to look for it—Blackbeard Island is now a national wildlife refuge.

Spanish. Led by an elderly chief, or *mico*, named Tomochichi, the Yamacraw enjoyed the area's natural bounty of shellfish, fruit, nuts, and small game.

A deft politician, Oglethorpe struck up a treaty and eventually a genuine friendship with Tomochichi. To the Yamacraw, Oglethorpe was a rare bird—a European who behaved with honor and was true to his word. The Native Americans reciprocated by helping the settlers and pledging fealty to the crown. Oglethorpe reported to the Trustees that Tomochichi personally requested "that we would Love and Protect their little Families."

In negotiations with local tribes using Mary Musgrove, a Creek-English settler in the area, as translator, the persuasive Oglethorpe convinced the coastal Creek to cede to the crown all Georgia land to the Altamaha River. Oglethorpe's impact was soon felt farther down the Georgia coast, as St. Simons Island, Jekyll Island, Darien, and Brunswick were settled in rapid succession, and with them the entrenchment of the plantation system and slave labor.

While the Trustees' utopian vision was largely economic in nature, like Carolina the Georgia colony also emphasized religious freedom. While to modern ears Charleston's antipathy toward "papists" and Oglethorpe's original ban of Catholics from Georgia might seem incompatible with this goal, the reason was a coldly pragmatic one for the time: England's two main global rivals, France and Spain, were both staunchly Catholic countries.

SPAIN VANQUISHED

Things heated up on the coast in 1739 with the so-called **War of Jenkins' Ear**, which despite its seemingly trivial beginnings over the humiliation of a British captain by Spanish privateers was actually a proxy struggle emblematic of changes in the European balance of power. A year later Oglethorpe cobbled together a force of settlers, Indian allies, and Carolinians to reduce the Spanish fortress at St. Augustine, Florida. The siege failed, and Oglethorpe retreated to St. Simons Island to await the inevitable counterattack. In 1742, a Spanish force invaded the island but was eventually turned back for good at the **Battle of Bloody Marsh.** That clash marked the end of Spanish overtures on England's colonies in what is now the United States.

Though Oglethorpe returned to England a national hero, things fell apart in Savannah. The settlers became envious of the success of Charleston's slave-based rice economy and began wondering aloud why they couldn't also make use of free labor. With Oglethorpe otherwise occupied in England, the Trustees of Georgia—distant in more ways than just geographically from the new colony—bowed to public pressure and relaxed the restrictions on slavery and rum. By 1753 the Trustees voted to return their charter to the crown, officially making Georgia the 13th and final colony of England in America. With first the French and then the Spanish effectively shut off from the American East Coast, the stage was set for an internal battle between England and its burgeoning colonies across the Atlantic.

REVOLUTION AND INDEPENDENCE

The population of the colonies swelled in the mid-1700s, not only from an influx of slaves but a corresponding flood of European immigrants. The interior began filling up with Germans, Swiss, Scottish, and Irish settlers. Their subsequent demands for political representation led to tension between them and the coastal inhabitants, typically depicted through the years as an Upcountry versus Lowcountry competition. It is a persistent but inaccurate myth that the affluent elite on the southeastern coast were reluctant to break ties with England. While the Lowcountry's cultural and economic ties to England were certainly strong, the **Stamp Act** and the **Townshend Acts** combined to turn public sentiment against the mother country here as elsewhere in the colonies.

South Carolinian planters like Christopher Gadsden, Henry Laurens, John Rutledge, and Arthur Middleton were early leaders in the movement for independence. Planters in what would be called Liberty County, Georgia, also strongly agitated for the cause. War broke out between the colonists and the British in New England, and soon made its way southward. The British failed to take Charleston—the fourth-largest city in the colonies—in June 1776, an episode that gave South Carolina its "Palmetto State" moniker when redcoat cannonballs bounced off the palm tree-lined walls of Fort Moultrie. The British under General Sir Henry Clinton successfully took the city in 1780, however, occupying it until 1782.

The British, under General Archibald Campbell, took Savannah in 1778. Royal Governor Sir James Wright returned from exile to Georgia to reclaim it for the crown, the only one of the colonies to be subsumed again into the British Empire. A polyglot force of colonists, Haitians, and Hessians attacked the British fortifications on the west side of Savannah in 1779 but were repulsed with heavy losses. Although the area's two major cities had fallen to the British, the war raged on throughout the surrounding area.

Indeed, throughout the Lowcountry, fighting was as vicious as anything yet seen on the North American continent. With over 130 known military engagements occurring here, South Carolina sacrificed more men during the war than any other colony—including Massachusetts, the "Cradle of the Revolution."

The struggle became a guerrilla war of colonists versus the British as well as a civil war between patriots and loyalists, or **Tories.** Committing what would today undoubtedly be called war crimes, the British routinely burned homes, churches, and fields and massacred civilians. Using Daufuskie Island as a base, British soldiers staged raids on Hilton Head plantations.

In response, patriots of the Lowcountry bred a group of deadly guerrilla soldiers under legendary leaders such as Francis Marion, "the Swamp Fox," and Thomas Sumter, "the Gamecock," who attacked the British in daring hit-and-run raids staged from swamps and marshes. A covert group of patriots called the **Sons of Liberty** met clandestinely throughout the Lowcountry, plotting revolution over pints of ale. Sometimes their efforts transcended talk, however, and atrocities were committed against area loyalists.

In all, four South Carolinians signed the Declaration of Independe[...]
Thomas Heyward Jr., Thomas Lynch Jr., Arthur Middleton, and Edw[...]
Rutledge.

HIGH COTTON

True to form, the new nation wasted no time in asserting its economic
strength. Rice planters from Georgetown north of Charleston on down to
the Altamaha River in Georgia built on their already impressive wealth,
becoming the new nation's richest men by far—with fortunes built on the
backs of the slaves working in their fields.

In 1786, a new crop was introduced that would only enhance the financial clout of the coastal region: cotton. A former loyalist colonel, Roger
Kelsal, sent some seed from the West Indies to his friend James Spaulding,
owner of a plantation on St. Simons Island, Georgia. This crop, soon to be
known as **Sea Island cotton** and considered the best in the world, would
supplant rice as the crop of choice for coastal plantations. At the height of
the Southern cotton boom in the early 1800s, a single Sea Island cotton harvest on a single plantation might go for $100,000—in 1820 dollars. While
Charleston was still by far the largest, most powerful, and most influential
city on the southeastern coast of the United States, at the peak of the cotton
craze Savannah was actually doing more business—a fact that grated to no
end on the Holy City's elite. Unlike Charleston, where the planters themselves dominated city life, in Savannah it was cotton brokers called **factors**
who were the city's leading class. During this time most of the grand homes
of downtown Savannah's historic district were built. This boom period, fu-
eled largely by cotton exports, was perhaps most iconically represented by
the historic sailing of the SS *Savannah* from Savannah to Liverpool in 29
days, the first transatlantic voyage by a steamship.

During the prosperous antebellum period, the economy of Charleston,
Savannah, and surrounding areas was completely dependent on slave labor,
but the cities themselves boasted large numbers of African Americans who
were active in business and agriculture. For example, the vending stalls at
the City Markets of both Charleston and Savannah were predominantly
staffed by African American workers, some of them free.

SECESSION

Much of the lead-in to the Civil War focused on whether slavery would
be allowed in the newest U.S. territories in the West, but there's no doubt
that all figurative roads eventually led to South Carolina. During Andrew
Jackson's presidency in the 1820s, his vice president, South Carolina's John
C. Calhoun, became a thorn in Jackson's side with his aggressive advocacy
for **nullification.** In a nutshell, Calhoun said that if a state decided the federal government wasn't treating it fairly—in this case with regard to tariffs
that were hurting the cotton trade in the Palmetto State—it could simply
nullify the federal law, superseding it with law of its own.

As the abolition movement gained steam and tensions over slavery rose,

Nathanael Greene and Mulberry Grove

Nathanael Greene's time in Savannah was short and mostly unfortunate. One of the American Revolution's greatest heroes, Greene rose from the rank of private in the Continental Army to become George Washington's right-hand man. As a brigadier general in the Rhode Island militia, Greene's innate military prowess caught Washington's eye during the siege of Boston, whereupon the future president gave Greene command of the entire Southern theater of the fight for independence. Greene's guerrilla tactics forced the English contingent to divide and hence weaken itself. It was Greene who sent General "Mad Anthony" Wayne in 1782 to free Savannah from the British. Greene insisted that no revenge be taken on Savannah's loyalists, instead welcoming them into the new nation as partners. For his service, Washington granted Greene a large estate on the banks of the Savannah River known as Mulberry Grove, known to history as the place where Eli Whitney would later invent the cotton gin while serving as tutor to the Greene children.

Mulberry Grove was less productive for Greene, who as a lifelong abolitionist refused to use slave labor on the plantation, and hence paid a steep financial price. The 44-year-old Greene had spent less than a year at Mulberry Grove, mostly worrying about finances, when he caught sunstroke on a particularly brutal June day in 1786 and died shortly thereafter.

At some point Greene's remains were said to have been lost after a family vault in Colonial Cemetery was vandalized by Union troops. Then in 1900 the Society of the Cincinnati of Rhode Island appointed a search committee to find and properly inter the general's long-lost remains. The remains were indeed found—right in the vault in Colonial Cemetery where they were supposed to have been, which you can see to this day. However, they were underneath someone else: After removing the coffin of one Robert Scott, excavators found "a mass of rotten wood and human bones mixed with sand," along with a rusty coffin plate reading, "Nathanael Greene / Obit June 19, 1786 / Aetat [Age] 44 Years." In 1902, Greene's remains were put to rest under his monument in Johnson Square—dedicated to him by the Marquis de Lafayette in 1825.

All buildings at Mulberry Grove were razed by Sherman's troops in 1864. The area entered industrial use in 1975 and is currently occupied by the Georgia Ports Authority. No full-scale archaeological dig has ever been done at the site, although the nonprofit Mulberry Grove Foundation (www.mulberrygrove.org) is working toward that as well as a plan to make part of the 2,200-acre parcel a wildlife preserve.

South Carolina congressman Preston Brooks took things to the next level. On May 22, 1856, he beat fellow senator Charles Sumner of Massachusetts nearly to death with his walking cane on the Senate floor. Sumner had just given a speech criticizing pro-slavery forces—including a relative of Brooks—and called slavery "a harlot." (In a show of support, South Carolinians sent Brooks dozens of new canes to replace the one he broke over Sumner's head.)

In 1860, the national convention of the Democratic Party, then the dominant force in U.S. politics, was held in—where else?—Charleston. Rancor over slavery and state's rights was so high that they couldn't agree on a single candidate to run to replace President James Buchanan. Reconvening in Maryland, the party split along sectional lines, with the Northern wing backing Stephen A. Douglas. The Southern wing, fervently desiring secession, deliberately chose its own candidate, John Breckinridge, in order to split the Democratic vote and throw the election to Republican Abraham Lincoln, an outspoken opponent of the expansion of slavery. During that so-called **Secession Winter** before Lincoln took office, seven states seceded from the Union, first among them the Palmetto State, followed by Mississippi, Florida, Alabama, Georgia, Louisiana, and Texas.

CIVIL WAR

Five days after South Carolina's secession on December 21, 1860, U.S. Army major Robert Anderson moved his garrison from Fort Moultrie on Sullivan's Island to nearby Fort Sumter in Charleston Harbor. Over the next few months and into the spring, Anderson would ignore many calls to surrender, and Confederate forces would prevent any Union resupply or reinforcement. The stalemate was broken and the Confederates finally got their casus belli when a Union supply ship successfully ran the blockade and docked at Fort Sumter. Shortly before dawn on April 12, 1861, Confederate batteries around Charleston—ironically none of which were at the famous Battery itself—opened fire on Fort Sumter for 34 straight hours, until Anderson surrendered on April 13.

In a classic example of why you should always be careful what you wish for, the secessionists had been too clever by half in pushing for Lincoln. Far from prodding the North to sue for peace, the fall of Fort Sumter instead caused the remaining states in the Union to rally around the previously unpopular tall man from Illinois. Lincoln's skillful management of the Fort Sumter standoff meant that from then on, the South would bear history's blame for initiating the conflict that would claim over half a million American lives.

After Fort Sumter, four more Southern states—Virginia, Arkansas, North Carolina, and Tennessee—seceded to join the Confederacy. The Old Dominion was the real prize for the secessionists, as Virginia had the South's only ironworks and by far the largest manufacturing base.

In November 1861, a massive Union invasion armada landed in Port Royal Sound in South Carolina, effectively taking the entire Lowcountry out of the war. Hilton Head was a Union encampment, and Beaufort became a major hospital center for the U.S. Army. The coast of Georgia was also blockaded, with Union forces using new rifled cannons in 1862 to quickly reduce Fort Pulaski at the mouth of the Savannah River. Charleston, however, did host two battles in the conflict. The **Battle of Secessionville** came in June 1862, when a Union force attempting to take Charleston was repulsed on James Island with heavy casualties.

The next battle, an unsuccessful Union landing on Morris Island in July 1863, was immortalized by the movie *Glory*. The 54th Massachusetts Regiment, an African American unit with Caucasian commanders, performed so gallantly in its failed assault on the Confederate **Battery Wagner** that it inspired the North and was cited by abolitionists as further proof that African Americans should be given freedom and full citizenship rights. Another invasion attempt on Charleston would not come, but the city was besieged and bombarded for nearly two more years (devastation made even worse by a massive fire, unrelated to the shelling, that destroyed much of the city in 1861).

Otherwise, the coast grew quiet. From Charleston to Brunswick, Southerners evacuated the coastal cities and plantations for the hinterland, leaving behind only slaves to fend for themselves. In many coastal areas, African Americans and Union garrison troops settled into an awkward but peaceful coexistence. Many islands under Union control, such as Cockspur Island, where Fort Pulaski sat, became endpoints in the Underground Railroad.

In Savannah, General William Sherman concluded his **March to the Sea** in Savannah in 1864, famously giving the city to Lincoln as a Christmas present. While staunch Confederates, city fathers were wise enough to know what would happen to their accumulated wealth and fine homes should they be foolhardy enough to resist Sherman's army of war-hardened veterans.

The only military uncertainty left was in how badly Charleston, the "cradle of secession," would suffer for its sins. Historians and local wags have long debated why Sherman spared Charleston, the hated epicenter of the Civil War. Did he fall in love with the city during his brief posting there as a young lieutenant? Did he literally fall in love there, with one of the city's legendarily beautiful and delicate local belles? We may never know for sure, but it's likely that the Lowcountry's marshy, mucky terrain simply made it too difficult to move large numbers of men and supplies. So Sherman turned his army inland toward the state capital, Columbia, which would not be so lucky.

For the African American population of Charleston and Savannah, however, it was not a time of sadness but the great Day of Jubilee. Soon after the Confederate surrender, African American Charlestonians held one of the largest parades the city has ever seen, with one of the floats being a coffin bearing the sign, "Slavery is dead."

As for the place where it all began, a plucky Confederate garrison remained underground at Fort Sumter throughout the war, as the walls above them were literally pounded into dust by the long Union siege. The garrison quietly left the fort under cover of night on February 17, 1865. Major Robert Anderson, who surrendered the fort at war's beginning, returned to Sumter in April 1865 to raise the same flag he'd lowered exactly four years earlier. Three thousand African Americans attended the ceremonies. Later that same night, Abraham Lincoln was assassinated in Washington DC.

RECONSTRUCTION

A case could be made that slavery need not have led the United States into the Civil War. The U.S. government had banned the importation of slaves long before, in 1808. The great powers of Europe would soon ban slavery altogether (Spain in 1811, France in 1826, and Britain in 1833). Visiting eign dignitaries in the mid-1800s were often shocked to find the prac in full swing in the American South. Even Brazil, the world center of sla ery, where four out of every 10 slaves taken from Africa were brought (les than 5 percent came to the United States), would ban slavery in 1888, suggesting that slavery in the United States would have died a natural death. Still, the die was cast, the war was fought, and everyone had to deal with the aftermath.

For a brief time, Sherman's benevolent dictatorship on the coast held promise for an orderly postwar future. In 1865 he issued his sweeping "40 acres and a mule" order seeking dramatic economic restitution for coastal Georgia's free African Americans. Politics reared its ugly head in the wake of Lincoln's assassination, however, and the order was rescinded, ushering in the chaotic Reconstruction era, echoes of which linger to this day.

Even as the trade in cotton and naval stores resumed to even greater heights than before, urban life and racial tension became more and more problematic. Urban populations swelled as freed slaves from all over the depressed countryside rushed into the cities. As one of them, his name lost to history, famously said: "Freedom was freer in Charleston."

RECONCILIATION

The opening of the exclusive Jekyll Island Club in 1886 marked the coming of the effects of the Industrial Revolution to the Deep South and the rejuvenation of regional economies. In Savannah, the Telfair Academy of Arts and Sciences, the South's first art museum, opened that same year. The cotton trade built back up to antebellum levels, and the South was on the long road to recovery.

The Spanish-American War of 1898 was a major turning point for the South, the first time since the Civil War that all citizens were joined in patriotic unity. The southeastern coast felt this in particular, as it was a staging area for the invasion of Cuba. President William McKinley addressed the troops bivouacked in Savannah's Daffin Park, and Charlestonians cheered the exploits of their namesake heavy cruiser the USS *Charleston,* which played a key role in forcing the Spanish surrender of Guam.

Charleston would elect its first Irish American mayor, John Grace, in 1911, who would serve until 1923 (with a break 1915-1919). Although it wouldn't open until 1929, the first Cooper River Bridge joining Charleston with Mount Pleasant was the child of the Grace administration, credited today for modernizing the Holy City's infrastructure.

The arrival of the tiny but devastating boll weevil all but wiped out the cotton trade on the coast after the turn of the century, forcing the economy to diversify. Naval stores and lumbering were the order of the day at the advent of World War I, the combined patriotic effort for which did wonders in repairing the wounds of the Civil War, still vivid in many local memories. A major legacy of World War I that still greatly influences life in the

untry is the Marine Corps Recruit Depot Parris Island, which began
s a small Marine camp in 1919.

ENAISSANCE AND DEPRESSION

n the Roaring '20s, that boom period following World War I, both
Charleston and Savannah entered the world stage and made some of their
most significant cultural contributions to American life. It was also the era
of Prohibition. Savannah became notorious as a major import center for
illegal rum from the Bahamas.

As elsewhere in the country, Prohibition ironically brought out a new ap-
preciation for the arts and just plain having fun. The "Charleston" dance,
originated on the streets of the Holy City and popularized in New York, would
sweep the world. The Jenkins Orphanage Band, credited with the dance, traveled the world, even playing at President William Howard Taft's inauguration.

In the visual arts, the "Charleston Renaissance" took off, specifically intended to introduce the Holy City to a wider audience. Key work included
the Asian-influenced art of self-taught painter Alice Ravenel Huger Smith
and the etchings of Elizabeth O'Neill Verner. Edward Hopper was a visitor to Charleston during that time and produced several noted watercolors.
The Gibbes Art Gallery, now the Gibbes Museum of Art, opened in 1905.
Recognizing the cultural importance of the city and its history, in 1920 so-
cialite Susan Pringle Frost and other concerned Charlestonians formed the
Preservation Society of Charleston, the oldest community-based historic
preservation organization in the country.

In 1924, lauded Charleston author DuBose Heyward wrote the locally set
novel *Porgy*. With Heyward's cooperation, the book would soon be turned into
the first American opera, *Porgy and Bess,* by George Gershwin, who labored
over the composition in a cottage on Folly Beach. Ironically, *Porgy and Bess,*
which premiered with an African American cast in New York in 1935, wouldn't
be performed in its actual setting until 1970 because of segregation laws.

In Savannah, the Roaring '20s coincided with the rise of Johnny Mercer,
who began his theater career locally in the Town Theater Group. In 1925,
Flannery O'Connor was born in Savannah, and the quirky, Gothic nature
of the city would mark her later writing indelibly.

The Depression hit the South hard, but since wages and industry were
already behind the national average, the economic damage wasn't as bad
as elsewhere in the country. As elsewhere in the South, the public works
programs of President Franklin D. Roosevelt's New Deal helped not only to
keep locals employed but contributed greatly to the cultural and archaeological record of the region. The Civilian Conservation Corps built much
of the modern state park system in the area.

WORLD WAR II AND THE POSTWAR BOOM

With the attack on Pearl Harbor and the coming of World War II, life on
the southeast coast would never be the same. Military funding and facilities swarmed into the area, and populations and long-depressed living

standards rose as a result. In many outlying Sea Islands of Georgia and South Carolina, electricity came for the first time.

The Charleston Navy Yard became the city's largest employer, and the city's population soared as workers swarmed in. The "Mighty Eighth" Air Force was founded and based in Savannah, and Camp Stewart, later Fort Stewart, was built in nearby Hinesville. In shipyards in Savannah and Brunswick, Georgia, hundreds of Liberty ships were built to transport cargo to the citizens and allied armies of Europe.

The postwar U.S. infatuation with the automobile—and its troublesome child, the suburb—brought exponential growth to the great cities of the coast. The first bridge to Hilton Head Island was built in 1956, leading to the first of many resort developments, Sea Pines, in 1961. With rising coastal populations came pressure to demolish more and more fine old buildings to put parking lots and high-rises in their place. A backlash grew among the cities' elites, aghast at the destruction of so much history.

The immediate postwar era brought about the formation of both the Historic Charleston Foundation and the Historic Savannah Foundation, which began the financially and politically difficult work of protecting historic districts from the wrecking ball. They weren't always successful, but the work of these organizations—mostly older women from the upper crust—laid the foundation for the successful coastal tourist industry to come, as well as preserving important U.S. history for the ages.

CIVIL RIGHTS

The ugly racial violence that plagued much of the country during the civil rights era rarely visited the Georgia and South Carolina coast. Whether due to the laid-back ambience or the fact that African Americans were simply too numerous there to be denied, cities like Charleston and Savannah experienced little real unrest during that time.

Contrary to popular opinion, the civil rights era wasn't just a blip in the 1960s. The gains of that decade were the fruits of efforts begun decades earlier. Many of the exertions involved efforts to expand African American suffrage. Though African Americans had secured the nominal right to vote years before, primary contests were not under the jurisdiction of federal law. As a result, Democratic Party primary elections—the de facto general elections because of that party's total dominance in the South at the time— were effectively closed to African American voters.

Savannah was at the forefront of expanding suffrage, and Ralph Mark Gilbert, pastor of the historic First African Baptist Church, launched one of the first African American voter registration drives in the South. In Charleston, the Democratic primary was opened to African Americans for the first time in 1947. In 1955, successful realtor J. Arthur Brown became head of the Charleston chapter of the NAACP and membership soared, bringing an increase in activism. In 1960, the Charleston Municipal Golf Course voluntarily integrated to avoid a court battle.

Martin Luther King Jr. visited South Carolina in the late 1960s, speaking in Charleston in 1967 and helping reestablish the Penn Center on St. Helena Island as not only a cultural center but a center of political activism as well. The hundred-day strike of hospital workers at the Medical University of South Carolina in 1969—right after King's assassination—got national attention and was the culmination of Charleston's struggle for civil rights. By the end of the 1960s, the city councils of Charleston and Savannah had elected their first African American aldermen, and the next phase in local history began.

A COAST REBORN

The decade of the 1970s brought the seeds of the future success of the region's coast. The historic tenure of Mayor Joe Riley began. The Irish American would break precedents and forge key alliances, reviving the local economy.

In the years 1970-1976, tourism in Charleston would increase by 60 percent. The resort industry, already established on Hilton Head, would hit Kiawah Island, Seabrook Island, and Isle of Palms with a vengeance.

The coast's combination of beautiful scenery and cheap labor proved irresistible to the movie and TV industry, which would begin filming many series and movies in the area in the 1970s and continuing to this day. Beaufort in particular would emerge from its stately slumber as the star of several popular films, including *The Great Santini* and *The Big Chill*.

Charleston received its first major challenge since the Civil War in 1989 when Hurricane Hugo—originally headed directly for Savannah—changed course at the last minute and slammed into the South Carolina coast just north of the Holy City. Charleston, including many of its most historic locations, was massively damaged, with hardly a tree left standing. In a testament to the toughness just beneath Charleston's genteel veneer, the city not only rebounded but came back stronger. The economic boom of the 1990s was particularly good to Charleston, whose port saw a huge dividend from increasing globalization.

Today Charleston is perennially ranked as one of the top U.S. cities for visitors as well as for residents. Attracted by the coastal region, artists, writers, and entrepreneurs continue to flock in, increasing the economic and social diversity of the area and taking it to new heights of livability.

People and Culture

Contrary to how the region is portrayed in the media, the coast from Charleston on down is hardly exclusive to natives with thick, flowery accents who still obsess over the Civil War and eat grits three meals a day. As you will quickly discover, the entire coastal area is heavily populated with transplants from other parts of the country, and in some areas you can actually go quite a long time without hearing even one of those Scarlett O'Hara accents. Some of this is due to the region's increasing attractiveness to professionals and artists, drawn by the temperate climate, natural beauty, and business-friendly environment. Part of it is due to its increasing attractiveness to retirees, most of them from the frigid Northeast. Indeed, in some places, chief among them Hilton Head, the most common accent is a New York or New Jersey one, and a Southern accent is rare.

In any case, don't make the common mistake of assuming you're coming to a place where footwear is optional and electricity is a recent development (though it's true that many of the islands didn't get electricity until the 1950s and 1960s). Because so much new construction has gone on in the South in the last quarter-century or so, you might find some aspects of the infrastructure—specifically the roads and the electrical utilities—actually superior to where you came from.

POPULATION

For demographic purposes, Charleston is part of the Charleston-North Charleston Metropolitan Statistical Area (MSA), which includes Berkeley, Dorchester, and Charleston Counties. In the 2010 census, it comprised about 664,000 people. The city of Charleston proper has a population of about 120,000. The Hilton Head-Beaufort MSA includes Beaufort and Jasper Counties and comprised about 180,000 people in the 2010 census. The town of Hilton Head had about 37,000 residents in 2010, and Beaufort had about 13,000.

Racial Makeup

Its legacy as the center of the U.S. slave trade and plantation culture means that the Charleston region has a large African American population. The Charleston MSA is about 31 percent African American. In the cities proper, the number is higher, about 35 percent in Charleston.

The Hispanic population, as elsewhere in the United States, is growing rapidly, but statistics can be misleading. Though Hispanics are growing at a triple-digit clip in the region, they still remain less than 3 percent of the state's population. Bilingual signage is becoming more common but is still quite rare.

RELIGION

This area is unusual in the Deep South for its wide variety of religious faiths. While South Carolina remains overwhelmingly Protestant—at least three-quarters of all Christians are members of some Protestant denomination, chief among them Southern Baptist and Methodist—Charleston's cosmopolitan, polyglot history has made it a real melting pot of faith.

Charleston was originally dominated by the Episcopal Church (known as the Anglican Church in other countries), but from early on it was also a haven for those of other faiths. Various types of Protestant offshoots soon arrived, including the French Huguenots and Congregationalists. The seeds of Methodism and the Great Awakening were planted along the coast.

Owing to vestigial prejudice from the European realpolitik of the

Voodoo and Hoodoo

The spiritual system called voodoo— the word is a corruption of various West African spellings—came to the Western Hemisphere with the importation of slaves. Voodoo is a clearly defined religion and is the dominant religion of millions of West Africans.

Like many ancient belief systems, voodoo is based on the veneration of ancestors and the possibility of continued communication with them. Up until fairly recently the African American Gullah and Geechee populations of the South Carolina and Georgia Sea Islands still had a common belief that the older slaves who were born in Africa could actually fly in spirit form to the continent of their birth and back again.

While voodoo has always been unfairly sensationalized—a notable recent example being the "voodoo priestess" Minerva in *Midnight in the Garden of Good and Evil*—it's not necessarily as malevolent in actual practice as in the overactive imaginations of writers and directors. The stereotypical practice of sticking pins in dolls to bring pain to a living person actually has its roots in European and Native American folklore.

Much of what the layperson thinks is voodoo is actually hoodoo, a body of folklore—not a religion—indigenous to the American South. Hoodoo combines elements of voodoo (communicating with the dead) and fundamentalist Christianity (extensive scriptural references). In the United States, most African American voodoo tradition was long ago subsumed within Protestant Christianity, but the Gullah populations of the Sea Islands of South Carolina and Georgia still keep alive the old ways. In the Gullah and Geechee areas of the Georgia and Carolina Sea Islands, the word *conjure* is generally the preferred terminology for this hybrid belief system, which has good sides and bad sides and borrows liberally from African lore and Christian folkways.

The old Southern practice of painting shutters and doors blue to ward off evil comes from hoodoo, where the belief in ghosts, or "haints," is largely a byproduct of poorly understood Christianity (Mediterranean countries also use blue to keep evil at bay, and the word *haint* is of Scots-Irish origin). You can still see this particular shade of "haint blue" on rural and vernacular structures throughout the Lowcountry.

Another element of hoodoo that you can still encounter today is the role of the "root doctor," an expert at folk remedies who blends together various indigenous herbs and plants in order to produce a desired effect or result. In *Midnight in the Garden of Good and Evil,* this role belongs to the fabled Dr. Buzzard, who teaches Minerva everything she knows about "conjure work." However, a root doctor is not to be confused with a "gifted reader," a fortune-teller born with the talent to tell the future. From the no-doubt embellished account in John Berendt's *Midnight,* scholars would put the late Minerva squarely into the category of root doctor or "conjurer" rather than the undeniably more compelling "voodoo priestess."

founding era, the Roman Catholic presence on the coast was late in arriving, but once it came, it was there to stay.

But most unusually of all for the Deep South, Charleston has a large Jewish population, which has been a key participant in the city from the very first days of settlement. Sephardic Jews of primarily Portuguese descent were among the first settlers.

MANNERS

The prevalence and importance of good manners is the main thing to keep in mind about the South. While it's tempting for folks from more outwardly assertive parts of the world to take this as a sign of weakness, that would be a major mistake. Southerners use manners, courtesy, and chivalry as a system of social interaction with one goal above all: to maintain the established order during times of stress. A relic from a time of extreme class stratification, etiquette and chivalry are ways to make sure that the elites are never threatened—and, on the other hand, that even those on the lowest rungs of society are afforded at least a basic amount of dignity. But as a practical matter, it's also true that Southerners of all classes, races, and backgrounds rely on the observation of manners as a way to sum up people quickly. To any Southerner, regardless of class or race, your use or neglect of basic manners and proper respect indicates how seriously they should take you—not in a socioeconomic sense, but in the big picture overall.

The typical Southern sense of humor—equal parts irony, self-deprecation, and good-natured teasing—is part of the code. Southerners are loath to criticize another individual directly, so often they'll instead take the opportunity to make an ironic joke. Self-deprecating humor is also much more common in the South than in other areas of the country. Because of this, conversely you're also expected to be able to take a joke yourself without being too sensitive.

Another key element in Southern manners is the discussion of money—or rather, the nondiscussion. Unlike some parts of the United States, in the South it's considered the height of rudeness to ask someone what their salary is or how much they paid for their house. Not that the subject is entirely taboo—far from it; you just have to know the code. For example, rather than brag about how much or how little was paid for a home, a Southern head of household will instead take you on a guided tour of the grounds. Along the way your guide will make sure to detail: (a) all the work that was done; (b) how grueling and unexpected it all was; and (c) how hard it was to get the contractors to show up.

Depending on the circumstances, in the first segment (a), you were just told either that the head of the house is made of money and has a lot more of it to spend on renovating than you do, or that this individual is a brilliant negotiator who got the house for a song. In part (b) you were told that you are not messing around with a lazy deadbeat here, but with someone who knows how to take care of things and can handle adversity with aplomb. And with part (c) you were told that the head of the house knows the best contractors in town and can pay enough for them to actually show up, and if you play your cards right, your guide might pass on their phone numbers to you with a personal recommendation. See? Breaking the code is easy once you get the hang of it.

Etiquette

As we've seen, it's rude here to inquire about personal finances, along with the usual no-go areas of religion and politics. Here are some other specific etiquette tips:

- **Basics:** Be liberal with "please" and "thank you," or conversely, "no thank you" if you want to decline a request or offering.

- **Eye contact:** With the exception of very elderly African Americans, eye contact is not only accepted in the South, it's encouraged. In fact, to avoid eye contact in the South means you're likely a shady character.

- **Handshake:** Men should always shake hands with a *very* firm, confident grip and appropriate eye contact. It's okay for women to offer a handshake in professional circles, but otherwise not required.

- **Chivalry:** When men open doors for women here—and they will—it is not thought of as a patronizing gesture but as a sign of respect. Accept graciously and walk through the door.

- **The elderly:** Senior citizens—or really anyone obviously older than you—should be called "sir" or "ma'am." Again, this is not a patronizing gesture in the South but considered a sign of respect. Also, in any situation where you're dealing with someone in the service industry, addressing them as "sir" or "ma'am" regardless of their age will get you far.

- **Bodily contact:** Interestingly, though public displays of affection by romantic couples are generally frowned upon here, Southerners are otherwise pretty touchy-feely once they get to know you. Southerners who are well acquainted often say hello or goodbye with a hug.

- **Driving:** With the exception of the interstate perimeter highways around the larger cities, drivers in the South are generally less aggressive than in other regions. Cutting sharply in front of someone in traffic is taken as a personal offense. If you need to cut in front of someone, poke the nose of your car a little bit in that direction and wait for a car to slow down and wave you in front. Don't forget to wave back as a thank-you. Similarly, using a car horn can also be taken as a personal affront, so use your horn sparingly, if at all. In rural areas, don't be surprised to see the driver of an oncoming car offer a little wave. This is an old custom, sadly dying out. Just give a little wave back; they're trying to be friendly.

THE GUN CULTURE

One of the most misunderstood aspects of the South is the value the region places on the personal possession of firearms. No doubt, the 2nd Amendment to the U.S. Constitution ("A well regulated Militia, being necessary to the security of a free State, the right of the people to keep and bear Arms, shall not be infringed") is well known here and fiercely protected, at the governmental and at the grassroots levels.

State laws do tend to be significantly more accommodating of gun owners here than in much of the rest of the country. It is legal to carry a concealed handgun in South Carolina with the proper permit, and you need no permit at all to possess a weapon in your house or car for self-defense. However, there are regulations regarding how a handgun must be conveyed in automobiles.

Walter Edgar's Journal

He's originally from Alabama, but you could call University of South Carolina (USC) professor Walter Edgar the modern voice of the Palmetto State. From the rich diversity of barbecue to the inner workings of the poultry business and the charms of beach music, Edgar covers the gamut of South Carolina culture and experience on his popular weekly radio show *Walter Edgar's Journal,* airing on South Carolina public radio stations throughout the state.

Currently director of the USC Institute of Southern Studies, the Vietnam vet and certified barbecue contest judge explains the show like this: "On the *Journal* we look at current events in a broader perspective, trying to provide context that is often missing in the mainstream media." More specifically, Edgar devotes each one-hour show to a single guest, usually a South Carolinian—by birth or by choice—with a unique perspective on some aspect of state culture, business, arts, or folkways. By the time the interview ends, you not only have a much deeper understanding of the topic of the show but of the interviewee as well. And because of Edgar's unique way of tying strands of his own vast knowledge and experience into every interview, you also leave with a deeper understanding of South Carolina itself.

In these days of media saturation, a public radio show might sound like a rather insignificant perch from which to influence an entire state. But remember that South Carolina Is a small close-knit place, a state of Main Street towns rather than impersonal metro areas. During any given show, many listeners in Edgar's audience will know his guests on a personal basis. And by the end of the show, the rest of the listeners will feel as if they do.

Listen to *Walter Edgar's Journal* each Friday at noon on South Carolina public radio, with a repeat each Sunday at 4pm. Hear podcasts of previous editions at www.scetv.org.

The state now has a so-called (and controversial) "stand your ground" law, whereby if you're in imminent lethal danger, you do not have to first try to run away before resorting to deadly force to defend yourself.

FESTIVALS AND EVENTS

Charleston is a festival-mad city, especially in the spring and early fall. And new festivals are being added every year, further enhancing the hedonistic flavor of this city that has also mastered the art of hospitality. Here's a look through the calendar at all the key festivals in the area.

January

Held on a Sunday in late January at historic Boone Hall Plantation in Mount Pleasant, the **Lowcountry Oyster Festival** (www.charlestonlow-country.com, 11am-5pm, $8, food additional) features literal truckloads of the sweet shellfish for your enjoyment. Gates open at 10:30am, and there's plenty of parking. Oysters are sold by the bucket and served with crackers and cocktail sauce. Bring your own shucking knife or glove, or buy them on-site.

February

One of the more unique events in town is the **Southeastern Wildlife Exposition** (various venues, 843/723-1748, www.sewe.com, $12.50 per day, $30 for 3 days, free under age 13). For the last quarter century, the Wildlife Expo has brought together hundreds of artists and exhibitors to showcase just about any kind of naturally themed art you can think of, in over a dozen galleries and venues all over downtown. Kids will enjoy the live animals on hand as well.

March

Generally straddling late February and the first days of March, the four-day **Charleston Food & Wine Festival** (www.charlestonfoodandwine.com, various venues and admission) is a glorious celebration of one of the Holy City's premier draws: its amazing culinary community. While the emphasis is on Lowcountry gurus like Donald Barickman of Magnolias and Robert Carter of the Peninsula Grill, guest chefs from as far away as New York, New Orleans, and Los Angeles routinely come to show off their skills. Oenophiles, especially of domestic wines, will be in heaven as well. Tickets aren't cheap—an all-event pass is over $500 pp—but then again, this is one of the nation's great food cities, so you might find it worth every penny.

Immediately before the Festival of Houses and Gardens is the **Charleston International Antiques Show** (40 E. Bay St., 843/722-3405, www.historic-charleston.org, admission varies), held at Historic Charleston's headquarters at the Missroon House on the High Battery. It features over 30 of the nation's best-regarded dealers and offers lectures and tours.

Mid-March-April, the perennial favorite **Festival of Houses and Gardens** (843/722-3405, www.historiccharleston.org, admission varies) is sponsored by the Historic Charleston Foundation and held at the very peak of the spring blooming season for maximum effect. In all, the festival goes into a dozen historic neighborhoods to view about 150 homes. Each day sees a different three-hour tour of a different area, at about $45 pp. This is a fantastic opportunity to peek inside some amazing old privately owned properties that are inaccessible to visitors at all other times. A highlight is a big oyster roast and picnic at Drayton Hall.

Not to be confused with the above festival, the **Garden Club of Charleston House and Garden Tours** (843/530-5164, www.thegardenclubofcharleston.com, $35) are held over a weekend in late March. Highlights include the Heyward-Washington House and the private garden of the late great Charleston horticulturalist Emily Whaley.

One of Charleston's newest and most fun events, the five-night **Charleston Fashion Week** (www.fashionweek.charlestonmag.com, admission varies) is sponsored by *Charleston* magazine and benefits a local women's charity. Mimicking New York's Fashion Week events under tenting in Bryant Park, Charleston's version features runway action under big tents in Marion Square—and, yes, past guests have included former contestants on *Project Runway*.

BACKGROUND
PEOPLE AND CULTURE

April

The annual **Cooper River Bridge Run** (www.bridgerun.com) happens the first Saturday in April (unless that's Easter weekend, in which case it runs the week before) and features a six-mile jaunt across the massive new Arthur Ravenel Bridge over the Cooper River, the longest cable span in the Western Hemisphere. It's not for those with a fear of heights, but it's still one of Charleston's best-attended events—there are well over 30,000 participants. The whole crazy idea started when Dr. Marcus Newberry of the Medical University of South Carolina in Charleston was inspired by an office fitness trail in his native state of Ohio to do something similar in Charleston to promote fitness. Participants can walk the course if they choose, and many do. The start is signaled with the traditional cannon shot. The race still begins in Mount Pleasant and ends downtown, but over the years the course has changed to accommodate growth—not only in the event itself but in the city. Auto traffic, of course, is rerouted starting the night before the race. Each participant in the Bridge Run now must wear a transponder chip; new "Bones in Motion" technology allows you to track a favorite runner's exact position in real time during the race. The 2006 Run had wheelchair participants for the first time. There's now a Kid's Run in Hampton Square the Friday before, which also allows strollers.

From 1973 to 2000—except for 1976, when it was in Florida—the **Family Circle Cup** (161 Seven Farms Dr., Daniel Island, 843/856-7900, www.familycirclecup.com, admission varies) was held at Sea Pines Plantation on Hilton Head Island. The popular Tier 1 women's tennis tournament in 2001 moved to Daniel Island's brand-new Family Circle Tennis Center (161 Seven Farms Dr., Daniel Island, 843/856-7900, www.familycirclecup.com, admission varies), specifically built for the event through a partnership between *Family Circle* magazine and the city of Charleston. Almost 100,000 people attend the multiple-week event. Individual session tickets go on sale the preceding January.

Mount Pleasant is the home of Charleston's shrimping fleet, and each April sees all the boats parade by the Alhambra Hall and Park for the **Blessing of the Fleet** (843/884-8517, www.townofmountpleasant.com). Family events and lots and lots of seafood are also on tap.

May

Free admission and free parking are not the only draws at the outdoor **North Charleston Arts Festival** (5000 Coliseum Dr., www.northcharleston.org), but let's face it, that's important. Held beside North Charleston's Performing Arts Center and Convention Center, the festival features music, dance, theater, multicultural performers, and storytellers. There are a lot of kids' events as well.

Held over three days at the Holy Trinity Greek Orthodox Church up toward the Neck, the **Charleston Greek Festival** (30 Race St., 843/577-2063, www.greekorthodoxchs.org, $3) offers a plethora of live entertainment, dancing, Greek wares, and, of course, fantastic Greek cuisine cooked by the congregation. Parking is not a problem, and there's even a shuttle to the church from the lot.

One of Charleston's newest annual events is the **Charleston International Film Festival** (843/817-1617, www.charlestoniff.com, various venues and prices). Despite being a relative latecomer to the film-festival circuit, the event is pulled off with Charleston's usual aplomb.

Indisputably Charleston's single biggest and most important event, **Spoleto Festival USA** (843/579-3100, www.spoletousa.org, admission varies) has come a long way since it was a sparkle in the eye of the late Gian Carlo Menotti three decades ago. Though Spoleto long ago broke ties with its founder, his vision remains indelibly stamped on the event from start to finish. There's plenty of music, to be sure, in genres that include orchestral, opera, jazz, and avant-garde, but you'll find something in every other performing art, such as dance, drama, and spoken word, in traditions from Western to African to Southeast Asian. For 17 days from Memorial Day weekend through early June, Charleston hops and hums nearly 24 hours a day to the energy of this vibrant, cutting-edge, yet accessible artistic celebration, which dominates everything and every conversation for those three weeks. Events happen in historic venues and churches all over downtown and as far as Middleton Place, which hosts the grand finale under the stars. If you want to come to Charleston during Spoleto—and everyone should, at least once—book your accommodations and your tickets far in advance. Tickets usually go on sale in early January for that summer's festival.

As if all the hubbub around Spoleto didn't give you enough to do, there's also **Piccolo Spoleto** (843/724-7305, www.piccolospoleto.com, various venues and admission), literally "little Spoleto," running concurrently. The intent of Piccolo Spoleto—begun just a couple of years after the larger festival came to town and run by the city's Office of Cultural Affairs—is to give local and regional performers a time to shine, sharing some of that larger spotlight on the national and international performers at the main event. Of particular interest to visiting families will be Piccolo's children's events, a good counter to some of the decidedly more adult fare at Spoleto USA.

June

Technically part of Piccolo Spoleto but gathering its own following, the **Sweetgrass Cultural Arts Festival** (www.sweetgrassfestival.org) is held the first week in June in Mount Pleasant at the Laing Middle School (2213 U.S. 17 N.). The event celebrates the traditional sweetgrass basket-making skills of African Americans in the historic Christ Church Parish area of Mount Pleasant. If you want to buy some sweetgrass baskets made by the world's foremost experts in the field, this would be the time.

July

Each year over 30,000 people come to see the **Patriots Point Fourth of July Blast** (866/831-1720), featuring a hefty barrage of fireworks shot off the

A Man, a Plan: Spoleto!

Sadly, Gian Carlo Menotti is no longer with us, having died in 2007 at the age of 95. But the overwhelming success of the composer's brainchild and labor of love, **Spoleto Festival USA,** lives on, enriching the cultural and social life of Charleston and serving as the city's chief calling card to the world at large.

Menotti began writing music at age seven in his native Italy. As a young man he moved to Philadelphia to study music, where he shared classes—and lifelong connections—with Leonard Bernstein and Samuel Barber. His first full-length opera, *The Consul,* would garner him the Pulitzer Prize, as would 1955's *The Saint of Bleecker Street.* But by far Menotti's best-known work is the beloved Christmas opera *Amahl and the Night Visitors,* composed especially for NBC television in 1951. At the height of his fame in 1958, the charismatic and mercurial genius—fluent and witty in five languages—founded the "Festival of Two Worlds" in Spoleto, Italy, specifically as a forum for young American artists in Europe. But it wasn't until nearly two decades later, in 1977, that Menotti was able to make his long-imagined dream of an American counterpart a reality.

Attracted to Charleston because of its long-standing support of the arts, its undeniable good taste, and its small size—ensuring that his festival would always be the number-one activity in town while it was going on—Menotti worked closely with the man who was to become the other key part of the equation: Charleston mayor Joe Riley, then in his first term in office.

Since then, the city has built on Spoleto's success by founding its own local version, **Piccolo Spoleto**—literally, "little Spoleto"—which focuses exclusively on local and regional talent.

Things haven't always gone smoothly. Menotti and the stateside festival parted ways in 1993, when he took over the Rome Opera. Making matters more uneasy, the Italian festival—run by Menotti's longtime partner (and later adopted son) Chip—also became estranged from what was intended to be its soul mate in South Carolina. (Chip was later replaced by the Italian Culture Ministry.) But perhaps this kind of creative tension is what Menotti intended all along. Indeed, each spring brings a Spoleto USA that seems to thrive on the inherent conflict between the festival's often cutting-edge offerings and the very traditional city that hosts it. Unlike so many of the increasingly generic arts "festivals" across the nation, Spoleto still challenges its audiences, just as Menotti intended it to. Depending on the critic and the audience member, that modern opera debut you see may be groundbreaking or gratuitous. The drama you check out may be exhilarating or tiresome.

Still, the crowds keep coming, attracted just as much to Charleston's many charms as to the art itself. Each year, a total of about 500,000 people attend both Spoleto and Piccolo Spoleto. Nearly one-third of the attendees are Charleston residents—the final proof that when it comes to supporting the arts, Charleston puts its money where its mouth is.

deck of the USS *Yorktown* moored on the Cooper River in the Patriots Point complex. Food, live entertainment, and kids' activities are also featured.

September

From late September into the first week of October, the city-sponsored

MOJA Arts Festival (843/724-7305, www.mojafestival.com, various venues and admission) highlights the cultural contributions of African Americans and people from the Caribbean with dance, visual art, poetry, cuisine, crafts, and music in genres that include gospel, jazz, reggae, and classical. In existence since 1984, MOJA's name comes from the Swahili word for "one," and its diverse range of offerings in so many media have made it one of the Southeast's premier events. Some events are ticketed, while others, such as the kids' activities and many of the dance and film events, are free.

For five weeks from the last week of September into October, the Preservation Society of Charleston hosts the much-anticipated **Fall Tours of Homes & Gardens** (843/722-4630, www.preservationsociety.org, $45). The tour takes you into more than a dozen local residences and is the nearly 90-year-old organization's biggest fund-raiser. Tickets typically go on sale the previous June, and they tend to sell out very quickly.

October

Another great food event in this great food city, the **Taste of Charleston** (1235 Long Point Rd., 843/577-4030, www.charlestonrestaurantassociation.com, 11am-5pm, $12) is held on a weekend in October at Boone Hall Plantation in Mount Pleasant and sponsored by the Greater Charleston Restaurant Association. Over 50 area chefs and restaurants come together so you can sample their wares, including a wine and food pairing, with proceeds going to charity.

Local company **Half Moon Outfitters** (280 King St., 843/853-0990; 425 Coleman Blvd., 843/881-9472, www.halfmoonoutfitters.com, Mon.-Sat. 10am-7pm, Sun. noon-6pm) sponsors an annual six-mile Giant Kayak Race at Isle of Palms Marina in late October, benefiting the Coastal Conservation League.

November

Plantation Days at Middleton Place (4300 Ashley River Rd., 843/556-6020, www.middletonplace.org, daily 9am-5pm, last tour 4:30pm, guided tour $10) happen each Saturday in November, giving visitors a chance to wander the grounds and see artisans at work practicing authentic crafts, as they would have done in antebellum days, with a special emphasis on the contributions of African Americans. A special treat comes on Thanksgiving, when a full meal is offered on the grounds at the Middleton Place Restaurant (843/556-6020, www.middletonplace.org, reservations strongly recommended).

Though the **Battle of Secessionville** actually took place in June 1862 much farther south, November is the time the battle is reenacted at Boone Hall Plantation (1235 Long Point Rd., 843/884-4371, www.boonehallplantation.com, $17.50 adults, $7.50 children) in Mount Pleasant. Call for specific dates and times.

December

A yuletide in the Holy City is an experience you'll never forget, as the **Christmas in Charleston** (843/724-3705, www.charlestoncity.info) events clustered around the first week of the month prove. For some reason—whether it's the old architecture, the friendly people, the churches, the carriages, or all of the above—Charleston feels right at home during Christmas. The festivities begin with Mayor Joe Riley lighting the city's 60-foot Tree of Lights in Marion Square, followed by a parade of brightly lit boats from Mount Pleasant all the way around Charleston up the Ashley River. The key event is the Sunday Christmas Parade through downtown, featuring bands, floats, and performers in the holiday spirit. The Saturday Farmers Market in the square continues through the middle of the month with a focus on holiday items.

Essentials

Transportation

GETTING THERE

Air

Way up in North Charleston is **Charleston International Airport** (CHS, 5500 International Blvd., 843/767-1100, www.chs-airport.com), served by AirTran (www.airtran.com), American (www.aa.com), Delta (www.delta.com), JetBlue (www.jetblue.com), Southwest (www.southwest.com), United Airlines (www.ual.com), and US Airways (www.usairways.com).

It'll take about 20 minutes to make the 12-mile drive from the airport to downtown, and vice versa. The airport is conveniently located just off the I-526/Mark Clark Expressway perimeter highway off of I-26. As in most cities, taxi service from the airport is regulated. This translates to about $30 for two people from the airport to Charleston Place downtown.

Car

There are two main routes into Charleston, I-26 from the west-northwest (which dead-ends downtown) and U.S. 17 from the west (called Savannah Highway when it gets close to Charleston proper), which continues on over the Ravenel Bridge into Mount Pleasant and beyond. There's a fairly new perimeter highway, I-526 (Mark Clark Expressway), which loops around the city from West Ashley to North Charleston to Daniel Island and into Mount Pleasant. It's accessible both from I-26 and U.S. 17.

Keep in mind that I-95, while certainly a gateway to the region, is actually a good ways out of Charleston, about 30 miles west of the city. Charleston is almost exactly two hours from Savannah by car, and about an hour's drive from Beaufort and Hilton Head.

Car Rentals

You don't have to have a car to enjoy Charleston, but to really explore the areas surrounding this city you'll need your own vehicle. Renting a car is easy and fairly inexpensive, as long as you play by the rules, which are simple. You need either a valid U.S. driver's license from any state or a valid International Driving Permit from your home country, and you must be at least 25 years old.

If you do not either purchase insurance coverage from the rental company or already have insurance coverage through the credit card you rent the car with, you will be 100 percent responsible for any damage caused to the car during your rental period. While purchasing insurance at the time of rental is by no means mandatory, it might be worth the extra expense just to have that peace of mind.

Previous: Arthur Ravenel Jr. Bridge; Broad Street from the Old Exchange and Provost.

Some rental car locations are in the city proper, but the vast majority of outlets are at the airport, so plan accordingly. The airport locations have the bonus of generally holding longer hours than their in-town counterparts.

Charleston International Airport has rental kiosks for **Avis** (843/767-7031), **Budget** (843/767-7051), **Dollar** (843/767-1130), **Enterprise** (843/767-1109), **Hertz** (843/767-4550), **National** (843/767-3078), and **Thrifty** (843/647-4389). There are a couple of rental locations downtown: **Budget** (390 Meeting St., 843/577-5195) and **Enterprise** (398 Meeting St., 843/723-6215). **Hertz** has a location in West Ashley (3025 Ashley Town Center Dr., 843/573-2147), as does **Enterprise** (2004 Savannah Hwy., 843/556-7889).

Train

Passenger rail service in the car-dominated United States is far behind other developed nations, both in quantity and quality. Charleston is served by the New York-Miami *Silver Service* route of the national rail system, Amtrak (www.amtrak.com), which is pretty good, if erratic at times—although it certainly pales in comparison with European rail transit. Charleston's Amtrak station (4565 Gaynor Street, 843/744-8263) is in a light industrial part of town, nowhere near the major tourist center.

GETTING AROUND

Taxi

The South is generally not big on taxis, and Charleston is no exception. The best bet is simply to call rather than try to flag one down. Charleston's most fun service is **Charleston Black Cabs** (843/216-2627, www.charleston-blackcabcompany.com), using Americanized versions of the classic British taxi. A one-way ride anywhere on the peninsula below the bridges is about $10 per person, and rates go up from there. They're very popular, so call as far ahead as you can or try to get one at their stand at Charleston Place. Two other good services are **Safety Cab** (843/722-4066) and **Yellow Cab** (843/577-6565).

You can also try a human-powered taxi service from **Charleston Rickshaw** (843/723-5685). A cheerful (and energetic) young cyclist will pull you and a friend to most points on the lower peninsula for about $10-15. Call 'em or find one by City Market. They work late on Friday and Saturday nights too.

Bus

Public transportation by the **Charleston Area Regional Transit Authority** (CARTA, 843/724-7420, www.ridecarta.com) is a convenient and inexpensive way to enjoy Charleston without the more structured nature of an organized tour. There's a wide variety of routes, but most visitors will limit their acquaintance to the tidy, trolley-like **DASH** (Downtown Area Shuttle) buses run by CARTA primarily for visitors. Each ride is $1.75 pp ($0.85 seniors). The best deal is the $6 one-day pass, which you get at the Charleston Visitor Reception and Transportation Center (375 Meeting St.). Keep in mind that DASH only stops at designated places. DASH has three routes: the 210, which runs a northerly circuit from the aquarium to the College of Charleston; the 211, running up and down the parallel Meeting and King Streets from Marion Square down to the Battery; and the 212 Market/Waterfront shuttle from the aquarium area down to Waterfront Park.

Boat

One of the coolest things about the Charleston area is the presence of the Intracoastal Waterway, a combined artificial and natural sheltered seaway from Miami to Maine. Many boaters enjoy touring the coast by simply meandering up or down the Intracoastal, putting in at marinas along the way. There's a website for Intracoastal information at wwww.cruiseguides.com and a good resource of area marinas at www.marinamate.com.

Parking

As you'll quickly see, parking is at a premium in downtown Charleston. An exception seems to be the large number of free spaces all along the Battery, but unless you're an exceptionally strong walker, that's too far south to use as a reliable base from which to explore the whole peninsula.

Most metered parking downtown is on and around Calhoun Street, Meeting Street, King Street, Market Street, and East Bay Street. That may not sound like a lot, but it constitutes the bulk of the area that most tourists visit. Most meters have three-hour limits, but you'll come across some as short as 30 minutes. Metered parking is free 6pm-6am and all day Sunday. On Saturdays, expect to pay.

The city has several conveniently located and comparatively inexpensive parking garages. I strongly suggest that you make use of them. They're located at: the aquarium, Camden and Exchange Streets, Charleston Place, Concord and Cumberland Streets, East Bay and Prioleau Streets, Marion Square, Gaillard Auditorium, Liberty and St. Philip Streets, Majestic Square, the Charleston Visitor Reception and Transportation Center, and Wentworth Street.

There are several private parking garages as well, primarily clustered in the City Market area. They're convenient, but many have parking spaces that are often too small for some vehicles. The city's website (www.charlestoncity.info) has a good interactive map of parking.

Travel Tips

TOURIST INFORMATION
Visitor Centers

I highly recommend a stop at the **Charleston Visitor Reception and Transportation Center** (375 Meeting St., 800/774-0006, www.charlestoncvb.com, Mon.-Fri. 8:30am-5pm). Housed in a modern building with an inviting, open design, the center has several high-tech interactive exhibits, including an amazing model of the city under glass. Wall after wall of well-stocked, well-organized brochures will keep you informed on everything a visitor would ever want to know about or see in the city. A particularly welcoming touch is the inclusion of the work of local artists all around the center. I recommend using the attached parking garage not only for your stop at the center but also anytime you want to see the many sights this part of town has to offer, such as the Charleston Museum, the Manigault and Aiken-Rhett Houses, and the Children's Museum. The big selling point of the center is the friendliness of the smiling and courteous staff, who welcome you in true Charleston fashion and are there to book rooms and tours and find tickets for shows and attractions. If for no other reason, you should go to the center to take advantage of the great deal offered by the **Charleston Heritage Passport** (www.heritagefederation. org), which gives you 40 percent off admission to all of Charleston's key historic homes, the Charleston Museum, and the two awesome plantation sites on the Ashley River: Drayton Hall and Middleton Place. You can get the Heritage Passport *only* at the Charleston Visitor Reception and Transportation Center on Meeting Street.

Other area visitors centers include the **Mount Pleasant-Isle of Palms Visitors Center** (99 Harry M. Hallman Jr. Blvd., 800/774-0006, daily 9am-5pm) and the new **North Charleston Visitors Center** (4975B Centre Pointe Dr., 843/853-8000, Mon.-Sat. 10am-5pm).

The Beaufort **Visitors Information Center** is within the Beaufort Arsenal building (713 Craven St., 843/986-5400, www.beaufortsc.org, daily 9am-5:30pm). In Hilton Head, get information, book a room, or secure a tee time just as you come onto the island at the **Hilton Head Island Chamber of Commerce Welcome Center** (100 William Hilton Pkwy., 843/785-3673, www.hiltonheadisland.org, daily 9am-6pm), in the same building as the Coastal Discovery Museum. You'll find Bluffton's visitors center in the **Heyward House Historic Center** (70 Boundary St., 843/757-6293, www. heywardhouse.org, Mon.-Fri. 10am-5pm, Sat. 10am-4pm).

Libraries

The main branch of the **Charleston County Public Library** (68 Calhoun St., 843/805-6801, www.ccpl.org, Mon.-Thurs. 9am-9pm, Fri.-Sat. 9am-6pm, Sun. 2pm-5pm) has been at its current site since 1998. Named for Sullivan's Island's most famous visitor, the **Edgar Allan Poe** (1921 I'on Ave., 843/883-3914, www.ccpl.org, Mon. and Fri. 2-6pm, Tues., Thurs., and Sat. 10am-2pm) has been housed in Battery Gadsden, a former Spanish-American War gun emplacement, since 1977.

The College of Charleston's main library is the **Marlene and Nathan Addlestone Library** (205 Calhoun St., 843/953-5530, www.cofc.edu), home to special collections, the Center for Student Learning, the main computer lab, the media collection, and even a café. The college's **Avery Research Center for African American History and Culture** (125 Bull St.,

Top: horse-drawn tour of Charleston. Bottom: environmentally friendly rickshaw service.

843/953-7609, www.cofc.edu/avery, Mon.-Fri. 10am-5pm, Sat. noon-5pm) houses documents relating to the history and culture of African Americans in the Lowcountry.

For other historical research on the area, check out the collections of the **South Carolina Historical Society** (100 Meeting St., 843/723-3225, www. southcarolinahistoricalsociety.org, Mon.-Fri. 9am-4pm, Sat. 9am-2pm). There's a $5 research fee for nonmembers.

ACCESS FOR TRAVELERS WITH DISABILITIES

While the vast majority of attractions and accommodations make every effort to comply with federal law regarding those with disabilities, as they're obliged to do, the very historic nature of this region means that some structures simply cannot be retrofitted for maximum accessibility. This is something you'll need to find out on a case-by-case basis, so call ahead. The sites administered by the National Park Service in this guide (Charles Pinckney National Historic Site, Fort Sumter, and Fort Moultrie) are as wheelchair-accessible as possible.

Some special shuttles are available. In Charleston, call the **"Tel-A-Ride"** service (843/724-7420). A couple of cab companies in town to check out are **Express Cab Company** (843/577-8816) and **Flag A Cab** (842/554-1231). For the visually impaired, in Charleston there's the **Association for the Blind** (1071 Morrison Dr., 843/723-6915, www.afb.org). Hearing-disadvantaged individuals can get assistance in Charleston at the **Charleston Speech and Hearing Center** (843/552-1212).

TRAVELING WITH CHILDREN

The Lowcountry is very kid-friendly, with the possible exception of some B&Bs that are clearly not designed for younger children. If you have any doubts about this, feel free to inquire. Otherwise, there are no special precautions unique to this area. There are no zoos per se in the region, but animal lovers of all ages will enjoy **Charles Towne Landing** in Charleston. Better still, take the kids on nature outings to the amazing National Wildlife Refuges in the area.

WOMEN TRAVELING ALONE

Women should take the same precautions they would anywhere else. Many women traveling to this region have to adjust to the prevalence of traditional chivalry. In the South, if a man opens a door for you, it's considered a sign of respect, not condescension. Another adjustment is the possible assumption that two or three women who go to a bar or tavern together might be there to invite male companionship. This misunderstanding can happen anywhere, but in some parts of the South it might be slightly more prevalent. Being aware of it is the best defense; otherwise no other steps need to be taken.

SENIOR TRAVELERS

Both because of the large proportion of retirees in the region and because of Southerners' traditional respect for the elderly, the area is quite friendly to senior citizens. Many accommodations and attractions offer a slight senior discount, which can add up over the course of a trip. Always inquire about such discounts before making a reservation, however, as checkout time is too late to do so.

GAY AND LESBIAN TRAVELERS

Contrary to many media portrayals of the region, Charleston is quite open to gays and lesbians, who play a major role in arts, culture, and business. As with any other place in the South, however, it's generally expected that people—straights as well—will keep personal matters and politics to themselves in public settings. A key local advocacy group is the **Alliance for Full Acceptance** (29 Leinbach Dr., Suite D-3, 843/883-0343, www.affa-sc.org). The **Lowcountry Gay and Lesbian Alliance** (843/720-8088) holds a potluck the last Sunday of each month. For the most up-to-date happenings, try the Gay Charleston blog (http://gaycharleston.ccpblogs.com), part of the *Charleston City Paper.*

TRAVELING WITH PETS

While the United States is very pet-friendly, that friendliness rarely extends to restaurants and other indoor locations. More and more accommodations are allowing pet owners to bring pets, often for an added fee, but inquire before you arrive. In any case, keep your dog on a leash at all times. Some beaches in the area permit dog-walking at certain times of the year, but as a general rule, keep dogs off of beaches unless you see signage saying otherwise.

RECREATION
Beaches

Some of the best beaches in the United States are in the region covered by this guide. While the upscale amenities aren't always there and they aren't very surfer-friendly, the area's beaches are outstanding for anyone looking for a relaxing, scenic getaway.

By law, beaches in the United States are fully accessible to the public up to the high-tide mark during daylight hours, even if the beach fronts private property and even if the only means of public access is by boat. While certain seaside resorts have over the years attempted to make the dunes in front of their properties exclusive to guests, this is actually illegal, although it can be hard to enforce. On federally run National Wildlife Refuges, access is limited to daytime hours, sunrise to sunset.

It is a misdemeanor to disturb the **sea oats,** those wispy, waving, wheatlike plants among the dunes. Their root system is vital to keeping the beach intact. Also, never disturb a turtle nesting area, whether it is marked or not.

The barrier islands of the Palmetto State have seen more private development than others in the region. Some Carolina islands, like Kiawah, Fripp, and Seabrook, are not even accessible unless you are a guest at their affiliated resorts, which, of course, means that the only way to visit the beaches there if you're not a guest is by boat, which I really don't advise. Charleston-area beaches include **Folly Beach, Sullivan's Island,** and **Isle of Palms.** Folly Beach has a county recreation area with parking at **Folly Beach County Park.** Isle of Palms has a county recreation area with parking at **Isle of Palms County Park.**

Moving down the coast, some delightful beaches are at **Edisto Island** and **Hunting Island,** which both feature state parks with campgrounds. **Hilton Head Island** has about 12 miles of beautiful family-friendly beaches, and while most of the island is devoted to private golf resorts, the beaches remain accessible to the general public at four convenient points with parking: **Driessen Beach Park, Coligny Beach Park, Alder Lane Beach Access,** and **Burkes Beach Road.**

Surfing

By far the most popular surfing area in the region is the **Washout** at Charleston's Folly Beach. The key surf shop on Folly is **McKevlin's.** For Folly surf conditions, go to www.mckevlins.com or www.surfline.com.

Kayaking and Canoeing

Some key kayaking and canoeing areas in the Charleston area are **Cape Romain National Wildlife Refuge, Shem Creek, Isle of Palms, Charleston Harbor,** and the **Stono River.** The best outfitter and tour operator in the area is **Coastal Expeditions.** Farther south in the Lowcountry are the Ashepoo, Combahee, and Edisto blackwater rivers, which combine to form the **ACE Basin.** Next is **Port Royal Sound** near Beaufort; a good outfitter and tour operator in this area is **Carolina Heritage Outfitters.** The Hilton Head/Bluffton area has good kayaking opportunities at Hilton Head's **Calibogue Creek** and Bluffton's **May River.** The best outfitter and tour operator here is **Outside Hilton Head.**

Fishing and Boating

Because of the large number of islands and wide area of salt marsh, life on the water is largely inseparable from life on the land in the Lowcountry. Fishing and boating are very common pursuits here, with species of fish including spotted sea trout, channel bass, flounder, grouper, mackerel, sailfish, whiting, shark, amberjack, and tarpon. Farther inshore you'll find largemouth bass, bream, catfish, and crappie, among many more. While entire books can be and are devoted to the area's fishing opportunities, here is an overview.

It's easy to fish on piers, lakes, and streams, but if you're over age 16, you have to get a nonresident fishing license from the state. These are inexpensive and available in hardware stores, marinas, and tackle shops anywhere. In South Carolina, a nonresident seven-day license is $11. Go to www.dnr.sc.gov for more information or to purchase a license online.

The most popular places for casual anglers are the various public piers throughout the area. There are public fishing piers at **Folly Beach** and **Hunting Island.** Two nice little public docks are at the **North Charleston Riverfront Park** on the grounds of the old Charleston Navy Yard and the **Bluffton public landing** on the May River. Many anglers cast from abandoned bridges, unless signage dictates otherwise. Fishing charters and marinas are ample throughout the region, for both inshore and offshore trips.

Golf and Tennis

The first golf club in the country was formed in Charleston, and the area has more than its share of fine courses. As far as quality is concerned, the consensus pick for best course in South Carolina is definitely the Pete Dye-designed Ocean Course at the **Kiawah Island Golf Resort,** which is open to guests of the club. Coming in second would almost certainly be **Harbour Town** on Sea Pines Plantation in Hilton Head. Not coincidentally, both courses host PGA events.

The premier tennis facility in the Charleston area is the new **Family Circle Cup Tennis Center** on Daniel Island, home of the eponymous women's event and some great public courts.

Hiking and Biking

Due to the flat nature of the Lowcountry, hiking and biking here are not very strenuous. However, the great natural beauty and prevalence of a rich range of plant and animal life make hiking and biking very rewarding experiences. Probably the best trails can be found at state parks in the region, such as **Edisto Beach State Park** and **Hunting Island State Park.** Many National Wildlife Refuges (NWRs) in the area also feature excellent trails, such as **Pinckney Island NWR** and **Cape Romain NWR.**

A "rails to trails" projects that might appeal is the **James Island Trail** outside Charleston. Some areas are almost defined by the plethora of bike and pedestrian trails running nearly their entire length and breadth, such as Hilton Head Island.

Wide beaches, very conducive to biking on the sand, are one of the great pleasures of this area. Most bikes you rent in the area will have fat enough tires to do the job correctly. The best beach rides are on **Sullivan's Island** and **Hilton Head Island.**

COMMUNICATIONS
Newspapers

The daily newspaper of record is the *Post and Courier* (www.charleston.net). Its entertainment insert, *Preview,* comes out on Thursdays. The free alternative weekly is the *Charleston City Paper* (www.charlestoncitypaper.

Clockwise from top left: Folly Pier; Kiawah Golf Resort; Charleston's Waterfront Park.

com), which comes out on Wednesdays and is the best place to find local music and arts listings. A particularly well-done and lively metro glossy is *Charleston* magazine (www.charlestonmag.com), which comes out once a month.

Radio and Television

The National Public Radio affiliate is the South Carolina ETV radio station WSCI at 89.3 FM. South Carolina ETV is on television at WITV. The local NBC affiliate is WCBD, the CBS affiliate is WCSC, the ABC affiliate is WCIV, and the Fox affiliate is WTAT.

Health and Safety

CRIME

While crime rates are indeed above national averages, especially in inner-city areas, incidents of crime in the more heavily trafficked tourist areas are no more common than anywhere else. In fact, these areas might be safer because of the amount of foot traffic and police attention.

By far the most common crime against visitors here is simple theft, primarily from cars. (Pickpocketing, thankfully, is rare in the United States.) Always lock your car doors. Conversely, only leave them unlocked if you're absolutely comfortable living without whatever's inside at the time. As a general rule, I try to lock valuables—such as CDs, a recent purchase, or my wife's purse—in the trunk. (Just make sure the "valet" button, allowing the trunk to be opened from the driver's area, is disabled.)

Should someone corner you and demand your wallet or purse, just give it to them. Unfortunately, the old advice to scream as loud as you can is no longer the deterrent it once was, and in fact may hasten aggressive action by the robber.

If you are the victim of a crime, *always call the police.* Law enforcement wants more information, not less, and at the very least you'll have an incident report in case you need to make an insurance claim for lost or stolen property.

POLICE

For nonemergencies in Charleston, West Ashley, and James Island, contact the **Charleston Police Department** (843/577-7434, www.charlestoncity.info). You can also contact the police department in Mount Pleasant (843/884-4176). North Charleston is a separate municipality with its own police department (843/308-4718, www.northcharleston.org). Of course, for emergencies always call **911.**

AUTO ACCIDENTS

If you're in an auto accident where there's injury or damage to one or both cars, you must at minimum exchange insurance information with the other driver. It's always prudent to wait for police. Unless there is a personal injury involved, you should move your car just enough to clear the way for other traffic if able to do so.

Since it's illegal to drive in these states without auto insurance, I'll assume you have some. And because you're insured, the best course of action in a minor accident, where injuries are unlikely, is to patiently wait for the police and give them your side of the story. In my experience, police react negatively to people who are too quick to start making accusations against other people. After that, let the insurance companies deal with it; that's what they're there for. If you suspect any injuries, call 911 immediately.

ILLEGAL DRUGS

Marijuana, heroin, methamphetamine, and cocaine and all its derivatives are illegal in the United States with only a very few select exceptions, none of which apply to the areas covered by this guide. The use of ecstasy and similar mood-elevators is also illegal. The penalties for illegal drug possession and use in South Carolina are quite severe.

ALCOHOL

The drinking age in the United States is 21. Most restaurants that serve alcoholic beverages allow those under 21 inside. Generally speaking, if only those over 21 are allowed inside, you will be greeted at the door by someone asking to see identification. These people are often poorly trained and anything other than a state driver's license may confuse them, so be forewarned.

Drunk driving is a problem on the highways of the United States, and South Carolina is no exceptions. Always drive defensively, especially late at night, and obey all posted speed limits and road signs—and never assume the other driver will do the same. You may never drive with an open alcoholic beverage in the car, even if it belongs to a passenger.

As far as retail purchase goes, in South Carolina you may only buy beer and wine, not hard liquor, on Sundays.

MEDICAL SERVICES

Unlike most developed nations, the United States has no comprehensive national health care system (although there are programs for the elderly and the very poor, as well as the new Affordable Care Act, or "Obamacare," for those who work but have no access to insurance). Visitors from other countries who need nonemergency medical attention are best served by going to freestanding medical clinics. The level of care is typically very good, but unfortunately you'll be paying out of pocket for the service. For emergencies, however, do not hesitate to go to the closest hospital emergency room, where the level of care is generally also quite good, especially for trauma. Worry about payment later; emergency rooms in the United States are required to take true emergency cases whether or not the patient can pay for services. Call 911 for ambulance service.

Hospitals

If there's a silver lining in getting sick or injured in Charleston, it's that there are plenty of high-quality medical facilities available. The premier institution is the **Medical University of South Carolina** (171 Ashley Ave., 843/792-2300, www.muschealth.com) in the northwest part of the peninsula. Two notable facilities are near each other downtown: **Roper Hospital** (316 Calhoun St., 843/402-2273, www.roperhospital.com) and **Charleston Memorial Hospital** (326 Calhoun St., 843/792-2300). In Mount Pleasant there's **East Cooper Regional Medical Center** (1200 Johnnie Dodds Blvd., www.eastcoopermedctr.com). In West Ashley there's **Bon Secours St. Francis Hospital** (2095 Henry Tecklenburg Ave., 843/402-2273, www.ropersaintfrancis.com).

Pharmaceuticals

Unlike many other nations, antibiotics are available in the United States only on a prescription basis and are not available over the counter. Most cold, flu, and allergy remedies are available over the counter. While homeopathic remedies are gaining popularity in the United States, they are nowhere near as prevalent as in Europe.

Drugs with the active ingredient ephedrine are available in the United States without a prescription, but their purchase is tightly regulated to cut down on the use of these products to make the illegal drug methamphetamine.

STAYING HEALTHY
Vaccinations

As of this writing, there are no vaccination requirements to enter the United States. Contact your embassy before coming to confirm this before arrival, however. In the autumn, at the beginning of flu season, preventive influenza vaccinations, simply called "flu shots," often become available at easily accessible locations like clinics, health departments, and even supermarkets.

Humidity, Heat, and Sun

There is only one way to fight the South's high heat and humidity, and that's to drink lots of fluids. A surprising number of people each year refuse to take this advice and find themselves in various states of dehydration, some of which can land you in a hospital. Remember: If you're thirsty, you're already suffering from dehydration. The thing to do is keep drinking fluids *before* you're thirsty as a preventative action rather than a reaction.

Always use sunscreen, even on a cloudy day. If you do get a sunburn, get a pain-relief product with aloe vera as an active ingredient. On extraordinarily sunny and hot summer days, don't even go outside between the hours of 10am and 2pm.

HAZARDS
Insects

Because of the recent increase in the mosquito-borne West Nile virus, the most important step to take in staying healthy in the Lowcountry—especially if you have small children—is to keep **mosquito bites** to a minimum. Do this with a combination of mosquito repellent and long sleeves and long pants, if possible. Not every mosquito bite will give you the virus; in fact, chances are quite slim that one will. But don't take the chance if you don't have to.

The second major step in avoiding insect nastiness is to steer clear of **fire ants,** whose large gray or brown dirt nests are quite common in this area. They attack instantly and in great numbers, with little or no provocation. They don't just bite; they inject you with poison from their stingers. In short, fire ants are not to be trifled with. While the only real remedy is the preventative one of never coming in contact with them, should you find yourself being bitten by fire ants, the first thing to do is to stay calm. Take off your shoes and socks and get as many of the ants off you as you can. Unless you've had a truly large number of bites—in which case you should seek medical help immediately—the best thing to do next is wash the area to get any venom off, and then disinfect with alcohol if you have any handy. Then a topical treatment such as calamine lotion or hydrocortisone is advised. A fire ant bite will leave a red pustule that lasts about a week. Try your best not to scratch it so that it won't get infected.

Outdoor activity, especially in woodsy, undeveloped areas, may bring you in contact with another unpleasant indigenous creature, the tiny but obnoxious **chigger,** sometimes called the redbug. The bite of a chigger can't be felt, but the enzymes it leaves behind can lead to a very itchy little red spot. Contrary to folklore, putting fingernail polish on the itchy bite will not "suffocate" the chigger, because by this point the chigger itself is long gone. All you can do is get some topical itch or pain relief and go on with your life. The itching will eventually subside.

Threats in the Water

While enjoying area beaches, a lot of visitors become inordinately worried about **shark attacks.** Every couple of summers there's a lot of hysteria about this, but the truth is that you're much more likely to slip and fall in

A far more common fate for area swimmers is to get stung by a jellyfish, or sea nettle. They can sting you in the water, but most often beachcombers are stung by stepping on beached jellyfish stranded on the sand by the tide. If you get stung, don't panic; wash the area with saltwater, not freshwater, and apply vinegar or baking soda. A product called Jellyfish Squish is also available and seems to work well.

Lightning

The southeastern United States is home to vicious, fast-moving thunderstorms, often with an amazing amount of electrical activity. Death by lightning strike occurs often in this region and is something that should be taken quite seriously. The general rule of thumb is that if you're in the water, whether at the beach or in a swimming pool, and hear thunder, get out of the water immediately until the storm passes. If you're on dry land and see lightning flash a distance away, that's your cue to seek safety indoors. Whatever you do, do not play sports outside when lightning threatens.

Resources

Suggested Reading

NONFICTION

Fraser, Walter J. Jr. *Charleston! Charleston! The History of a Southern City.* Columbia, SC: University of South Carolina Press, 1991. Another typically well-written and balanced tome by this important regional historian.

Gessler, Diana Hollingsworth. *Very Charleston: A Celebration of History, Culture, and Lowcountry Charm.* Chapel Hill, NC: Algonquin Books, 2003. A quick, visually appealing insider's perspective with some wonderfully whimsical cartoon-style illustrations.

Klein, Maury. *Days of Defiance: Sumter, Secession, and the Coming of the Civil War.* New York: Vintage, 1999. A gripping and vivid account of the lead-up to war, with Charleston as the focal point.

Rogers, George C. Jr. *Charleston in the Age of the Pinckneys.* Columbia, SC: University of South Carolina Press, 1980. This 1969 history is a classic of the genre.

Rosen, Robert. *A Short History of Charleston.* Columbia, SC: University of South Carolina Press, 1997. Quite simply the most concise, readable, and entertaining history of the Holy City I've found.

Woodward, C. Vann, ed. *Mary Chesnut's Civil War.* New Haven, CT: Yale University Press, 1981. The Pulitzer Prize-winning classic compilation of the sardonic and quietly heartbreaking letters of Charleston's Mary Chesnut during the Civil War.

General Background

Aberjhani and Sandra West. *Encyclopedia of the Harlem Renaissance.* New York: Checkmark Books, 2003. A brilliantly researched account of the great African American diaspora out of the South that eventually gave birth to the Charleston dance craze of the 1920s.

Lewis, Lloyd. *Sherman: Fighting Prophet.* Lincoln, NE: University of Nebraska Press, 1993. Though first published in 1932, this remains the most thorough, insightful, and well-written biography of General William Sherman in existence.

Robinson, Sally Ann. *Gullah Home Cooking the Daufuskie Island Way.* Chapel Hill, NC: University of North Carolina Press, 2007. Subtitled "Smokin' Joe Butter Beans, Ol' 'Fuskie Fried Crab Rice, Sticky-Bush Blackberry Dumpling, and Other Sea Island Favorites," this cookbook by a native Daufuskie Islander features a foreword by Pat Conroy.

Stehling, Robert. *Hominy Grill Recipes.* Charleston, SC: Big Cartel, 2009. This humble, hand-illustrated, self-published little tome features 23 great recipes from one of Charleston's most respected Southern cooking joints, Hominy Grill on Rutledge Avenue. At only $12.95, one of the best cookbooks for the money you'll find.

FICTION

Berendt, John. *Midnight in the Garden of Good and Evil.* New York: Vintage, 1999. Well, not exactly fiction, but far from completely true, nonetheless this modern classic definitely reads like a novel while remaining one of the unique and most readable travelogues of Savannah.

Conroy, Pat. *The Lords of Discipline.* New York: Bantam, 1985. For all practical purposes set at The Citadel, this novel takes you behind the scenes of the notoriously insular Charleston military college.

Conroy, Pat. *The Water is Wide.* New York: Bantam, 1987. Immortal account of Conroy's time teaching African American children in a one-room schoolhouse on "Yamacraw" (actually Daufuskie) Island.

Hervey, Harry. *The Damned Don't Cry.* Marietta, GA: Cherokee Publishing, 2003. The original *Midnight,* this bawdy 1939 potboiler takes you into the streets, shanties, drawing rooms, and boudoirs of real Savannahians during the Depression.

O'Connor, Flannery. *Flannery O'Connor: Collected Works.* New York: Library of America, 1988. For a look into the South's conflicted, paradoxical soul, read anything by this native-born writer, so grounded in tradition yet so ahead of her time even to this day. This volume includes selected letters, an especially valuable (and entertaining) insight.

Internet Resources

RECREATION
Dozier's Waterway Guide
www.waterwayguide.com
A serious boater's guide to stops on the Intracoastal Waterway, with a lot of solid navigational information.

South Carolina Department of Natural Resources
www.dnr.sc.gov
More than just a compendium of license and fee information—though there's certainly plenty of that—this site features a lot of practical advice on how best to enjoy South Carolina's great outdoors, whether you're an angler, a kayaker, a bird-watcher, a hiker, or a biker.

South Carolina State Parks
www.southcarolinaparks.com
Ditto for this site all about South Carolina's state parks.

NATURE AND ENVIRONMENT
Ocean Science
http://oceanscience.wordpress.com
A blog by the staff of Savannah's Skidaway Institute of Oceanography, focusing on barrier island ecology and the maritime environment.

CUISINE AND ENTERTAINMENT
Charleston City Paper blogs
http://ccpblogs.com
The collected staff blogs of the *Charleston City Paper,* dealing with the latest foodie news in town and entertainment options.

HISTORY AND BACKGROUND
South Carolina Information Highway
www.sciway.net
An eclectic cornucopia of interesting South Carolina history and assorted background facts, which makes for an interesting Internet portal into all things Palmetto State.

TOURISM INFORMATION
Charleston Convention and Visitors Bureau
www.charlestoncvb.com
This very professional and user-friendly tourism site is perhaps the best and most practical Internet portal for visitors to Charleston.

Restaurants Index

Nightlife Index

Hotels Index

Photo Credits

title page: traditional sweetgrass baskets © Martha Snider /123rf.com; page 2 (top left) Magnolia Cemetery in Charleston © Jim Morekis, (top right) the flag of South Carolina © Kcphotos | Dreamstime.com, (bottom) Waterfront Park's fountain illuminated at dusk © Cvandyke | Dreamstime.com; page 12 (top left) horse-drawn carriage tour © Jerry Coli | Dreamstime.com, (top right) Arthur Ravenel Jr. Suspension Bridge © Daveallenphoto | Dreamstime.com, (bottom) aerial view of Charleston's harbor © lofoto | Dreamstime.com; page 13 hitching post © Paladex | Dreamstime.com; page 14 © Kzlobastov | Dreamstime.com; page 15 © Jim Morekis; page 16 © Jim Morekis; page 17 © Yibbish | Dreamstime.com; page 18 © Reb3times | Dreamstime.com; page 19 © Cvandyke | Dreamstime.com; page 20 © Jim Morekis; page 21 © Visions Of America LLC/123rf.com; page 22 © Jerry Coli | Dreamstime.com; page 23 © Katie Smith/123rf.com; page 25 (both) © Jim Morekis; page 30 © Jim Morekis; page 34 (top left) © dndavis/123rf.com, (top right) © Jim Morekis, (bottom) © Jim Morekis; page 41 (all) © Jim Morekis; page 43 © Jim Morekis; page 48 (top left) © Jim Morekis, (top right) © Liane Harrold, bottom © Jim Morekis; page 59 (all) © Jim Morekis; page 62 (top left and right) © Jim Morekis, (bottom) © Brooke Becker/123rf.com; page 75 (top left) © Katie Smith/123rf.com, (top right) © Jim Morekis, (bottom) © Jim Morekis; page 77 (top) © Jim Morekis, (bottom) courtesy of Circa 1886; page 82 (top left) © Jim Morekis, (top right) © Maverick Southern Kitchens, (bottom) © Andrew Cebulka; page 90 (top) courtesy of Hyman's Seafood, (bottom) courtesy of Circa 1886; page 95 (top left) © Sherry Lee / courtesy of EVO Pizzeria, (top right) © Squire Fox, (bottom) © Andrew Cebulka; page 101 (top) courtesy of BLU Restaurant & Bar, (bottom) courtesy of The Chart Group; page 104 (top) © Jerry Coli | Dreamstime.com, (bottom) courtesy of Robert Lange Studios; page 110 (top) © Jerry Coli | Dreamstime.com, (bottom) © Abigail Marie; page 113 (both) © Jim Morekis; page 120 (top) © Aneese | Dreamstime.com, (bottom) © Kiawah Island Golf Resort; page 125 © Jim Morekis; page 131 (top) © Kiawah Island Golf Resort, (bottom) © Pattersonville | Dreamstime.com; page 135 (top left) © Kiawah Island Golf Resort, (top right) © Judith Bicking | Dreamstime.com, (bottom) © Pattersonville | Dreamstime.com; page 137 (top) © Jim Morekis, (bottom) © Kiawah Island Golf Resort; page 142 (top left) courtesy of The Vendue, (top right) courtesy of French Quarter Inn, (bottom) courtesy of HarbourView Inn; page 144 (top left) courtesy of Kings Courtyard Inn, (top right) © Jim Morekis, (bottom) © Jim Morekis; page 147 (top) courtesy of John Rutledge House Inn, (bottom) © Kiawah Island Golf Resort; page 150 (top) © Mark Vandyke | Dreamstime.com, (bottom) © Jim Morekis; page 159 (all) © Jim Morekis; page 175 (all) © Jim Morekis; page 185 (all) © Jim Morekis; page 204 (all) © Jim Morekis; page 212 (top) Mark Vandyke | Dreamstime.com, (bottom) © Charlescurtis | Dreamstime.com; page 220 (top) © Jack Nevitt/123rf.com, (bottom) © daveallenphoto/123rf.com; page 226 (both) © Jim Morekis; page 258 (top) © John R. Amelia | Dreamstime.com, (bottom) © Jim Morekis; page 263 (top) © Jerry Coli | Dreamstime.com, (bottom) © Cvandyke | Dreamstime.com; page 268 (top left) © Anthony Heflin | Dreamstime.com, (top right) © Kiawah Island Golf Resort, (bottom) © Fotoluminate | Dreamstime.com